CULTURE
STRUCTURE
& AGENCY

TITLES OF RELATED INTEREST FROM PINE FORGE PRESS AND SAGE PUBLICATIONS

DAVID RUBINSTEIN

CULTURE STRUCTURE & AGENCY

TOWARD A TRULY MULTIDIMENSIONAL SOCIETY

Sage Publications
International Educational and Professional Publisher
Thousand Oaks ▪ London ▪ New Delhi

For information:

Pine Forge Press
Sage Publications, Inc.
2455 Teller Road
Thousand Oaks, California 91320
E-mail: order@sagepub.com

Sage Publications Ltd.
6 Bonhill Street
London EC2A 4PU
United Kingdom

Sage Publications India Pvt. Ltd.
M-32 Market
Greater Kailash I
New Delhi 110 048 India

Printed in the United States of America

Library of Congress Cataloging-in-Publication Data

Rubinstein, David.
    Culture, structure, and agency: Toward a truly multidimensional sociology / by David Rubinstein.
        p.   cm.
    Includes bibliographical references and index.
    ISBN 0-7619-1928-7 (pbk.: alk. paper)
    1. Sociology. 2. Social structure. 3. Culture. I. Title.
    HM585 .R868   2000
    301—dc21   00-010037

01   02   03   04   05   06   07   7   6   5   4   3   2   1

Acquiring Editor:	Steve Rutter
Editorial Assistant:	Ann Makarias
Production Editor:	Denise Santoyo
Copy Editor:	Linda Gray
Typesetter/Designer:	Barbara Burkholder
Indexer:	Teri Greenberg
Cover Designer:	Ravi Balasuriya

We are not lumps of clay, and what is important is not what people make of us but what we ourselves make of what they have made of us.

Jean-Paul Sartre, Saint Genet

CONTENTS

◆◆◆

PREFACE

◆◆◆ ───────────────────────────────

This book engages a long-standing controversy in sociological theory: the debate between those who believe that behavior is mainly controlled by cultural training and those who emphasize the priority of social structure. The conclusion that a synthetic, or "dialectical," approach is required is not new. While some insist on the controlling power of culture or social structure "in the final analysis," many theorists advocate synthesis.

But this goal remains elusive. While a synthesis sounds right to many, saying just what this means is difficult. Part of the problem is confusion about the term *social structure.* The ordinary understanding of culture (attitudes, values, rules, commonsense understandings, etc.) is pretty close to the social scientists'. But while the concept of social structure is ubiquitous in the sociological literature, its meaning remains elusive. I have resolved this obstacle by arguing that most often the term means the structure of opportunity—that is, the array of costs and benefits available to the actor. Many sociologists will doubt that this is what social structure "really" means. But I cite much theoretical and empirical work to defend the claim. My task, then, is to find a synthesis between cultural explanations of behavior and those that emphasize opportunities, or costs and benefits.

The main problem in previous attempts is that they have failed to understand culture and social structure in a way that allows their synthesis. As a result, many synthetic efforts remain what I call *additive:* Structure and culture are drawn on to explain action, but their "interpenetration" is missed. I will show how these two components of action can be conceived to reveal how they shape or "mutually constitute" one another. Highlighting this process should facilitate research on how it happens—that is, how ordinary actors synthesize culture and social structure in their everyday lives.

A second concern here is the problem of agency, which, simply put, is the degree to which persons are authors of their own conduct or are controlled by "external" social forces: cultural training and/or the structure of costs and benefits. This problem is ancient: Most philosophers have had something to say about freedom and determinism. Rather than engaging this vast literature, I will comment on agency in sociological terms by showing how autonomy can be conceived in relation to cultural and structural determinism. I will argue that a synthetic conception of structure and culture *requires* agency—that is, that to an important degree, social actors constitute each in light of the other. These two issues will thus be brought together in an effort to solve the problems of synthesis and agency together.

Theoretical commentary on culture, structure, and agency is often esoteric. My hope is that I have made these topics accessible to nonspecialists. To this end, I present many examples of empirical work in which these issues arise to demonstrate their significance for doing sociology rather than theorizing about it. There are, alas, points in the text, especially Chapter 7, where some theoretical nit-picking is unavoidable: The notion of dialectics is especially difficult. But the main lines of my argument can be followed without getting tangled in the fine distinctions between my position and those of others. Some of the fussier points have been placed in endnotes.

While parts of the book will mainly interest specialists, it will update the general sociologist on the state of these arguments. It can also be a useful resource for teaching. The issues of culture, structure, and agency are hard to avoid, not just in theory courses, but in empirical studies. The many examples, drawn from various fields, demonstrate the relevance of these issues to substantive explanations. For example, in studies of social inequality, one quickly encounters the claim that values are the key—and the response that structural variables, especially the structure of opportunity, explains unequal outcomes. In the latter view, values are seen as irrelevant or merely adaptive to opportunity. For example, blocked opportunities are alleged to encourage the "short-term hedonism" that cultural explanations claim inhibit success. Hence, the structure of opportunity is considered to be "more basic" than culture. But advocates of the priority of culture contend that it is an independent force in behavior and sometimes argue that it is not possible to conceptualize opportunities apart from the cultural resources that are needed to exploit them. I hope to show that this chicken-and-egg argument can be solved by a synthetic approach. A hint of what I mean by this can be found in considering these two propositions: Poor opportunities may indeed encourage short-term hedonism, but short-term hedonism may obviate opportunities.

Noticing how often this debate appears in ordinary discourse will help students to follow the arguments. A newspaper reader will quickly encounter the claim that dysfunctional values inhibit success—and the familiar riposte that, compared with opportunities, the effect of values is trivial or that enhanced opportunities will change them. The claim that crime is caused by disordered values and the counterclaim that it is a "reasonable" or "rational" response to blocked opportunities are common. Everyone knows about the debate between conservatives who "blame the victim" for their misfortune by stressing the lack of "family values" and liberals who see "the system" as the cause of crime and low economic attainment and argue that opening up opportunities will cure these and other social problems. Similarly, while some claim that women are "different"—because of their early socialization or perhaps genetic dispositions—others respond that such differences are an adaptive response to limited economic opportunities that channel women toward domestic roles and encourage the development of suitable values.

There has been a great deal of controversy about the role of genetics in human behavior. Traditionally, social scientists have seen such claims as a rival to their emphasis on the role of "social facts": cultural training and/or costs and rewards. This prejudice is becoming untenable. For example, several studies have found that the personalities of twins, especially identical twins, raised apart are strikingly similar. In a recent article surveying the role of genetics in happiness Edward Diener, a psychologist at the University of Illinois, said that "identical twins separated from birth are more similar in how happy they are than fraternal twins who grew up together" (quoted in Belluck, 1999, p. 18).[1]

In Chapter 8, I argue that recognition of presocial behavioral dispositions need not threaten a sociological perspective because such dispositions are profoundly shaped, even "constituted," by the social context. The project of synthesis is thus expanded to include this aspect of human behavior. Again, this issue appears in ordinary discourse. The press routinely reports studies on the genetics of alcoholism and mental illness, differences between men and women, the biology of sexual orientation, and so on. Unusual crimes that defy explanation in terms of training or economic motives inspire research about personality traits that antedate socialization.

General readers, and students, may find comments on some new theoretical approaches informative. There is a major buzz about what has been called the pop psychology of the 1990s: evolutionary psychology. The theory that human psychology ought to be understood in an evolutionary perspective is sketched in Chapter 8. Mention is made of economic psychology: the use of cost-benefit analysis to explain emotional life. Network theory, rational choice theory, postmodernism, and the new cultural studies are also touched on.

At several points, I draw on the ideas of Ludwig Wittgenstein, an Austrian-born philosopher who taught at Cambridge University in England. Although he is widely regarded as one of the greatest philosophers of the twentieth century, his work is largely unknown to sociologists. I use his ideas on rule following and on the nature of "inner" feelings to solve some important problems in social science. Wittgenstein was a pioneer in philosophy, and many of his ideas seem strange and puzzling. But my own teaching suggests that much of what he says can be made accessible to nonspecialists. While I address some of the finer points of his thought, the main lines of his arguments can be easily followed.

1

Culture, Structure, and Social Explanation

A n enduring debate in sociology has been over cultural versus structural
understandings of action. This debate can be traced to Marx's distinction between "material substructures" and "ideological superstructures,"
and nearly every major sociological thinker has had something to say about
the locus of social causation. Various philosophical issues are implicated,
such as objectivism and subjectivism, materialism and idealism, freedom
and determinism, and so on. Also, there is a political subtext to the debate
that sometimes comes to the foreground. While the linkages are not inevitable, advocates of structural explanation tend to be on the left, whereas conservatives usually favor cultural explanation.[1] This issue has been reinvigo-
rated in recent years in the debate between rational choice theory and the
new cultural studies.

DEFINING CULTURE AND STRUCTURE

There are many definitions of culture[2] and disputes about how it is to be analyzed, but the basic program—at least in mainstream American sociology—
is relatively clear: systems of belief—norms and values, attitudes, world-
views, and so on—are adduced to explain conduct. Conceptions of culture
proliferate and can be complex, but they usually approximate Sharon
Hays's (1994) definition: "systems of meaning . . . including not only the
beliefs and values of social groups, but also their language, forms of

knowledge, and common sense, as well as the material products, inter-actional practices, rituals, and ways of life established by these" (p. 65). Bennett Berger (1991) defines culture simply as "the realm of symbols and meanings (p. 5), and Robert Wuthnow et al. (1984) define it as "the sym-bolic-expressive dimension of social life" (p. 259). Clifford Geertz's (1973) concept of culture is especially influential: "an historically transmitted pat-tern of meanings embodied in symbols, a system of inherited conceptions expressed in symbolic forms by means of which men communicate, perpet-uate, and develop their knowledge about and attitudes toward life" (p. 89). Talcott Parsons and A. L. Kroeber's (1958) definition of culture is not signif-icantly different: "transmitted and created content and patterns of values, ideas, and other symbolic-meaningful systems" (p. 116).

While there are intense debates about nearly all aspects of cultural anal-ysis, these examples show that it is possible to find approximate consistency in definitions of culture. But this cannot be done for social structure. There is a striking degree of obscurity and confusion over a concept that is widely regarded as defining the sociological perspective. William Sewell (1992) be-gins his analysis of the term by describing the familiar embarrassment felt by teachers when asked by a student to define *structure* (p. 1). It is often im-possible to derive a clear definition even from extended discussions of the term. Hays (1994) points out that, in a careful analysis, Anne Kane (1991) "never actually defines the term social structure" (p. 67, n. 10). While Anthony Giddens (1977, p. 117) criticized Robert Merton and Arthur Stinchcombe for failing to define the term precisely, Sewell (1992) finds that "'structure'"—the central term of Giddens's theory—"remains frustrat-ingly underspecified" (p. 5).

Social structure can mean "relations between groups" "configurations of social roles," "the degree of inequality in society," the "world capitalist system," the "relations of production," etc. etc. Berger (1991) defines struc-ture as "patterns of action" (p. 5) and Hays (1994) as "systems of social rela-tions" (p. 65) or "patterns of social life" (p. 60) that are not reducible to and are durable enough to withstand the inclinations of individuals. Definitions of structure thus range from a concreteness that precludes generality—"the degree of inequality"—to an abstractness that threatens vacuity—"patterns of action." Despite her effort to clarify, Hays reproduces the incoherence of the concept by including a farrago of examples of social structures: "capitalism" (p. 61), "gender and racial hierarchies" (p. 63), "the centralized state" (p. 63), and so on. Like many others, Hays complicates the concept, and challenges the distinction I have introduced, by incorporating culture or "systems of meaning" (p. 65), "language" (p. 61), and "moral rules" (p. 61). While devoting close attention to the concept throughout his work, Jeffrey Alexander's (1984) notion is equally diffuse. In one article, he describes "a certain distribution of resources and a certain relationship of bargainers to one another" as "economic and political structures" (p. 9) and goes on to include "the concentration of private wealth" (p. 10), "bureaucracy" (p. 11), and "the material context" (p. 14). Like Hays, Alexander also includes culture by adding elements "within the actor," such as "emotional bonds" and "symbolic codes of social morality" (p. 15) as kinds of structure.

Chris Jencks (1993) is admirably blunt about how wide a net structural sociology casts: "Structure provides the supra-individual source of causality in sociological reasoning whether it is experienced by members, or constituted by theorists, as economic, political, moral, cognitive or even physical in its orientation" (p. 119). Sometimes it seems that the concept of social structure is ritually invoked to affirm a sociological perspective. But the extra-individual source of determinism may not even be social. Gary Fine (1992) describes walls, as in prison walls, as a structural variable.

This range of factors suggests that little more than the principle of social determinism is being invoked. But if everything and anything that bears on behavior can be a structural variable, the term, rather than providing an organizing principle of explanation, approaches meaninglessness. The diffuseness of the term is greatly amplified with the inclusion of culture. Indeed, by calling culture a structure, a rival theory of action is introduced under a unifying rubric. Sewell's embarrassment is well warranted.

While there has been little agreement about concrete definitions of social structure, there is agreement on the *type* of concept sociologists are looking for. Structure is usually conceived as "external" and "objective" features of social order that are thought to have controlling power over culture and action. This explanatory program echoes Marx's (1964) conception of "the economic structure of society" as "the real foundation on which rise legal and political superstructures and to which correspond definite forms of social consciousness" (p. 51). Wuthnow et al. (1984) aver that "in standard social scientific discussions of culture the human world is divided in two, objective social structure on the one hand, subjective thoughts and perceptions on the other" (p. 5). Hays (1994) agrees that structure is usually conceived as "a pattern of material, objective, and external constraints" (p. 58), the "hard and solid . . . independent variables . . . that in some manner conditions or determines thoughts and actions" (p. 61). In this view, Hays says that "culture and agency are simply assimilated to each other, sharing their opposition to structure as conceptual underdogs" (p. 58). In this approach, structures, rather than culture and consciousness, ultimately control social process.

Because culture is durable and constrains individual conduct, some theorists, such as Hays, advocate "a conception of culture as a part of social structure" (p. 58). Sewell (1992) believes that Giddens offers "an essentially rule-based notion of structure" (p. 9). Wuthnow et al. (1984) also include culture as a structure, emphasizing its constraining and, in some extended sense, exterior and objective nature (p. 250). Reflecting the Parsonian conception of structure as normative, Alexander (1984, p. 15) incorporates "symbolic codes of social morality" as a kind of structure, and Emirbayer and Mische (1998) also expand the term to include culture (p. 970, n. 5). This view of culture traces to Durkheim's (1950) inclusion of norms as "social facts," which are "external to the individual" and "endowed with coercive power, by virtue of which they impose themselves upon him, independent of his individual will" (p. 2). But as Hays notes, most sociologists try to separate the two (at least analytically) and argue that the rock bottom of explanation is to be found in "objective" and in some sense "material" structures.

Because it involves a substantially different model of action and explanation, the notion of culture as a structure will be considered separately in Chapter 4. My preliminary focus will be on "standard" sociology, where culture and structure are separated and the former is seen to be epiphenomenal or even irrelevant to conduct, a view illustrated in Leo Schnore's (1958) concept of "shared norms and values" as "mere 'emanations' of underlying social morphology or structure" (p. 632). In this approach, culture is often assigned the role of "reflecting" social position— that is, a means of legitimating structurally determined, usually material, interests. Sewell (1992) also notes that "structure, in normal sociological usage, is thought of as 'hard' or 'material' and therefore as primary and determining, whereas culture is regarded as 'soft' or 'mental' and therefore as secondary or derived" (p. 2).

Structural sociology thus seeks to reproduce the spirit of Marx's (1964) aphorism: "It is not the consciousness of men that determines their social existence, but rather, their social existence which determines their consciousness" (p. 51). Durkheim's comment on Marx affirms this principle: "I consider extremely fruitful this idea that social life should be explained, not by the notions of those who participate in it, but by more profound causes which are unperceived by consciousness, and I think also that these causes are to be sought mainly according to which the associated individuals are grouped" (quoted in Winch, 1958, p. 23).

My strategy here is to consider these issues by, initially, stepping around much of the metatheoretical debate about the concept of social structure. In addition to being vague—a consequence of trying to incorporate the myriad features mentioned above—theoretical discussions of social structure are often disconnected from concrete sociological work. Instead, attention will be focused on the concepts of social structure that drive the discipline—that is, those used in mid-range theory and empirical research. Lessons learned here will be applied to more theoretical questions.

Once attention is directed away from high theory, substantial agreement and relative precision about the concept of social structure emerges. For a striking number of sociologists, and across a wide range of literatures, the "supra-individual source of causality," the "material, external, objective constraints" that control conduct and belief is the array of *opportunities*. Amidst variety in specific definitions of structure, there is considerable agreement that they ultimately control conduct via the costs and benefits they present to actors. This concept of structure is central to studies often cited as emblematic of the sociological perspective and used as staples of undergraduate teaching, such as Rosabeth Kanter's (1977) *Men and Women of the Corporation,* William Julius Wilson's (1987) *The Truly Disadvantaged,* and Merton's (1938) theory of crime.

The centrality of this concept has been noticed by Barry Hindess (1988): "Social structure ... provides for each actor the pattern of costs, incentives and opportunities that characterize the situation in which action is to take place" (p. 43). He contends that various definitions of social structure, such as "systems of social relations," implicitly explain action in terms of costs and benefits: "Their location within sets of social relations affects actors only through the incentives, opportunities, and costs presented to them" (Hindess, 1984, p. 267). Daniel Little (1989) has also noted the pervasiveness of this model: "Social institutions and practices are regulative systems that define opportunities and constraints that guide, limit, and inspire individual action" (p. 220). While not explicitly defining structure as opportunity, Hays (1994) summarizes the various examples she surveys as "structurally provided possibilities and structurally maintained constraints" (p. 69). Derek Layder (1985) defines structure as "an ongoing set of reproduced relations between particular social groups" (p. 132) and concretizes structural power in organizations as "the provision of positive incentives for 'proper' behavior" (p. 145). In structural sociology, opportunity is seen to drive behavior, while, as Bennett Berger (1991) put it, "Pieces of culture are treated as dependent variables" (p. 7). This can have various meanings. Often, culture is seen as adaptive to the opportunity structure as, for example, scanty economic opportunities depress aspirations or encourage fatalism and short-term hedonism. Culture is sometimes interpreted as providing a legitimating moral smokescreen for actions that are materially motivated. Sometimes it is dismissed as largely irrelevant to behavior—in Hays's imagery: "the decorations on the walls" as opposed to the "hard and solid . . . girders" of social structure (p. 61). Douglas Porpora (1987) characterizes this conception of culture as "Standard American Sociology" (p. 12).

The concept of social structure as opportunity is necessarily tied to a commensurate model of the actor as, in Alexander's (1984) terminology, "instrumental," while cultural sociology sees the individual as mainly norm driven. Lindenberg (1985) contrasts these two models as "calculating" versus "role playing" man. With this emphasis on opportunity, structural sociology has, despite frequent disavowals, adopted an essentially *economic* notion of action—that is, a conception of actors as calculators of costs and benefits. Knottnerus and Prendergast (1994) have noticed this odd convergence of disciplinary rivals, claiming that rational choice has become the "common sense psychology for structural theorizing" (p. 9). Considering the impact of Marxism on structural sociology might dampen the surprise of finding an economic actor at its heart.

Because many readers may doubt that social structure often means the array of opportunities, Chapters 2 and 3 will demonstrate the ubiquity of this concept—even to the point of some tedium. It will be argued that this version, while far from universal, captures a great deal of emphatically structural analysis. Indeed, if Jon Elster (1990) is correct that "there are really just two basic motivations of human behavior"(p. 243)—rationality and social norms—then noncultural explanations *must* ultimately account for behavior in terms of costs and benefits. Using this definition has the important advantage of sufficient clarity to allow understanding of how structure constrains behavior, which is a prerequisite of the synthetic project that is the ultimate aim of this book.

Before proceeding to the project of synthesis, it will be argued in Chapter 3 that the adoption of a virtual twin of homo economicus is not just unexpected: it subverts the structural view of social order. An important difference between neoclassical economics and structural sociology is that the latter sees opportunity as structured. While this term can have various meanings, it generally implicates the exercise of collective power. In Layder's work, power and structure are nearly inseparable. But because strictly economic actors do not easily form "distributive coalitions"—that is, alliances that advantage members—it will be argued that an economic concept of the individual cannot be combined with a conception of social order as structured by collective action. Chapter 3 will conclude with a brief evaluation of the explanatory value of structural sociology.

The main focus here will be on substantive work. But the conception of social structure as opportunity has played an important role in major sociological theories. According to Alexander (1984), "instrumental structuralism," which includes Marx, Weber, and their followers, is based on the premises that "individual action is strongly affected by the material context in which it occurs" and that "actors are efficient calculators of their own material environments" (p. 14). It will be argued in Chapters 2 and 3 that structures of opportunity are central to the work of Giddens, Pierre Bourdieu, Peter Blau, and Randall Collins and that they are central to exchange and network theory, and so on.

SYNTHESIS

The debate between cultural and structural explanation has been one of the most enduring in sociological theory. Weber is routinely seen as introducing a cultural emphasis as an antidote to Marx's materialism. Indeed, much debate about Marx has been about the relationship between the strains of idealism and materialism in his work. Durkheim aimed at providing a normative alternative to economics and social contract theory, and Parsons similarly championed normative explanation over the utilitarian model of action. Much post-Parsonian sociology, especially network theory, has re-emphasized the priority of structural relations over norms.

In recent years, polarities have sharpened, especially in the debate between rational choice theory and various cultural sociologies. But calls for a synthetic approach have also become more urgent. While there are unyielding advocates of the priority of norms, on one hand, and instrumental reason, on the other, many theorists—such as Alexander (1984), Sewell (1992), George Ritzer (1992), Hays (1994), Ann Swidler (1986), Emirbayer and Goodwin (1994), and Kane (1991)—have sought a way to incorporate both normative and instrumental dimensions of action. Postone et al. (1993) describe Bourdieu's work as aimed at "escaping the dualism of objectivist and subjectivist views" (p. 8), a dualism that largely overlaps that of culture and social structure.

The appeal of a synthetic approach is encouraged by several factors. First, each position can present hard cases. The autonomous power of culture is often argued with examples of individuals sacrificing self-interest by adhering to norms of fairness or by contributing to "public goods," such as donating money to a museum, when "free-riding"—benefiting from other's generosity—is the "rational" choice. The importance of culture is often demonstrated with cases in which individuals respond differently to the same "objective" situation. On the other hand, structuralists argue the priority of instrumental reason by, for example, showing that following a norm, even a moral rule, provides strategic advantages. They frequently cite examples in which inconvenient norms are opportunistically modified or rejected. Viktor Vanberg (1988) argues for the business advantages of a reputation for following norms of honesty, and Samuel Popkin (1979) shows how "traditionalist" peasants readily abandon norms when it suits them.

Another spur to synthetic efforts is the oft-noted difficulty of maintaining the conceptual distinction between structural and cultural factors. Hays (1994) illustrates the implication of culture in structure: "The modern family consists of a system of hierarchically arranged positions, at the same time as each of those positions is culturally defined" (p. 66, n. 7).[3] In this view, we cannot say what a social structure is without incorporating the beliefs of actors. Paul DiMaggio (1990) argues that Parsons's analytical distinction between culture and social structure is "artificial" in that "patterns of cognition are deeply implicated in the constitution of social structure" (p. 113). Breaking with his earlier acultural bias (see White et al., 1976), Harrison White (1992) has recognized that "social networks are phenomenological realities. . . . A social network is a network of meanings" (pp. 65, 67). This insight is incorporated in Emirbayer and Goodwin's (1994) critique of the network theorists' aspiration to formulate a strictly "objectivist" notion of networks "independent of the actor's wills, beliefs, and values" (p. 1417).

The problem of conceptual interpenetration has confounded the culture-structure dichotomy from its origin in Marx because "superstructural" elements, such as the law, are implicated in "substructures," such as relations of property. As Karl Renner (1949) put it, "Legal and economic institutions, though not identical, are but two aspects of the same thing, inextricably interwoven" (p. 59). The problem of dichotomizing culture and structure is illustrated in Marx's aphorism cited above because "social existence" and "consciousness" cannot be disentangled. This problem is reproduced in Durkheim's comments on Marx in that it is difficult, as Peter Winch (1958, p. 23) points out, to separate how "the associated individuals are grouped" from their ideas.[4] In many cases, "grouping"—for example, being a Protestant or a member of a political party—is *constituted* by actors' ideas.

In fact, despite his objectivist rhetoric, Marx (1971), unsurprisingly, affirmed a dialectical relationship of substructures and superstructures: "Every form of production creates its own legal relations, forms of government, etc. The crudity and the shortcomings of the conception [of bourgeois economists] lies in the tendency to see only an accidental reflective connection in what constitutes *an organic union*" (p. 21). Susan James (1985) points out that, noticing the dependence of the economy on law, Althusser contended "that certain aspects of economic practice depend upon the so-called superstructure" (p. 146).

A survey of variables alleged to be rigorously structural shows that they are saturated with culture. Blau (1974, p. 620) claims that "values" and "cultural traditions" and "norms" should be excluded from structural analysis. In another work, he includes variables such as status, ethnicity, kinship, and authority in the structural lexicon. But it would be impossible to define these terms apart from the "cultural and psychological orientations" he aims to exclude (Blau, 1977, p. 38). Denying "that norms determine role behavior" White et al. (1976, p. 1390) emphasize the explanatory power of network relations. But as White (1992) eventually acknowledged, network ties—such as "friendship"—are in large measure culturally established. Even Blau's master variable—group size—is a "cultural" fact because it is determined by social members' rules of inclusion. Because few structural variables can be articulated apart from cultural meanings, they are commonly kicked out the front door only to be smuggled back in.

The problem of conceptual interpenetration can also be seen in the difficulty of separating instrumental from normative action because what is "rational" depends on values. As Marshall Sahlins (1976) puts it, "It is culture which constitutes utility" (p. viii). The intertwining of values and costs and benefits is illustrated by the religious ascetic whose beliefs define material deprivations as moral gains. This is why Parsons and Shils (1951) emphasized the role of culture in utility: "Instrumental actions are subsidiary in the sense that the desirability of the goal is given by patterns of value-orientations, as is the assessment of cost" (p. 165).

The parallel problems of dichotomizing cultural and structural variables and distinguishing between normative and interest-driven action is a sure sign that a synthetic approach is called for. But synthesis, or "multidimensionality," often means an ad hoc deployment of both "ideal" and "material" factors. This improves on a one-sided approach but can result in what Bourdieu (1993) calls an "eclectic pseudo-synthesis" (p. 12) which invites controversy about why an actor is sometimes instrumental and sometimes normative.

By using terms such as *synthesis, dialectic,* and *interpenetration,* Alexander's (1984) "multidimensional" approach signals an attempt to go beyond eclecticism. But it is not clear that he has. At points, he pursues the logic of "the missing variable"—that is, incorporating both normative and instrumental dimensions of action: "Any given act must . . . be viewed as combining internal and external elements: every impinging condition is mediated by the actor's reference to an interpretive norm" (Alexander, 1982, p. 67). An additive, rather than synthetic, approach is implied in Alexander's (1984) description of Weber's Protestant ethic thesis as illustrating how "interpretive norms" mediate "impinging conditions" (p. 19).

Weber's (1946) work is often cited as a model of multidimensional analysis that incorporates both normative and instrumental dimensions of action. His frequently cited comment on this issue is regarded by many as the key to a synthetic sociology: "Not ideas, but material and ideal interests, directly govern men's conduct. Yet very frequently the 'world images' that have been created by 'ideas' have, like switchmen, determined the tracks along which action has been pushed by the dynamic of interest" (p. 280). This sort of synthesis is implied by the effort of socioeconomics to introduce what Etzioni (1988) calls "the moral dimension" to economic analysis.

But a real synthesis of structure and culture is not captured in Weber's formulation. Setting aside the odd distinction between "ideal interests" and "ideas," and the questionable pairing of the former with "material interests," Weber seems to say that our ideas, such as religious beliefs, determine how we address our interests. This interpretation is suggested by the closing remark in *The Protestant Ethic and the Spirit of Capitalism* (Weber, 1958) that his aim is not to counter Marx's materialism with an "equally onesided idealism" (p. 183) but to incorporate both. This seems to be Alexander's (1984) understanding of the Weberian synthesis. In his view, Weber contended that "the labor performed by different classes makes them more or less susceptible to different ideological orientations, but he insisted that any particular orientation must be viewed as the product of specific religious and cultural factors in the class environment" (p. 19).

But the relationship between culture and structure is more intimate than this. What is required is not just to show how values shape responses to structured interests—as though they were separate things, one "internal" and the other "external," but to show how social structures are *constituted through* culture and how culture is, in turn, *structurally constituted*. A full synthesis requires that the distinction between culture and structure, and between normative and instrumental action, be eroded, if not entirely dissolved. It will be argued (mainly in Chapter 7) that Alexander's and other synthetic efforts fail to articulate the nature of the interpenetration of culture and structure and hence cannot show *how* it happens. As a result, important areas of empirical research are underdeveloped because the process of interpenetration is not examined.

A second problem with previous efforts is that a synthetic approach is often abandoned for the temptations of unidimensionality and/or an inclination to prioritize material or moral factors. Alexander (1982) notes the persistent ambivalence between a synthetic and a unidimensional approach: "A multidimensional position has been rejected, in part or in whole, by every major theoretical tradition. At the same time, every tradition has also, at one time or another, accepted it as its primary theoretical goal" (p. 124). It will be argued in Chapter 7 that Alexander suffers the same equivocation. While calls for a multidimensional sociology pervade his work, he ultimately backs away from a synthetic position by prioritizing culture. Sewell's initially promising effort at synthesis mirror's Alexander by subordinating culture to instrumental reason.

Drawing on concrete examples of sociological explanation, it will be argued that structure and culture are essential in *constituting* one another. This requires that both be reconceptualized. To this end, it will be shown that culture cannot be understood apart from structures of opportunity because, as structuralists argue, culture emerges and is articulated in a practical context. The core claim is that culture is, in part, instrumentally devised and, more interestingly, its content is indeterminate and hence open to opportunistic "reading" by the practical actor. Culture is not *merely* instrumental. But it is formulated and reformulated by actors engaged in practical situations that consist, importantly, in the structure of opportunity. Culture, as Marx (1967b) argued, must be brought to earth; its relation to "material practice," both in its formulation and its interpretation, must be recognized: "Men are the producers of their conceptions, ideas, etc.—real active men as they are conditioned by a definite development of their productive forces. . . . Consciousness can never be anything else than conscious existence and the existence of men is their actual life-process" (p. 1). The intrication of culture and consciousness with practical exigencies will be introduced in Chapter 2 with examples of culture adapting to opportunity. These illustrations of the malleability of culture will be underpinned, in Chapter 4, with Wittgenstein's (1953, para. 143, 195) argument that the meaning of a rule must be determined by practical actors.

But in an important qualification of this argument it will be shown in Chapter 5 that culture, while intricated with practical reason, cannot be absorbed into it or treated as epiphenomenal. There are multiple dimensions to the partial, or relative, autonomy of culture. While there are compelling examples of culture adapting to structure, there are also abundant examples of rule following that subvert instrumental advantage, such as tipping in a restaurant one will never return to or casting a vote unlikely to decide an election. Also, as Alexander's interpretation of Weber implies, it is rare that structural circumstances are "single exit" situations that *require* a particular response: there are almost always alternative "adaptive" responses to practical exigencies, and culture dictates the choice of sometimes radically different courses of action. The autonomy of culture from instrumental reason will be emphasized with some striking examples of culture subverting instrumental goals.

The familiar claim that culture is partially autonomous of practical interests will be amplified in Chapter 6 with a more fundamental argument that culture is essential to the *constitution* of opportunity. This point has been broached insofar as cultural meaning is implicated in structures: for example, family structure is culturally defined. It can be expanded by recognizing that opportunities are not "objective" or "external" conditions to which actors react. They exist, as Bourdieu's concept of "habitus"—the mental categories through which actors engage the world—suggests, only in relation to actors who can draw on appropriate cultural resources. To this end, some studies of the role of culture in opportunity will be described. Here, the logic of *inter*penetration, or "organic union," will be introduced. Structural sociologists can show that culture is adaptive to opportunity. But *just as culture is "read" in light of opportunities, opportunities are read through the lens of culture.* In Chapter 7, culture and opportunity will be described as dialectically interdependent insofar as opportunity appears in relation to cultural resource, which are devised and articulated in light of opportunities.

The meaning of dialectical will be clarified with Bertell Ollman's (1971) interpretation of Marx. Also, James Gibson's (1979) concept of "affordances" will be introduced to conceptualize both the autonomy and the interpenetrations of culture and opportunity. Dialectical logic will be used to address the problem of conflation described by Margaret Archer (1988) in which, in some synthetic efforts, the components of action are merged so thoroughly as to preclude theorizing their interplay. A dialectical approach allows a way to conceptualize interpenetration without conflation.

AGENCY

The structural approach has commonly been tied to the search for a "supra-individual source of causality . . . ultimately independent of the will or caprice of particular individuals" (Jencks, 1993, p. 119). While a cultural approach can support agency, it too can emphasize determinism. According to Durkheim (1966), "It is society which, fashioning us in its image, fills us with religious, political, and moral beliefs that control our actions" (p. 212). In recent years, the project of theorizing agency, without succumbing to a voluntarism in which the notion of structural constraint is lost, has become more urgent (see Emirbayer & Mische, 1998; Hays, 1994; Sewell, 1992). But there is little agreement on how to do this. The Parsonian tradition, drawing on Kant's belief that moral law is the locus of freedom, sees culture as the arena of choice insofar as values provide autonomy from material constraints and the imperatives of biological drives. In contrast, structural advocates of agency see constraint in culture and find autonomy in the capacity of actors to cast off their training and calculate their advantages.

It will be argued in Chapter 7 that the dialectic of structure and culture suggests an actor who, while subject to both cultural and structural constraint, is in thrall to neither—that is, is neither a cultural nor a structural dope. Insofar as actors can read their culture in light of their practical needs, they are not, in Marx's term, mere "trager," or bearers, of culture. Wittgenstein's emphasis on the role of agency in rule following will be used to challenge the notion of culture as a locus of constraint. But because opportunities and costs and benefits are culturally constituted, neither are actors practical or behavioral dopes, driven by instrumental advantage in a strictly material environment. Generally, agency is sought in culture *or* structure. Here, agency will be grounded in the *interplay* of the two. The issues of synthesis and agency will thus be dovetailed. In this view, because culture and structure are constituted by actors, each in light of the other, both are *essentially* agential and *essentially* interpenetrating.

Throughout, global conclusions about the relations of action, culture, and structure will be avoided in preference to idiographic variation. There are several dimensions to this. The notion of partial autonomy implies that sometimes culture, and sometimes practical interests, may dominate action. Similarly, agency will be portrayed as contingent in two senses. First, *both* culture and instrumental calculation can, depending on circumstances, provide agency and, second, the *degree* of agency varies. But in an apparent *reversal* of these arguments, it will also be argued that, in limiting cases, actors can be appropriately described as structural or cultural dopes.

DESIRES ETC.

The debate between structural and cultural explanation has implicitly conceptualized the actor as an empty vessel: a conduit of structural and/or cultural forces. But this sociologistic concept of the person as a tabula rasa is implausible and increasingly so as a growing body of research shows that individuals have distinct temperaments and dispositions, inscribed both genetically and by early training. Michael Levin (1987) describes heirs of Hegel, who see persons as entirely products of historical culture, and behaviorists, who believe that learning fully controls conduct, as "The New Creationists" because they except humans from what we know to be true of all other animals: that they have behavioral dispositions not reducible to social experience. Dennis Wrong (1994) has recently amplified his critique of the oversocialized actor, arguing that persons have "wants, feelings and impulses" that are partially autonomous of structural and cultural forces and "that undergird and set in motion the whole process of human interaction" (p. 59).

The failure of previous synthetic attempts to consider presocial traits of persons will be remedied by introducing, in Chapter 8, a third component of action: "desires etc." I have reluctantly settled on this vague term to encompass the various traits of persons that are thought to antedate their training: temperamental dispositions, emotions, needs, impulses, and so on. While theoretical precision is of course preferable, the unsettled nature of this subject precludes closure on this issue.

Drawing on recent developments in evolutionary psychology, it will be argued that humans carry various inclinations and behavioral dispositions. But the logic of interpenetration will be maintained. That is, desires etc. will be shown to be a component of action, but one that must be treated sociologically—that is, as intricated with culture and opportunity. The actor will be conceptualized as "reading" desires etc. in light of culture and opportunity. This analysis will incorporate research in the sociology of emotions, a field that emphasizes the cultural dimension of emotions, and research on economic psychology, which highlights their strategic aspects.

Just as it is necessary to reconceptualize culture and structure to understand their interpenetration, desires etc. will be reconceived with Wittgenstein's ideas about the bearing of cultural training and practical calculation on "inner" experience. Fears that a sociological perspective is threatened by admitting nonsocial sources of behavior can be assuaged by emphasizing the role of social factors in constituting "feelings." But just as culture and social structure, while interpenetrating, cannot be collapsed into one another, the (partial) autonomy of desires etc. will be maintained. Following the established logic, culture and opportunity will also be seen as constituted or read by the actor in light of desires etc. The implications of this full schema for agency will be discussed in terms of a conception of the actor as a "reader" of culture, opportunity, and desires etc.

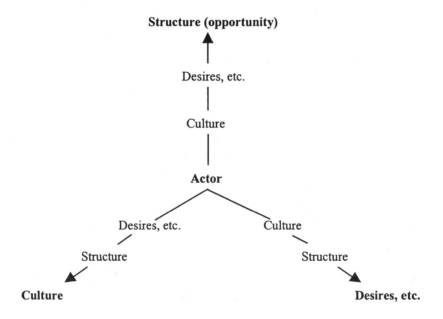

Figure 1.1

This project focuses on what has been underconceptualized in previous synthetic efforts: the *ways* in which actors engage opportunity, culture, and desires etc. Their fixity and autonomy will be challenged by showing how actors constitute each in relation to the others. The aim is to provide a concrete description of *how* a synthesis of the components of action occurs. Figure 1.1, which will be explained in Chapter 9, illustrates the interactions to be portrayed.

PART I

◆◆◆

Structural Explanation

2

Structured Opportunity and Social Explanation

STRUCTURE AS OPPORTUNITY

Because it has emerged in a piecemeal way, few sociologists realize that structured opportunity has become a kind of master variable in the discipline. This chapter will try to convince skeptics that social structure usually means the array of opportunities by showing how central this variable is to explaining crime, poverty, social inequality, differences between men and women, and so on.

A paradigmatic example of structural explanation is Robert K. Merton's theory of deviance as driven by structures of opportunity. Often cited as emblematic of the sociological method, Merton's 1938 article was found to be the most frequently cited and reprinted in the history of American sociology (Cole, 1975, p. 175). Merton (1938) argued that differences between individuals—in biology, personality, or values—do not distinguish criminal "innovators" from "conformists." He also doubted that there are differences in skills between the two. Rather, "anomie" theory considers "blockage" in the "legitimate opportunity structure" to be the main factor in the preponderance of lower-class crime, which is seen to be "normal," that is, a rational response to blocked opportunity (p. 672).

Richard Cloward and Lloyd Ohlin's (1960) version of anomie theory recognized the role of "features of lower class socialization" such as an "inability to defer gratification" (p. 99, n. 27). But they argued, "Although these cultural orientations, once crystallized, persist as major obstacles to the utilization of opportunity, it should be remembered that they emerged initially as adaptive responses to socially structured deprivations" (p. 103). In anomie theory, the essential features of structural explanation are in place. Opportunities are portrayed as the "external" and "objective" features of social structure that control individual conduct, whereas culture and personality are treated as adaptive or epiphenomenal to the context of incentives.

Another study widely considered emblematic of sociological explanation, Rosabeth Kanter's (1977) *Men and Women of the Corporation,* follows this logic closely. She contends that unequal opportunity, not personality or culture, explains women's unequal attainment and accounts for various behavioral and attitudinal differences between men and women. Acknowledging that women have less ambition and job commitment and focus more on peer relations than do men, Kanter explains these traits as adaptive: "The very lack of opportunity the group faces creates a self-defeating cycle and puts pressure on members to limit their aspirations. . . . When women seem to be less motivated or committed, it is probably because their jobs carry less opportunity" (p. 159). Kanter is emphatic that differences between men and women are not ingrained: "what appear to be 'sex' differences in work behavior emerge as responses to structural conditions" (p. 262). Rejecting explanations based on "either biologically based psychological attributes or characteristics developed through a long socialization to a 'female sex role' " (p. 262), Kanter argues that men placed in circumstances typically faced by women behave like them: "Men with low opportunities look more like the stereotype of women in their orientations toward work . . . they limit their aspirations . . . emphasize leisure and consumption, and create sociable peer groups in which interpersonal relationships take precedence over other aspects of work" (p. 161). An array of personal traits and conduct are thus seen to emerge in response to structures of opportunity. Individuals are portrayed as cultivating the personalities and cultural orientations that suit their available opportunities.

Kanter's understanding of women is reiterated by Randall Collins (1988). Arguing "the power of social structure in producing cultures, including gender cultures" (p. 123), he claims: "The ideology is not autonomous; one is not stuck in a given traditional set of sex and gender roles; instead these change with structural shifts in the line-up of resources" (p. 122). The task for sociology is to account for cultural differences "not in terms of intrinsic sexual differences, or deep-seated early childhood experience, but of variations in social structure," which Collins specifies as opportunities and "economic leverage" (p. 122). Because persons are seen to quickly shed values and personality traits in response to changed opportunities, Kanter and Collins deny the inertia that Cloward and Ohlin (1960) attribute to socialization. Persons are virtual mirrors of opportunity structures.

The emphasis on the role of opportunity in shaping norms and values dominates various sociological literatures. It has become the canonical sociological view of poverty. Herbert Gans (1968) argues that "some behavioral norms are more persistent than others, but over the long run, all of the norms and aspirations by which people live are nonpersistent: they rise and fall with changes in situations" (p. 124). Charles Valentine (1968) contends that "through culture men collectively adapt themselves to environmental conditions and circumstances" (p. 5), and he believes that personality also reflects access to opportunities: "impulse control and gratification deferral vary situationally and may be maximized when a future reward can be realistically predicted" (p. 13). Stanley Lieberson (1980) denies that "cultural or normative explanations can go very far in accounting for the origins of Black-new European gaps" (p. 363) in attainment and argues that if, for example, blacks are less committed to schooling, it is because of "less incentive or reward for schooling" (p. 252).

Loic Wacquant (1993) offers a radicalized version of Merton's theory to explain black crime. Arguing that various ghetto behaviors "obey a social rationality that takes stock of past experiences and is well adapted to their immediate socioeconomic context," Wacquant minimizes the *differentness* of ghetto criminals: "Ghetto dwellers are not a distinctive breed of men and women; they are ordinary people trying to make a living and improve their lot as best they can under the unusually oppressive circumstances imposed upon them" (p. 15). Drug selling and the like reveal, not "behavioral and cultural deficiencies of inner-city residents" (p. 34), but that "most ghetto residents have little choice" (p. 22). Even a "survival strategy of last result"—in the words of a resident—to "Steal, knock old ladies down and take their pension checks. . . . Turn tricks, sell drugs, anything" is interpreted as an adaptation to economic exigencies (p. 23). Crime directed at fellow ghetto residents is situationally compelled by the visibility of blacks: "You got to burglarize your own people" (p. 18). The "culture of terror that engulfs many inner-city streets" is "a business requirement" for dealing drugs (p. 24).

This interpretation of ghetto life as an adaptation to restricted opportunity is dominant in the sociological literature. James Montgomery (1990) contends that some of the most famous ethnographies of inner-city life, including Kenneth Clark's (1965) *Dark Ghetto,* Elliott Liebow's (1967) *Talley's Corner,* Ulf Hannerz's (1969) *Soulside,* and Lee Rainwater's (1970) *Behind Ghetto Walls* are guided by the idea "that ghetto behavior stems from blocked opportunities" (p. 3). Montgomery believes that these studies can be readily translated into rational choice terms.

Many critics of the culture of poverty, like Wacquant, dismiss it as a pernicious myth. But William Julius Wilson (1987) acknowledges that the poor have distinctive values that affect their conduct. However, arguing that "group variations in behavior, norms, and values often reflect variations in group access to channels of privilege and influence" (p. 75), he contends that "ghetto-specific culture is a response to these structural constraints and limited opportunities" (p. 137). In this view, violence, for example, is a means of gaining esteem in the absence of more conventional opportunities, fatalism is a metaphorical representation of real powerlessness, and unwillingness to defer gratification is an adaptation to unpredictable futures. Like Kanter, Wilson believes that, if opportunities were made available, the culture of poverty would quickly fade. Norms and values are not "the ultimate sources of the problem" (p. 76) and hence can be remediated by "changes in the structures of opportunities for the disadvantaged" (p. 75).

Elijah Anderson's (1990) frank and sometimes harrowing portrait of ghetto life similarly acknowledges the pathologies of the ghetto underclass: criminal predation, an aversion to work and family life, exploitative gender relations, and so on. Like Wilson, he describes these patterns as adaptations to limited opportunities: "When no good jobs are available the work ethic loses its force" (p. 110). The almost sporting efforts of young men to seduce and impregnate girls "is a mean adaptation to blocked opportunities and profound lack, a grotesque form of coping" (p. 110). And when young mothers use welfare checks to gain economic leverage over males, this too is adaptive: "Thus girls and boys alike scramble to take what they can from each other, trusting only their own ability to trick the other into giving them something that will establish their version of the good life—the best life they can put together in their environment" (p. 135).

Merton (1938) extended his theory of blocked opportunity to explain various behaviors that cannot be "rationalized" as alternate paths to conventional goals, such as the "retreatism" of drug users. This approach is routinely used to explain noninstrumental "adaptations."[1] In a study of homicide and social inequality, Blau (1982) argues that "if there is a culture of violence, its roots are pronounced economic inequality" (p. 114). Harold Finestone's (1957) interpretation of heroin addicts, "Cats, Kicks, and Color," described a way of life that seems to demonstrate indifference and even hostility toward conventional goals. The display of unique taste in clothes and music, the "aristocratic disdain for work," the attempt to make life "a gracious work of art" (p. 4), and of course, the pursuit of the heroin "kick" suggests a radically different set of values. But at base, such values reflect blocked opportunities:

> The context for such a movement must include the broader community, which, by its policies of social segregation and discrimination, has withheld from individuals of the colored population the opportunity to achieve or to identify with status positions in the larger society. The social type of the cat is an expression of one possible type of adaptation to such blocking and frustration. (p. 6)

Actors, even when they champion deviant values, still reflect their structural disadvantage: "Insofar as the social type of the cat represents a reaction to a feeling of exclusion from access to the means towards the goals of our society . . . it can be confidently expected that the cat as a social type will tend to disappear as such opportunities become more prevalent among the colored population. (p. 13)

As might be expected, opportunity is central in the status attainment literature. While the "Wisconsin school" stresses the role of social psychological and human capital variables, the more distinctively sociological approach focuses on opportunity, rather than culture, psychology, or even skill. Arthur Stinchcombe (1986) has noticed this emphasis and the attendant derogation of culture and psychology: "The causes [of inequality] were not variations in subjective processes (such as how much people valued prestige versus money returns, or security versus higher average income) but rather variations in the situations that determined people's possibilities" (p. 140).

This perspective informs much empirical research. Marta Tienda and Haya Stier's (1991) conclusion to a study of joblessness and shiftlessness among Chicago's poor is representative: "Our survey has shown not the absence of a work ethic, but limited opportunities to secure employment" (p. 153). In many cases, the controlling power of opportunity is simply assumed. Raymond Boudon (1974) claims that inequality of outcome is a virtual measure of unequal opportunity: "A society is characterized by a certain amount of inequality of social opportunity if the probability of reaching a high social status is smaller for . . . a worker's son than for a lawyer's son" (p. xi). Beck et al. (1978) similarly treat inequality as a measure of unequal opportunity: "Analysts in the structural tradition interpret the existence of sex and race differences in earnings as indicative of systematic forces involving differential opportunity structures which are embedded in the socioeconomic order" (p. 709). They consider that "sex and race could be included within the human capital framework by assuming that sex and race differences reflect basic inequalities in job-related capacities." But they aver that "few sociologists would make such an assumption" (p. 708). In an empirical study, Albert Szymanski (1976) measures racism as inequality: "As the indication of racism, the ratio of third world [nonwhite] to white median earnings are sought" (p. 406). In this view, racial inequality is an index of variation in structures of opportunity. According to Michael Smith (1990), structural explanations of social inequality have become increasingly dominant.

Like Kanter, Wilson, and others, structural theorists explain differences in values as adaptations. Arguing that "market segmentation [the dual economy] is not a *product* of variations in the quality of labor or other attributes of workers, rather it is the *cause* of differences in the composition or quality of labor," Horan et al. (1980) claim that "job instability is not a personality characteristic of the worker but a characteristic of the sectoral organization of production" (p. 283). Challenging the claim that different labor markets segments have different, culturally ingrained decision-making protocols, Granovetter (1985) argues that "When the social situation of those in nonprofessional labor markets is fully analyzed, their behavior looks less like the automatic application of 'cultural' rules and more like a reasonable response to their present situation" (p. 506).

The structural theory of culture and personality as adaptive is expressed in the conception of aspiration as a mirror of opportunities rather than an ingrained trait. The concept of cognitive dissonance is often invoked as the mechanism through which aspirations are matched to opportunities. Like Kanter, Alan Kerckhoff (1984) sees aspirations as reflecting opportunity: "It is possible to interpret . . . ambition . . . as indicating the individual's understanding of probable outcomes" (p. 143). Even when real differences in human capital—or skills—are found, opportunity is considered to be the ultimate cause. Margaret Marini (1989) argues that gender differences in skill reflect "the effects of labor market discrimination on the acquisition of worker qualifications and tastes" (p. 357).

In this view, skills and even personality traits ("tastes") are seen as investments that match available opportunities. Baron and Hannon (1994) also believe that opportunity shapes personality, values, and skills:

> Sociologists tend to posit opportunity structures—inherited by virtue of social class background, other ascribed statuses, network position, educational attainment, and the like—in terms of which individuals form preferences and tastes. The image is one of social constraints inducing preferences and aptitudes, rather than actors sorting themselves into social roles based on tastes and abilities. (p. 1117)

Those with low opportunities will not cultivate skills that will not be rewarded nor will they develop values or personalities incompatible with their "objective" situations. To explain the paradox of blacks expressing high commitment to education, but performing badly in school, Roslyn Mickelson (1990) argues that "black youths, for quite rational reasons, perceive the opportunity structure differently from middle class white youths and consequently tend to put less effort and commitment into their school work" (p. 45).[2]

The controlling power of opportunity is also invoked to explain differences in the development of nations. World systems and dependency theory deny that different rates of development emerge from cultural differences between nations. Underdevelopment reflects variations in opportunities presented by the (capitalist) world system. Claiming that "opportunity structures condition human behavior" (p. 113), Valenzuela and Valenzuela (1984) argue that

> it is not inappropriate attitudes which contribute to the absence of entrepreneurial behavior or to institutional arrangements reinforcing underdevelopment. Dependent, peripheral development produces an opportunity structure such that personal gain for dominant groups and entrepreneurial elements is not conducive to the collective gain of balanced development. (p. 107)

Stinchcombe (1986) believes that this is the dominant assumption in this perspective: "The world systems tradition displaces attention from subjective matters entirely, since its central concepts are structural relations between societies rather than relations between social action and what goes on inside the minds of individuals" (p. 137). Irving Kristal's (1983) belief that "everyone, whether economist or not, is quite certain that if India or Peru were inhabited by Swiss and Dutchmen, they would be fairly prosperous countries" (p. 174) must except Immanuel Wallerstein (1974) who argues that "Portugal, because of its geography, had no choice" in its economic destiny (p. 47).[3]

In most of these examples, the claim that culture and conduct adapt to opportunity is largely inferential. There are more finely grained accounts of the process by which this happens. Like Kanter (1977), Kathleen Gerson (1985) argues in *Hard Choices* that the availability of jobs, not socialization or childhood aspirations, is the main factor determining the choice women make between homemaking and paid labor. Her main evidence, derived from reconstructed life histories, is the finding that women who were "traditionally" oriented early in their lives frequently developed career commitments later in life and vice versa. Women who encountered suitable domestic situations—well-employed husbands supportive of child bearing—were drawn to homemaking, while the pull of good job opportunities, or the push of financial or domestic troubles, guided women into paid careers, largely independently of how they were brought up and even of their early adult values. (Gerson's study will be examined in Chapter 6.)

Gresham Sykes's (1958) study of prisons also provides a processual account of how structured incentives constrain behavior. His aim is to explain the pervasive corruption in prisons whereby the administration "retreats to the walls" and allows prisoners to virtually run the inner life of the prison. Sykes stresses that this outcome has little to do with the intentions of guards and everything to do with situational constraints. The main administrative imperative, imposed by political forces, is to prevent the sorts of trouble that provoke public concern—such as riots and escapes. But administrators have few ways to legitimately induce prisoner compliance. Unrestrained violence against prisoners is no longer tolerated and legitimate punishments, such as solitary confinement, are often shrugged off by the hard cases. Moreover, the guard who frequently asks for extraordinary interventions is suspected of not being able to do his job without making demands on supervisors. Illegitimate punishments risk legal sanctions and can provoke dangerous reactions: each guard must fear the day when the tables are turned and he needs the goodwill of the inmates. The best resource the guard has to induce cooperation is a willingness to overlook deviance. The upshot is that guards allow various sorts of infractions, such as nonstandard clothing, time out of cells, homosexual trysts, preying on the weak, and pervasive drug and alcohol use. This system of collusion to subvert institutional rules works because everybody gains: it allows the guard easy time, relaxes the pains of imprisonment for inmates, and permits the administration to present a quiet prison to the public. Although Sykes does not use the language of rational choice, his book is essentially an account of the process by which calculations of costs and benefits overwhelm rules and intentions.

INTERPRETING CULTURE

The examples cited so far portray culture as adaptive to the array of opportunities and hence nearly irrelevant as a cause of conduct. Wilson, Kanter, and many other structural theorists employ a hard instrumentalism in which opportunity alone explains conduct and cultural training is seen to fall easily away. In this approach, it is not clear why persons even *have* culture—that is, what role it plays in behavior, a question often addressed to Marx's theory of ideology. There is an alternate structural approach in which culture is given significant weight. In this view, culture is seen to be *interpreted* by actors in light of their opportunities. The emphasis is on the flexibility and/or ambiguity of rules rather than on their irrelevance. As Daniel Little (1991b) describes this approach: "Normative systems are inherently ambiguous and subject to revision over time. Consequently we should expect that opportunistic agents will find ways of adapting given social norms more comfortably to the pursuit of self-interest" (p. 153).

A study of changes in the Chinese concept of filial piety among immigrants (Lin, 1985) illustrates the flexibility of culture. The core of traditional Chinese values requires the devotion of children to parents. They must provide love and comfort, especially to their aged parents. Nearly as central is the obligation to bring honor to the family by occupational achievement. In the American context, the latter duty becomes more salient because opportunities for professional advancement are richer and the display of devotion is more difficult because parents typically remain in Taiwan or China. Also, career demands render personal service more difficult even if parents are in America. Immigration, then, brings two codes of conduct into conflict. The characteristic response is to de-emphasize the love and personal service component of filial devotion and to focus instead on career advancement in the name of family honor. Changed opportunities induce a change in which values are emphasized.

In contrast to the arguments of Wilson and others that culture has little staying power in relation to the push and pull of opportunity, Lin shows the durability of cultural legacies while portraying the actor as able to adapt them to suit altered circumstances. David Matza and Gresham Sykes (1957) take a middle position by arguing that, although values make a difference, actors can deflect rules far from their original intentions. Their analysis of delinquent subcultures challenges the claim that juveniles, surrounded by conventional culture, are capable of devising or sustaining their own values. Rather, they contend that "the delinquent does not necessarily repudiate the imperatives of the dominant normative system, despite his failure to follow them" (p. 669). Noting that "social rules or norms calling for valued behavior seldom if ever take the form of categorical imperatives" (Matza & Sykes 1957, p. 666), Matza (1964) argues that the delinquent interprets conventional values to suit his purposes: "He hears, distorts, and capitalizes on" aspects of mainstream culture that are useful in "negating offense" (p. 91). For example, conventional norms of loyalty are adapted to legitimate participation in peer delinquency. Even carefully crafted rules can be opportunistically reinterpreted. The principal of self-defense is stretched beyond its narrow legal definitions to include "preventative aggression in anticipation of provocation" (p. 80). Similarly, the legal doctrine of home defense is expanded to include the gangster's turf. Rather than radically opposing conventional morality, "The delinquent viewpoint flourishes when it receives sustenance from conventional sources" (p. 83). For Matza and Sykes, the delinquent project involves " 'bending' the dominant normative system—not 'breaking' it" (p. 669).

A study of Mormons and the gambling industry of Nevada also illustrates the adaptability of moral norms. Although it is doctrinally prohibited, Mormons not only tolerate gambling but actively participate. The main justification is, unsurprisingly, practical necessity. In the words of one church leader, "We can't eliminate the only industry in the state which most people work in." This defense is supported by the profession of democratic values. Since Mormons are a small minority in Nevada, one spokesman "believe[s] that the people of Nevada have a right to do as they please" (Galliher & Cross, 1983, p. 77). But Mormons not only tolerate gambling, they are active participants. This is rationalized by maintaining a discrete distance from forbidden activities: "If you are directly involved in gaming, you can't be fully involved in the church. By direct involvement I mean the action itself as a dealer or pit boss or cocktail waitress" (p. 78). The most ingenious, or disingenuous, defense is an eccentric definition of what those involved in gambling are actually doing. Because the house is virtually guaranteed to win, "On the house side it isn't gambling" (p. 82).

The structure of opportunity, then, is the key variable in a number of studies widely regarded as displays of sociological virtuosity. Various social outcomes—especially inequality—and various traits of actors—their aspirations, values, and personality traits—are thought to reflect structures of opportunity. Thus far, I have cited mainly mid-range, empirically based sociology. But this concept of structure is the core of various theoretical approaches. While Bourdieu's thought defies easy characterization, structures of opportunity are central. The controlling power of opportunities over habitus is the main instrument of the reproduction of inequality. Specifically, lowered aspiration, which induces "the educational mortality of the working classes," is a reaction to limited opportunities (Bourdieu & Passeron, 1977, p. 156). Blau (1987) argues that the aim of his emphatically structural approach is "not to account for behavior on the basis of the motives inducing it but . . . on the basis of the external constraints and opportunities" (p. 75). Homans's (1987) behaviorism, which he equates with rational choice theory, also explains individual conduct as constrained by costs and benefits and minimizes the importance of values (p. 75). In *Conflict Sociology* (1975), Collins advises that we "think of people as animals maneuvering for advantage, susceptible to emotional appeals, but steering a self-interested course toward satisfactions and away from dissatisfactions" (p. 60). He summarizes his approach by modeling the actor in a way that highlights the determinative force of opportunities: "The basic premises of the conflict approach are that everyone pursues his own best line of advantage according to the resources available to him and to his competitors" (p. 89). Collins (1986) draws on this perspective to explain the heterogeneity of sociological perspectives. The rapid increase in the number of sociologists in the 1960s packed the profession so densely that individuals needed to differentiate themselves to gain visibility. Sociologists turned to phenomenology, ethnomethodology, existentialism, and so on, not in response to vexing intellectual puzzles, but in search of an ecological niche.

CONCLUSION

My objective in this chapter has been to demonstrate that social structure often means the array of opportunities. This does not encompass all definitions of the term. But no definition *could* do this. I hope I have been persuasive that a synthesis based on this concept of structure is a worthwhile enterprise because without some concrete definition of the term, a synthesis would be impossible. It will be argued later that vagueness about the concept of structure has undermined other synthetic efforts. But before proceeding to this, Chapter 3 will consider some implications of the sociological adoption of an essentially economic notion of social action.

3

The Structural Actor
and Homo Economicus

◆◆◆────────────────────────────────

Having argued that social structure often means the structure of opportunities, my intent now is to highlight the parallels between structural
sociology and economics. This is meant to shock insofar as these disciplines
have conventionally been portrayed as rivals. I then argue that the combination of an economic actor and the concept of social order as structured raises
a serious conceptual problem because the latter cannot be derived from the
former. The chapter concludes with a brief survey of data on the role of opportunity in social inequality and crime.

HOMO SOCIOLOGICUS AND HOMO ECONOMICUS

The individual of structural sociology is curiously empty in that culture
and personality drop away entirely or are reduced to adaptive responses.
In the examples cited, significant differences between men and women,
criminals and the law-abiding, rich and poor individuals and nations,
are denied, and values are considered to be adaptations to circumstances
with little autonomous effect on behavior—in Marx's (1967b) words,
"phantoms formed in the human brain" (p. 14). Structural theories are particularly insistent that behavior is controlled by *present* circumstances
rather than by what Kanter (1977) calls "the dim past." Having no durable

histories, actors are not full persons but fungible mirrors of their situations. Bruce Mayhew (1980) roots his radical structuralism in Mancur Olson's dictum: "from the point of view of social organization all individuals are interchangeable" (p. 349).

Despite disavowals of psychology, there is an implicit, if rudimentary, theory of motivation in structural sociology: individuals are seen as making the best of their situations. As indicated in the last chapter, Wacquant (1993) describes ghetto residents as trying to "improve their lot as best they can" (p. 15), and Anderson (1990) portrays his subjects as aiming for "the best life they can put together in their environment" (p. 135). This is a common assumption in theories of inequality. As Stinchcombe (1986) put it, "A decade ago the status attainment literature assumed that everyone got the highest occupational status they could, so it assumed uniformity of values (although they never discussed what they were assuming)" (p. 140). The claim that aspirations reflect opportunities, and hence that open opportunities will induce higher aspirations, implies this inclination to maximize.

Given the long rivalry between economics and sociology, usually described in terms of a normative versus a rational conception of action, the adoption of a near twin of homo economicus—a self-interested rational maximizer—is surprising. By many accounts, sociology was invented, in large measure, to challenge the economic view of action in which "Culture . . . is strangely absent" (DiMaggio, 1990, p. 115).[1] But Ludwig Von Mises's description of homo economicus suggests the actor of structural sociology: "To buy in the cheapest market and to sell in the dearest is, other things being equal, not conduct which would presuppose any assumptions concerning the actor's motives and morality. It is merely the necessary offshoot of any action under the conditions of market exchange" (quoted in Latsis, 1976, p. 24). This derogation of cultural and psychological factors is part of a programmatic effort in economics to ignore the traits of actors and to explain action situationally—that is, as constrained by costs and rewards. Von Mises's denial of the role of motives and morality is echoed by Popper's (1950) claim that the "'psychological' part of the explanation is very often trivial, as compared with the detailed determination of action by what we may call 'the logic of the situation.' . . . The analysis of the situation . . . is, in fact, *the* method of economic analysis" (pp. 289-290). Popper (1976) believed that situational explanation "can be developed independently of all subjective or psychological ideas" (p. 102).

Insofar as the actors of economics and structural sociology are portrayed as maximizing in light of their costs and benefits and insofar as the role of culture and psychology is minimized, their explanatory paradigms are substantially identical. This has been occasionally noticed. Alan Wolfe (1989) argues that Blau's structuralism "collapses sociology into economics" (p. 193). Alex Callinicos (1985) contends that Giddens has adopted the neoclassical actor: "His is a remarkably economic conception of practice, in which agents use scarce resources to achieve their ends. There seems to me no way of genuinely distinguishing this position from Popper's, whose methodological individualism is precisely a generalization of neo-classical economics's model of rational action" (p. 144).

Bourdieu and Wacquant (1992) allow an array of noneconomic interests in their understanding of action, such as the pursuit of distinction, and at one point claimed that "economism is a form of ethnocentrism" (p. 115, n. 68). But incorporating the pursuit of noneconomic goods does not preclude a fundamentally economic, or calculating, concept of action. Thomas Hobbes' proto-economic understanding of actors (1985) included among various human motivations the "competition for Honour and Dignity" (p. 225), and Gary Becker (1976) insists that "the economic approach is clearly not restricted to material goods and wants" (p. 6). Craig Calhoun (1993) contends that because of his emphasis on strategic calculation, "Bourdieu does indeed share a good deal with Gary Becker and other rational choice theorists" (p. 71). Alexander (1995) also detects Becker's project in Bourdieu's work: "to carry out in full what economics does only partially, and to extend economic calculation to all the goods, material and symbolic, without distinction, that present themselves as rare and worthy of being sought" (p. 157).

Like economists, structural sociologists admit culture only by subordinating it to instrumental purpose. This is how Collins (1975) replicates Popper's derogation of the role of "motives and morality": "Ideals and beliefs likewise are to be explained in terms of the interests which have the resources to make their viewpoint prevail" (p. 61). Blau (1994) is similarly stingy in allowing a role for culture: "Cultural traditions legitimate forms of social organization and structure and thereby perpetuate them" (p. 203).

The bridge between the traditional domain of economics and a more general understanding of social behavior was crossed, most famously, by Becker's (1976) aim to extend economic thinking to "all human behavior" (p. 8). Like structural sociologists, he rejects explanations based on "values and their frequent unexplained shifts, custom and tradition, the compliance somehow induced by social norms" (Becker, 1979, p. 18). This poaching on sociological turf has resulted in explanations nearly indistinguishable from those of structural sociologists. Merton's (1938) theory of crime matches Becker's (1976) argument that "some persons become 'criminals'... not because their basic motivation differs from that of other persons, but because their benefits and costs differ" (p. 46). Both deny that there are significant differences between criminals and the law-abiding and explain their different conduct situationally. Kanter's (1977), Gerson's (1985), and Collins's (1975) understanding of women's participation in the labor force replicates Becker's (1981) argument that the rise in female employment in recent years is mainly due to changes in opportunity—"the growth in the earning power of women" (p. 245)—rather than shifts in values. And Arthur Okun's (1975) critique of the culture of poverty parallels that of structural sociologists. Rejecting the "present-orientedness of the lower class ... as a psychological mystery requiring some deep explanatory structure," he argues that "many of the poor act like there's no tomorrow because their main problem is surviving today. Saving and investment are hardly rational at the cost of survival" (p. 80).

An economic view of action is evident in Porpora's (1989) examples of structure. He cites "job opportunities" as a "causal force that people's material circumstances exert on their behavior" (p. 202). His economism emerges from a neomarxist understanding of actors as "motivated to act in their interests, which are a function of their social position" (p. 208). Such actors are little different from the homines economici of neoclassical theory.

In its more radical versions, network theory purports indifference to the traits of individuals, especially their norms, values, attitudes, and "internalized drives" (Wellman & Berkowitz, 1988, p. 6). All the explanatory action is to be derived from network relations: what counts is not *who* but *where* you are. Wellman (1988) is emphatic that sociology should "treat norms as effects of structural location, not causes" (p. 33). Granovetter (1988) introduces the book series "Structural Analysis in the Social Sciences" rejecting "explanations stressing the causal primacy of abstract concepts such as ideas, values, mental harmonies, and cognitive maps" (n.p.).

But in eliminating the cultural and psychological components of behavior, network theory unavoidably adopts a rational actor: as Elster (1990, p. 243) argues, this is really the only alternative. So networks effectively become networks of opportunities. Indeed, some network theorists have explicitly adopted at least a close kin of homo economicus. Granovetter (1985) allows that "insofar as rational choice arguments are narrowly construed as referring to atomized individuals and economic goals [but see Becker on p. 35], they are inconsistent with the embeddedness position presented here. In a broader formulation of rational choice, however, the two views have much in common" (p. 505). He goes on to argue that "while the assumption of rational action must always be problematic, it is a good working hypothesis that should not be easily abandoned. What looks to the analyst like nonrational behavior may be quite sensible when situational constraints, especially those of embeddedness, are fully appreciated" (p. 506).

This approach is common. According to Nan Lin (1982), network theory "focuses on those instrumental actions that are for the purpose of gaining valued resources" (p. 132). Marsden and Lin (1982) further claim that "Networks are created in part by the self-interested efforts of actors to pursue interests" (p. 175). Here, the refusal to model an actor is traded for a concept of networks as intentionally constructed to maximize benefits. Comparing blockmodeling and market theory, Harrison White (1988) claims that both approaches "assume that all are rationally motivated" (p. 230). He goes on to say that "My approach makes minimal changes in older Marshallian assumptions about behavior in markets" (p. 232), and he concludes by noting that "all of the major technical pieces of the model presented here were already in the economics literature" (p. 255). A clear economism underpins Wellman's (1988) description of network theory as focused on "the ways in which variations in structured access to scarce resources determine opportunities and constraints for behavior" (p. 33). Ronald Burt (1992) suggests that traits commonly attributed to culture are epiphenomenal to opportunity: "I will treat motivation and opportunity as *one and the same*" because "the network is its own explanation of motive" (p. 36). This extravagant claim replicates David Ricardo's belief that "The will is seldom wanting when the power exists" (quoted in Gudeman, 1986, p. 51). Both see motivation as unproblematic: where there is a way, a will can be presumed. In this program, network theory suggests Robert Solow's (1995) description of homo economicus: "Academic economics likes to pretend that economic behavior is pretty much the same, always and everywhere, almost uninfluenced by socially conditioned perceptions and norms" (p. 37).

Insofar as the actors of economics and structural sociology are seen as maximizing in light of their costs and benefits, their explanatory paradigms are substantially identical. Both turn inquiry away from the traits of the actor, such as values and preferences, and toward the environment of rewards. The explicit adoption of economic thinking into sociology has, in recent years, taken the form of rational choice and network theory. But this form of analysis has long been a—largely unacknowledged—staple of structural sociology. Emirbayer and Goodwin (1994) note the tendency among "structuralist instrumentalists," including network theorists, "to 'smuggle' conceptions into their investigations, whether overtly or covertly, from the domain of rational choice theory" (p. 1428).

It is strange to see homo economicus incorporated into the heart of sociology because sociologists have traditionally decried the deficiency of this model. In his critique of Spencer, Durkheim (1964) stressed the non-contractual foundation of social contracts, arguing contracts "only give rise to transient relations and passing associations" (p. 203). While there are important economic strains in his work, Weber (1966) introduced various concepts alien to economics, such as charisma, legitimacy, status groups, ultimate ends, and so forth. His portrayal of most action as traditional and of traditionalism as "almost automatic reaction to habitual stimuli" (p. 116) contrasts sharply with the economic emphasis on calculation. *The Protestant Ethic and the Spirit of Capitalism* (Weber, 1958) was written to show the importance of culture in economic life. Parsons similarly used a critique of economism as a linchpin of his thought.

In contrast to the assumption of economic rationality, most sociologists emphasize the importance of culture to action and social order. According to Lindenberg (1985), "Sociologists in particular have made it part of their tradition to argue against what they take to be the homo economicus" (p. 100). Paul Hirsch et al. (1987) claim that "the most basic difference between economics and sociology concerns their assumptions about human nature. The famous homo economicus is a rational, self-interested, instrumental maximizer with fixed preferences." But according to "one of the standard sociological criticisms of economics," "Actions follow from culturally given values, not just some pure (culture-free) calculation of self-interest" (p. 322). According to Michael Hechter (1983), "The importance of normative obligations, derived from societal membership, for individual action is the central axiom of sociological reasoning, distinguishing it in this respect from the atomism of economics" (p. 161). In contrast to the economic emphasis on incentives, Elster (1979) describes homo sociologicus as "propelled into certain channels by subculture-specific norms and values" (p. 75). This aversion to an economic model of action is expressed in the continuing unpopularity of rational choice theory. A survey of theoretical preferences found that just 6.8% of American sociologists identify with this perspective (Sanderson & Ellis, 1992, p. 33).

And yet, we find homo economicus at the center stage of sociological explanation. In structural sociology, persons are seen, not as bearers of variable cultural orientations, but as rational maximizers with homogeneous and stable preferences. This is why Boudon and Bourricaud (1989) have argued that "looking back, it appears that the contrast between [utilitarianism and the sociological tradition] must not be overemphasized. Perhaps sociology, not as it is often presented but as it really is, is based less on the categorical rejection of the utilitarian paradigm than on the refusal to narrowly define and apply that paradigm" (p. 421).

An economic logic can even be found in the most prominent advocate of cultural determinism. Despite his attacks on economism, Marshall Sahlins argues that Durkheim's functionalism attributed a utilitarian logic to "the social being" in that it "has needs of its own and among them the need for material things." Thus, society "institutes and organizes in order to satisfy these needs an economic activity which is not that of this or that individual or that of the majority of the citizens, but of the nation in its entirety" (Durkheim quoted in Sahlins, 1976, p. 109). Sahlins highlights a paradox in a theorist who relentlessly opposed utilitarian logic: "Durkheim was forced to reproduce at the level of society, viewed as a kind of supersubject, the same economism he refused as constituting [sic] at the level of the individual" (p. 108). Indeed, economism can be found in Durkheim's (1966) view of the individual. The concept of anomie describes persons as driven by an "inextinguishable thirst" (p. 247) little different than "the natural tendency to better our condition" that Adam Smith thought followed us to the grave.

STRUCTURED INEQUALITY AND POWER

Before proceeding to the project of synthesizing cultural and structural explanation, it is worth pausing to consider a conceptual difficulty in combining homo economicus with a portrait of social order as structured. As suggested above, various aspects of social organization bear on the distribution of opportunities. William Julius Wilson (1987) emphasizes the loss of manufacturing jobs and ecological barriers as constraints on the opportunities of ghetto blacks.

But most commonly, the structural concept of opportunity implicates the efforts of groups to exercise power on behalf of their own members and to constrict the opportunities of others. This is particularly evident in the domain where structural explanation is most emphatic: social inequality. In the structural view, dominant groups—such as men and ethnic majorities—attain greater success than those lacking in power—such as women and minorities—because of their social power, not their superior individual ability. The exercise of power is central to Wacquant's (1993) analysis of ghetto pathology. Intentional residential segregation, the disappearance of manufacturing jobs, and other features of the ghetto, emerge from "a mechanism of racial domination and economic oppression" (p. 14) that reflects "the political will of urban elites" (p. 24). Government, according to Wacquant, has "intentionally trapped and packed poor blacks in the poorest all-black areas of the central city" (p. 28).

While Wacquant is not a typical advocate of the structural perspective, his emphasis on power has become a benchmark of structural theories of inequality. Robert Rothman's (1978) definition of "structural inequality" is representative: "those forms of inequality which are allocated on the basis of group membership or position in the social organization of society" (p. 3). In understanding differences between men and women, Kanter (1977) suggests "that what look like sex differences may really be power differences" (p. 202).

Because of this emphasis on power, the homo economicus of structural sociology is combined with a portrait of social order at odds with the "atomism" of neoclassical economics. In the neoclassical view, social order is composed of disaggregated and competing *individuals:* something like a market. But in structural sociology, society is seen as a system of competing *groups* exercising collective power. Men, whites, employers, union members, and others are portrayed as colluding to enhance the prospects of their members. A nearly constitutive claim of structural sociology is that the exercise of power, rather than individual differences, explains social inequality. Bibb and Form (1977) underline this difference between economic and sociological views of inequality: "The human capital model suggests that groups disadvantaged by ethnicity, race, or sex, are denied access because they are unproductive. The structural theory, in contrast, suggests that they are denied access by purposive social action on the part of employers, unions, and other dominant groups" (p. 978).

This conception of society as divided into competing power groups can be found in nearly every structural theory of social inequality. According to Kalleberg (1989), structural explanations of inequality "reject human capital explanations of earnings in favor of more structural theories that emphasized the power of workers to realize their interests in labor market exchanges." This approach is meant to distinguish sociology from economics: "Sociologists have developed their own, distinct, noneconomic, theoretical contributions to explaining economic inequality" (p. 589). A key claim of the "New Structuralist" approach, according to Michael Smith (1990) is that "earnings are profoundly affected by wage earners' bargaining power, especially their collective power" (p. 827). According to Kerckhoff (1984), the study of inequality is largely a study of "allocation"—that is, "the mechanisms by which people are channeled into class positions" (p. 144).

The emphasis on power is, of course, central to conflict theory, which Collins (1975) describes as "the analysis of stratification . . . in terms of a struggle between groups" (p. 435). Giddens (1981) also highlights "structures of domination" and has said, in response to critics, that "a preoccupation with power forms a leading thread" in his thought (p. 3). Porpora's (1989) preferred definition of structure as "systems of human relations among social positions" is mostly about power relations—for example, "patriarchy" and "racial modes of exclusion" (p. 199).

The conception of social order as composed of competing groups is pervasive in network theory. According to Wellman and Berkowitz (1988), structural analysts "argue that political behavior arises out of contentions for resources between interest groups" (p. 10). Granovetter and Tilly (1988) claim that "inequalities associated with labor result from bargaining and conflict among workers, capitalists, households, organizations and governments over the ranking of positions and the sorting of individuals into those ranked positions" (p. 213). In his network account of Canadian stratification, Tepperman (1988) contends that "ethnic groups create and maintain structures within which individual mobility takes place" (p. 406). And Nan Lin (1990) describes Burt's work as focused on "structural actions, actions taken by individuals who are at the same or neighboring positions to protect or promote their common resources and interests" (p. 263). While differential opportunities can have various causes, the interplay of competing groups is, for many sociologists, the chief factor in the structuring of opportunities. One of the recent iterations of this approach—closure theory—studies the techniques, such as the formation of unions and professional associations, occupational licensure, educational requirements, and so on by which groups protect their economic privileges.[2]

The sociological view of inequality as a product of competing groups challenges the economic view of social order as composed of atomized individuals.[3] As Friedland and Robertson (1990) have put it, "Power has no place in neoclassical theory" (p. 7), which is why neoclassical economics has denied the existence of social classes (p. 6). This difference is articulated by Huppes (1976): "The neoclassical paradigm may be characterized as utilitarianistic, rationalistic, and atomistic" while "the sociological concept is altogether different. Man as a social actor belongs to various groups" (pp. 28-29). Neoclassical economists recognize that markets are imperfect: there is "rent seeking" on the part of unions, cartels, and so on. But while economics sees coalitions as exceptional and fragile and individualism as "normal," structural sociology sees group action as ubiquitous and routine: aggregation is the most outstanding feature of social order. Aage Sorensen (1990) challenges the neoclassical "assumption of openness in labor markets" with the claim "that labor markets are in fact structured, full of barriers to movements" (p. 308). This emphasis on collusive power is as central to structural sociology as the concept of the actor as an acultural maximizer.

Society is seen as a kind of sorting machine—sorting on race, gender, class origins, and so on rather than by skill—and social power sets the dials.

This difference in perspective is not entirely theoretical. Karl Polanyi (1957) described capitalism as "disembedding" the economy from the social order—that is, allowing the market to override other institutions and cultural values. In a curious reversal, structural sociology argues that the market is *insufficiently* disembedded because economic inequalities are seen as following the tracks of other societal hierarchies: ethnic, racial, gender, and the like. Structural theories of social inequality are thus meant to be an implicit critique of capitalism insofar as the emphasis on power challenges the openness of markets and hence the fairness of social inequality. Baron and Hannon's (1994) survey of the differences between economics and sociology highlights the latter's understanding of "differences in socioeconomic outcomes" as a product of "systematic inequalities and structures of reproduction" (p. 1119). They tie this emphasis on power and domination to "sociologists' strong ideological egalitarianism and their tendency to attribute unequal outcomes to unfair social advantages" (p. 1118). For structural sociology power, not merit, explains unequal attainment.

By assuming that actors are equally inclined to maximize attainments and that differences in behavior are explained by differences in situational opportunities rather than by values, structural sociology has, for the most part implicitly, adopted the neoclassical actor. But this *economic* conception of the *individual* is paired with a *sociological,* that is, structural, conception of *social order.* Society is conceived as composed of rival "groups"—men and women, whites and blacks, and so on—who exclude or underreward others by exercising power on their own behalf. The leading edge of social structure—that is, the medium through which behavior is controlled—is the array of opportunities. The background from which these opportunities emerge is the power exercised by organized groups. While many aspects of economy and society bear on opportunity, it is characteristically seen as *structured* by power.

THE PROBLEM OF FREE RIDERS

But the combination of opportunity-driven individuals and society ordered into competing groups is problematic because it is difficult to derive cohesive groups from rational maximizers. This is the foundation of Durkheim's argument, reiterated by Parsons, that contract theory cannot solve the problem of social order because fidelity to contracts must be supported by normative consensus. There is a conceptual tie between the neoclassical view of the actor as a utility maximizer and the portrait of social order as disaggregated. The difficulty of deriving collective action, or "distributive coalitions," from economic actors is articulated in Mancur Olson's (1968) contention that maximizing individuals will not, except under specific conditions, act to secure "public goods": advantages from which noncontributors cannot be excluded. There are costs involved in creating, for example, clean air, and so the rational choice for homo economicus is to free ride on others' efforts. Hence, a self-interested worker will not contribute to the good of the working class even if he would benefit from its success. Paradoxically, shared interests do not lead to collective action. In the language of the prisoner's dilemma, the defecting option wins.

The free rider problem can be overcome, Olson argues, only under certain conditions. For one, the number of cooperators must be small enough so that an individual contribution will make a worthwhile difference. For example, if four soldiers are defending a position, the effort of each can be decisive. But if there are, say, four thousand defenders, the rational choice is cowardice. This holds even for the soldier who prefers that his side win because the contribution of each individual to that outcome is negligible. Hence, the personal benefits of contributing, by fighting bravely, are unlikely to exceed the cost of increased risk. With large numbers, rational individuals will contribute only if there are enforcement mechanisms—that is, ways of sanctioning noncontributors. But this can work only when individual contributions are visible and sanctions can be applied: "Only with the ability to monitor and sanction will solidarity be possible" (Turner, 1992, p. 315). While the military has ways to ensure contribution, "men" or "the capitalist class" do not. Furthermore, this solution only postpones the problem of collective action in that we must explain why some will accept the costs of sanctioning defectors. Sanctioners can be rewarded for their efforts. But the creation of resources to be used as rewards reintroduces the problem of collective action: it is not rational for a man to contribute to the collective good of "men."

Because it is difficult to meet the conditions of collective action, temptations to defect render alliances of rational egoists unstable. Even Adam Smith's (1976a) concern that "People of the same trade seldom meet together but the conversation ends in a conspiracy against the public, or in some diversion to raise prices" (p. 284) was, in this view, unwarranted in that each party to such agreements would be tempted to undercut rivals for personal benefit. This problem has subverted the efforts of OPEC to control oil prices because when restricted production raises the price, individual members are tempted to produce more than their designated share. This logic leads Michael Hechter (1990) to conclude that "one of the firmest conclusions of rational choice is that whereas the production of private goods is hardly problematic, in general public goods will not be produced at optimal levels, if they are produced at all" (p. 17).

It is difficult to see how structural theorists can reconcile two foundational claims of the perspective: an essentially neoclassical view of actors and the conception of opportunity as structured by competing power groups. Rational maximizers are, by definition, neither loyal nor prejudiced and hence are not inclined to sacrifice for the well-being of others. The problem, or oxymoron, of "collective instrumentalism" troubles various sociological literatures. Jean Cohen (1985) has highlighted the problem of deriving collective action from instrumental actors in "resource mobilization" theory. A central goal of Charles Tilly, Mayer Zald, and others is to challenge the "crowd" understanding of collective action as irrational outbursts. In contrast, "all versions of the resource-mobilization approach analyze collective action in terms of the logic of strategic interaction and cost-benefit calculations" (Cohen, 1985, p. 675). Furthermore, the role of values, culture, and ideology is scanted in favor of instrumental strategizing. While the free rider problem has been recognized in this school, Cohen argues that Parsons's critique of utilitarianism—the impossibility of deriving group solidarity from instrumental actors—has not been overcome: "an analytical perspective that focuses on strategic-instrumental action cannot provide an answer to the question of the origin and logic of group solidarity" (p. 677). Cohen is emphatic that solidarity cannot be an add-on to resource mobilization: "Only if one switches to a model of analysis which also looks at collective interaction from a nonstrategic standpoint can one find a solution to the free-rider problem" (p. 687).

The problem of "collective instrumentalism" is emphasized by Dennis Wrong's (1994) argument that the contemporary opposition between "consensus" and "conflict" theory is confounded because "the very existence of organized groups mobilized for conflicts indicates the achievement of consensus within them, so conflict and consensus can hardly be regarded as absolute contraries" (p. 209). He also notes that the individualism of Hobbesian "conflict theory" is decisively different from Marxian notions of *collective* conflict in that the latter presumes class solidarity, a concept that finds no foothold in Hobbes's (1985) belief that in the state of nature "every man is Enemy to every man" (p. 186). Conflict theorists have also failed to appreciate the problem Olson (1968) poses for their effort to combine an instrumental model of individual action with the idea of society as divided into competing groups.

In contrast, Allen Buchanan (1980) and Gordon Tullock (1971) have pointed out the difficulty of deriving a public good, like revolution, from the instrumental motivations of individual workers. Because individual contributions are unlikely to affect the outcome, a rational worker, even believing that revolution will provide benefits, would sit it out until the shooting stops rather than run the risks of participation. Whether the revolution succeeds or fails, defection, as in the prisoner's dilemma, is the maximizing option.[4]

Despite numerous efforts, confidence that collective action can be derived from instrumental individuals, except under narrow circumstances, has been elusive. The strategy of selective incentives, such as unions that provide cheap life insurance as a "side payment," is limited because an organization will not survive if individuals contribute to collective goods merely for selective benefits: costly side payments allow no "profit" for the organization to devote to collective goods. Instrumental cooperation based on Rapoport and Chammah's (1965) "tit for tat" strategy, or reciprocal altruism, can work only for sustained interactions in which behavior can be monitored and sanctioned. Another alternative, the Leviathan solution, involves a coercive agent who can act to control free riding. But as suggested above, this presumes that the collective action problem has already been solved in the creation of an authority with the resources to exert control. Furthermore, we must explain why the authorities do not turn their power and resources to their own benefit.

Some theorists believe that even a one-shot prisoner's dilemma can be solved by rational actors. Others have concluded that individualistic rationality rarely leads to cooperation and cite the substantial literature—historical, anthropological, and experimental—showing that persons are firmly gripped by norms of duty, fairness, and so forth that dictate cooperation when self-interest would motivate defection. Devoted advocates of rational choice theory, such as James Coleman (1990, chaps. 9-11), argue that norms that discourage free riding can be explained in rational choice terms. In contrast, Jon Elster (1989a) concludes that "the enforcement of social norms is not in general individually rational" (p. 101). A key difficulty in explaining norms via rational choice analysis is to show that self-interested actors will contribute to their enforcement. Even if another's compliance with a norm benefits an individual, this is a public good, and because enforcement efforts are usually costly, the self-interested choice is to free ride on others' enforcement efforts. A willingness to sanction can be based on fear of sanctions. But to avoid an infinite regress, "Some sanctions must be performed for motives other than the fear of being sanctioned" (p. 133). This is why Elster doubts that "many cases of successful collective action can be explained by stipulating selfish rationality alone" (p. 186).

It is not possible here to review this vast and intricate literature or to show conclusively that the problem of collective action resists a rational choice solution. But this is not required in order to see that combining homo economicus with a social order dominated by distributive coalitions confounds structural sociology. For even if it can be shown that homines economici can sustain collective action under certain conditions, such demonstrations cannot explain the *ubiquity* of distributive coalitions that structural sociologists see at the heart of social order. The problem is especially acute for the diffuse and amorphous "groups" (or pseudogroups) such as "men" and "workers" of structural sociology. A system of monitoring and sanctioning that could constrain free riding among "capitalists" or "white people" through rational choice mechanisms is unimaginable.

There is a good deal of debate on who, if anyone, profits from discrimination: employers, majority workers, and so on (see Reich, 1994). But however this debate is resolved, the problem of explaining why *individuals* contribute to securing alleged group advantages remains. As Milton Friedman (1982, chap. 7) argues, the employer who breaks ranks with discriminatory practices can benefit by drawing on an underpaid pool of labor. Thus, even maximal success in resolving collective action problems in rational choice terms would not sustain the structural understanding of social order as composed of competing groups that are composed of maximizing individuals.

The cavalier combination of homo economicus with the idea of structured inequality stands in contrast to the respect others have shown the problem of collective action, which Coleman (1986) characterizes as "this most theoretically intractable realm of social phenomena" (p. 2). He describes the problem of "how individuals, each acting in his own self-interest, can nevertheless make collective decisions, function as an ongoing society, and survive together without a 'war of all against all' " as "the most difficult of all intellectual problems in the functioning of a society" (p. 318). Because of these difficulties, Michael Smith (1990), in a critique of structural theories of inequality, believes that "no modern writer on the organization of interest groups would neglect the free rider problem" (p. 837, n. 12). But this problem is routinely slighted, even ignored, in structural sociology. Granovetter (1981) criticizes economists' understanding of income inequality for an insufficient attention to "the exercise of social power" (p. 37). He also considers obsolete their conception of sociology as focused on the role of values in behavior, contending that post-Parsonian sociology has incorporated the insights of rational choice theory. But he does not engage the tension between adopting rational choice and conceiving "the organization of interest groups" (p. 36) as the key to income inequality.

The problem of deriving collective action from homo economicus has been masked by the tendency of actors to use the "rhetoric of reason" to legitimate nonutilitarian action. In contemporary society, as Sahlins puts (1976) it, "Rationality is our rationalization" (p. 72). There is prestige in appearing to be calculating and this can mislead social science interpretation. For example, workers may cite instrumental motives—"immigrants are taking our jobs"—to sustain exclusionary alliances that are held together by other sorts of motives, such as xenophobia or racism. The readiness of social science to accept such rhetoric as explanatory is enhanced by the fact that exclusionary alliances may indeed result in material benefits. But because of the advantages of free riding, these benefits cannot explain the *individual* decision to contribute. Environmental activists may personally benefit from cleaner air and so on, but this cannot explain their choice to contribute rather than free ride.

In contrast to the instrumentalism of much of his work, Collins (1993) has argued that the display of solidarity can even be more important to striking workers than higher wages and that the latter can even be subordinate to the former: "Material interest itself becomes a collective symbol of group solidarity" (p. 223). But he does not appreciate the implications of this insight for his instrumentalist theory of action. Indeed, the role of noninstrumental motives can be amply documented; workers, especially older ones, often fail to recoup the costs of lengthy strikes. An extreme example of the dominance of extra-rational motives in seemingly instrumental action is the self-immolation of several workers during the Korean labor conflicts of the 1980s—in pursuit of better wages and working conditions! A particularly bizarre use of the rhetoric of reason is the claim of some Nazi ideologists that the mass extermination of millions of productive human beings made economic sense. Omer Bartov (1999) notes that the "ethnocrats" of the SS devised "ingenious arguments to justify killing as an economically sound means to prevent overpopulation and to bring about a modernization of the economy and a Germanization of the Reich's Lebensraum in the East." But of course, "There can be no doubt that, from the standpoint of the German war effort, this was a disastrous decision" (p. 51).

It is easy to imagine a man acting on behalf of men, or workers sacrificing for the working class, by adding norms of loyalty, a sense of fairness, and so forth. Interestingly, extra-rational explanations are selectively deployed by structural sociologists. Kanter (1977) portrays women as responding rationally to restricted opportunity and scoffs at explanations based on "deep-seated" personality traits. But male hostility toward women is interpreted in rather different terms: "Freud wrote of the need for men to handle women's sexuality by envisioning them either as 'madonnas' or 'whores' " (p. 233). To explain men's exclusion of women she adduces "group solidarity" (p. 222). Similarly, although Gerson (1985) explains women's choices in terms of their opportunities, she attributes *restrictions* on women's opportunities to the traditionalist values of men, families, and employers. While explaining crime in terms of blocked opportunity, Merton (1938) offers no "rational" reason for class and ethnic-based exclusion from the legitimate opportunity structure. Wilson and O'Sullivan (1988) explain the behavior of underclass blacks as adaptive, but elsewhere they reject rational choice explanation: "The extensive research on racism indicates the determinative impact of ideology in fostering group preferences in situations where greater benefits would be secured from intergroup alliances" (p. 229).

The ad hoc introduction of extra-rational motives to explain restrictions on opportunity is a common "solution" to the problem of deriving exclusionary alliances from economic actors. In a study of religious affiliation and choice of academic field, Debra Friedman (1983), a rational choice theorist, concludes that structural factors—such as group size, the time of entrance into academia, and the growth of academic fields—fully explain differences in areas of specialization. The values of different religious groups, such as a Catholic affinity for the humanities or a Jewish preference for social science, are dismissed as far less significant than the opportunity structure the group faces. But Friedman also acknowledges that the structure of opportunities that control occupational choice can have extra-rational roots: "Jews and Catholics entered academia at a later time than Protestants due in part to discrimination in academia against individuals on the basis of religion" (p. 100). While Friedman purports to rely "solely on an analysis of external constraints" (p. 112), she claims that the structure of opportunity that explains choice of profession emerges from irrational collective action. Similarly, while adopting rational choice, Granovetter and Tilly (1988) cite "the collective action of organized groups" (p. 190) as the main dynamic of social inequality.

I have not undertaken the fool's errand of denying that distributive coalitions exclude outsiders.[5] Collective power often controls opportunity by excluding outsiders who, in turn, often succeed in collectively challenging such coalitions. Even Becker (1976) acknowledges that some employers have a "taste for discrimination" (p. 19) that they can indulge under conditions of limited competition. Structural theorists are persuasive that various groups collude to restrict the opportunities of others. But they cannot, in most cases, account for these processes with the model of the actor they have adopted. This problem is often resolved by an ad hoc introduction of nonrational motivations, such as prejudice or loyalty. The result is a dualistic view in which "excluders" are modeled with motivations fundamentally different from the excluded. (The contradictory views of dominant groups and the dominated will be examined in Chapter 9.)

THE NEW ECONOMICS

It is curious that sociologists have adopted an extreme, if inconsistent, economism that is now widely challenged within economics. For example, Herb Simons (1987) recommends that "we stop debating whether a theory of substantive rationality and the assumption of utility maximization provides a sufficient base for explaining and predicting human behavior. The evidence is overwhelming that they do not" (p. 39). As Friedland and Robertson (1990) put it, "It seems perverse that economics is tightening its grip on other branches of social science at a time when an increasing number of economists are themselves questioning its theoretical adequacy" (p. 7).

A major theme in the new economics has been doubts about scanting the role of culture in economic conduct. Amartya Sen (see especially 1977) advocates the central role of moral, personal, and political commitments in human conduct, and many economists agree. While neoclassical economists treat strictly rational choice explanations as scholarly trophies, only the most extreme believe that culture and personality are otiose, or merely adaptive tools. Even Gary Becker, "the great neoclassical dogmatist" (Friedland & Robertson, 1990, p. 23), after pushing economic analysis as far as he can, concedes that "social norms" can play a role in explanation (Becker, 1979, p. 18) and agrees that "how preferences have become what they are, and their perhaps slow evolution over time, [is] obviously relevant in predicting and understanding behavior" (p. 19). Becker expands explanatory options considerably (and runs the risk of tautology) by allowing a role for "psychic costs" (p. 11). The economism of structural sociology is a case of identifying with an increasingly chimerical enemy.

Michael McPherson (1984) argues that what is missing from economics is just those factors that structural sociology aims to purge: "economists have recognized that morality plays a central role within the economy and that the moral ideas of the participants in the economy themselves—their willingness to restrain their pursuit of self-interest within morally prescribed limits—is essential to normal economic functioning" (p. 71). Indeed, the "new economics" is not all that new. Adam Smith, the "other" Adam Smith (1976b) of *The Theory of Moral Sentiments,* was emphatic about the fundamentally social nature of man: "Nature, when she formed man for society, endowed him with an original desire to please, and an original aversion to offend his brethren.... She rendered their approbation most flattering and most agreeable to him for its own sake; and their disapprobation most mortifying and most offensive" (quoted in Robinson, 1962, p. 8). Sociological critiques of atomism and materialism in economics have often been addressed to straw figures.[6]

I have argued that the power of distributive coalitions to restrict opportunity cannot emerge from a Hobbesian war of all against all: structured inequality requires collective action, which in turn requires norms of loyalty. As Wrong (1994) puts it, "Conflict groups depend on some degree of underlying solidarity uniting their members" (p. 183). The importance of cultural factors has been recognized by some economists as essential to solving the free rider problem. In contrast to Olson's (1982) strained efforts to explain how societies can be overwhelmed by distributive coalitions in rational choice terms, Douglass North (1984) argues that "many distributive coalitions got their start as 'productive' institutions, or because of ideological conviction that overcame initial free riding" (p. 39) and concludes that "it is necessary to construct a theory of ideology to resolve the free rider problem" (North, 1986, p. 258). In out-economizing economists, structural sociologists have not only adopted an increasingly challenged model of individual action; they have cut the ground from under their conception of social order. Insofar as distributive coalitions require nonopportunistic behavior, the very idea of structured opportunity contradicts the obsolete economism of the structural concept of the actor.

ADDENDUM ON STRUCTURAL EXPLANATION: THE EVIDENCE

Before proceeding to the theoretical issues that are the main focus of this book, it is worth considering the empirical validity of structural explanation. Perhaps the contradiction between the conception of social order as structured by collective power and the adoption of homo economicus is a harmless theoretical anomaly. But some of the most well-elaborated fields of structural explanation suggest that the adoption of homo economicus impedes substantive work. It is not easy to show this in a systematic way. An evaluation of the power of structures of opportunity to explain crime, status attainment, the progress of nations, personality formation, and so on would be a daunting undertaking. But it can be suggested that structured opportunity is not the decisive factor it is often thought to be. There are two main issues at stake. The first is the validity of the claim that social order is controlled by collective power. The second, related, claim is that individual conduct is mainly guided, not by cultural training, but by the availability of opportunities.

There are many ways these claims can be challenged. The success of various ethnic groups raises doubts about both the irrelevance of culture to attainment and the argument that power controls opportunity. Fifty years ago Japanese-Americans were, arguably, the *least* powerful group in America: they were unable to prevent the mass imprisonment of innocents. But within a generation, and with scant involvement in politics, they were near the top of the income and status hierarchy (Sowell, 1983, p. 187) with family incomes averaging 30% more than white families (O'Neill, 1987, p. 175). Jewish Americans, mostly the sons and grandsons of immigrants, are just 2% of the population but about 23% of America's wealthiest 400 individuals are Jewish (Feagin, 1989, p. 159). While more politically engaged than the Japanese, their rapid assent was not a product of politics. According to Lieberson (1980, p. 86), Jewish political representation was, until recently, proportionate to their numbers in the population. There are many other examples of politically powerless but upwardly mobile ethnic groups. Light and Bonacich (1988) found that Korean immigrants have prospered in impoverished areas of Los Angeles. Indeed, Thomas Sowell (1983) suggests that political involvement may work *against* economic progress. Despite their remarkable success in big city politics, "As late as 1890, 42% of all Irish Americans were servants." While 50 of 110 presidents of the AFL unions were of Irish ancestry, they were rarely businessmen (p. 70, 71).

The differential success of ethnic groups in the world economy similarly challenges the claim of Wallerstein and others that power, not culture, conditions development. P. T. Bauer (1979) and David Landes (1998) show that some ethnic groups flourish even when politically and culturally repressed. Perhaps the most striking contemporary example is the Chinese of Southeast Asia. Small and often ruthlessly persecuted minorities, their economic dominance is remarkable. Gordon Redding (1993) finds that Chinese entrepreneurs have an uncanny ability to succeed almost anywhere, including places where governments and populations sharply, and at times brutally, restrict their legal rights and economic opportunities. For example, although making up only about 2% of the population of Indonesia, "The Chinese own, at the very least, 70%–75% of private domestic capital" (p. 25). This success is replicated throughout Southeast Asia.

STRUCTURED INEQUALITY

Perhaps the most apposite venue in which to evaluate structural explanation is the field of status attainment. Structural theorists of inequality typically cite examples in which the "human capital" of, for example, women or minorities seems to be underrewarded in labor markets, which is taken to be evidence that social inequality is structured by the power of dominant groups. A major defect of such studies is that they usually rely on limited measures of human capital: mainly years of education and work experience. When additional controls are applied, pay gaps narrow dramatically.[7] Most important, just as examples of exceptional minorities are of uncertain significance, selected examples of underrewarded groups cannot support the more general claim that inequality is controlled by power. This requires more comprehensive studies of status attainment.

As noted earlier, in contrast to the claim of functionalism and human capital theory that "placement is a reflection of the worker's basic value to the system" (Beck et al., 1978, p. 705), structural theorists argue that inequality is allocated by social power: "Rather than differential attainment being seen as due to variations in learned motives and skills, as in a socialization model, an allocation model views attainment as due to the application of structural limitations and selection criteria" (Kerckhoff, 1984, p. 143). The claim that opportunity is structured by the power of dominant groups often underpins a critique of capitalism, which, it is implied, does not and, perhaps, cannot guarantee "free entry"—that is, unrestricted access to economic opportunities. Challenging "liberal laissez faire ideology" (p. 129), Pease et al., describe "structural realism" as stressing "socially created arrangements that maintain economic, political and social inequality" (p. 128). Emphasizing the reproduction of inequality across generations, Bourdieu and Wacquant (1992) challenge "the enduring myth of America as the paradise of social mobility" (p. 78). The structural emphasis on group power is also meant to challenge the functionalist claim that inequality reflects an individual's value to society: "It is the society that does the allocation of property, and it proceeds to allocate and distribute, according to the sentiments it has for the individual and moved too, by the way it calculates the value of his services" (Durkheim, 1958, p. 219). In contrast to both functionalist and market approaches, Baron and Hannon (1994) describe sociologists as "more likely to trace large observed differences in labor market outcomes between groups (defined by gender, race/ethnicity, and so forth) to structural constraints on the demand side" (p. 1120).

But the claim that rewards are allocated by group power is undermined by numerous studies that find high levels of intergenerational social mobility. This is an appropriate test of the structuralist thesis because if social inequality is determined by power rather than skills, it would likely result in intergenerational continuity: guaranteeing the success of their children would presumably be a high priority for the powerful. A landmark study in this literature is Blau and Duncan's (1967) *The American Occupational Structure,* which found that the correlation between a father's and son's occupational status was about .40. That is, just 16% of the variation in son's status is explained by father's status. This means that if all we knew about a man was his father's status, we could predict his occupational status only 16% better than if we knew nothing about him. In *Inequality,* Christopher Jencks (1972, p. 148) described the continuity of status with this illustration: if two fathers differ in occupational status by 20 points (on a 100-point) scale, their sons will, on average, differ by 10 points. Because there is so much dispersion between generations, Jencks (1979) concluded in *Who Gets Ahead?* that brothers "display about 75 percent of the inequality in occupational status of unrelated individuals" (p. 297). That is, most of the range of status inequality in the American occupational structure can be found between children of the same family.

When the focus is shifted to income, the results are more striking. In *Who Gets Ahead?* Jencks estimated that all family background variables combined explain about 48% of the variation in son's occupational status but only 15% to 35% of the variation in incomes (p. 81). The disparity in income between individuals born in the same family is revealed by the finding that the brothers of men earning twice the average typically earn 1.15 to 1.35 more than average (p. 217). Startlingly, Jencks (1973) claims that there is "almost as much income inequality among people born in the same circumstances . . . as in the larger population" (p. 151; see also p. 149). In his later book, Jencks (1979) found that the differences in brother's income are on average 84% to 89% of those found between random pairs of men (p. 299). Jencks (1992) has recently affirmed the validity of these findings:

> Most subsequent studies suggested that family background explained more of the variation in mature men's incomes than Duncan's initial study of twenty-five- to thirty-four-year-olds had, but no national survey suggested that family background explained more than a fifth of the variation in annual income at any age. (p. 238)

Currently, the most direct study of social mobility is the University of Michigan's Panel Survey on Income Dynamics. Sidestepping the daunting problems of measuring intergenerational mobility, this study has followed the lives of 5,000 American families since 1968, and the results challenge the structural portrait of inequality. The most striking contradiction to the structural thesis is the remarkable level of "churning"—that is, movement between income quintiles. Only 5% of those who were in the bottom fifth of earners in 1975 were still there in 1991. A majority of them made it to the top three-fifths of the income distribution and almost 30% of the bottom fifth earners entered the top fifth by 1991 (Cox & Alm, 1999, p. 73). This finding must be qualified because much of the movement represents the gains of recent college graduates. But the Michigan study has consistently revealed substantial dynamism in social inequality.

The mobility process has, in recent years, incorporated historically excluded groups. It is easily shown that the opportunities of minorities and women have been subject to severe structural constraints. But these barriers have been dissolving. This is not the place to examine the vast and complicated literature on this topic, but the change is undeniable. A turning point on this issue was William J. Wilson's (1987) finding that

> while the socioeconomic status of the most disadvantaged members of the minority population has deteriorated rapidly since 1979, that of the advantaged members has significantly improved. . . . The number of blacks in professional, technical, managerial, and administrative positions increased by 57 percent . . . from 1973 to 1982, while the number of whites in such positions increased by only 36 percent. (p. 109)

The rate of ascent of blacks into the middle class continues to outpace that of whites. In 1970 1.5% of black households earned over $75,000. By 1990, this figure more than doubled to 3.8%. While of course a greater percentage of white households earn this much, their *rate* of increase in this period was slower, moving from 6.1% to 10.4% (Hurst, 1995, p. 20). The pace of this change quickly renders data obsolete. In the 1995 edition of the Hurst book (p. 21), married-couple black families earned 80% of similar white families: in the 1998 edition this figure had climbed to 89% (p. 24). Indeed, with certain variables controlled, some argue that there is little evidence of ongoing racial discrimination. June O'Neill (1987) found that in 1980 college-educated black males outside the South earned 97% of their white counterparts. She also cites findings that "holding schooling, region, and other factors constant, there were no differences in earnings between Chinese-Americans and white men" and that "after adjusting for ability to speak and use English in addition to schooling . . . there was no significant difference between the earnings of Hispanics and white non-Hispanics in the U.S." (pp. 179-180).

The progress of women has also been striking. Between 1973 and 1996 the median earnings of full-time women workers rose from about $20,000 to about $24,000; during the same period the median earnings of men *fell* from about $38,000 to about $32,000 (Marger, 1999, p. 313). In 1970, only 13% of Ph.D.s went to women. In 1995, the figure was 40%. Female law school graduates went from 5% to 45% and medical degrees increased from 8% to 38% (Furchtgott-Roth & Stolba, 1996, pp. 18-20).

Overall, the wage gap between men and women has gone from the 59 cents cited by feminists in the 1960s to 75 cents today. But because many crucial variables are uncontrolled, this figure does not fully capture the change. The "adjusted wage gap"—adjusted for age, occupation, experience, education, and time in the workforce is considerably narrower. For example, a study of men and women employed by the federal government found that among college graduates under the age of 35, about 70% of the gap could be explained by degree level, years of government experience, and college major, leaving an unexplained gap of 5% (O'Neill, 1987, p. 185).

Because of the rapid changes in recent years, it is important to control for age. According to Furchtgott-Roth and Stolba (1999, p. 14), younger women, whose work experience began under the new gender regime, are approaching parity: women aged 16 to 29 rose from 77% to 92% of men between 1974 and 1993, a figure that is still not controlled for the various differences between men and women, such as college major and so on. While this gap will likely grow later in the life cycle, largely because of work interruptions for child rearing, women between the ages of 27 and 33 with no children now earn 98% of men (p. 14).

An important issue in mobility studies is the mechanisms through which family background affects occupational attainment, for it is here that the role of culture in attainment emerges. Jencks (1979, p. 82) has concluded that half the background effect on son's occupational attainment is via the impact of family on cognitive skills and education. Gregory Duncan (1984) similarly finds that "parental status operates to affect children's status primarily by determining the level of education of the child" (p. 114). This figure is open to interpretation since—for example, genetic endowment, family wealth, or socialization could be involved. But many researchers argue that money has relatively little to do with the family impact on education and that training is decisive. Otto and Haller (1979) of the "Wisconsin School" contend that "parental SESs [socioeconomic status] are transmitted to sons by way of social psychological mechanisms" (p. 888). Bielby (1980) estimates that one-third of the occupational status and perhaps half of the earnings advantage shared by brothers is due to "subtle ways that are largely unrelated to parent's standing in occupational or social class hierarchies" (p. 755). In a review of this literature, Richard Campbell (1983) concluded that "no study to date has seriously challenged the basic empirical findings of the Wisconsin model" (p. 49).

The role of education in attainment further challenges the structural perspective. In an influential book, Bowles and Gintis (1976) argued that by favoring the cultural resources of the privileged, schools are mainly transmitters of extant inequalities. This claim is eroded by the finding cited above that parental income has little to do with their ability to support their children's success in school. It is further challenged by Blau and Duncan's (1967) finding that educational credentials overwhelm the effect of background. That is, if two men have acquired equal education, the continuing influence of differences in their fathers' status is small: "The number of years of school a man finishes accounts for twice as much of the variation in his career prospects as does his father's occupational status" (Jencks, 1979,

p. 19). As Kahl and Gilbert (1987) put it, "Once young men get into college . . . the payoff of higher education is almost as great for those from poorer families as it is for others" (p. 183).

Insofar as educational attainment largely controls status attainment and is mainly determined by parental influences other than money, the structuralist claim that culture has little effect on attainment is challenged. The decisive role of values in learning can be further illustrated by the role of school funding on education. The Coleman Report (1966) found that the resources devoted to school, however they are deployed, have little effect on children's learning. In Coleman's view, family background was far more decisive. Coleman (1974) later reiterated his belief that

> those resources under the control of the school were considerably less important than those which were intrinsic to the child's family background. That is, the resources brought to education from the home were considerably more important for achievement than those provided by the schools.(p. 750)

Coleman also believes that "parental inputs" have little to do with money. They consist in "the most intimate elements of a student's environment: the gentle encouragement of his mother, the painstaking hours that parents—some parents—spend in nurturing reading and spelling skills, the discussions that take place in some homes which stretch the child's mind" (p. 751).

Summarizing research on educational attainment, Bielby (1981) concluded that "none of the teacher behaviors and administrative procedures examined so far contributes to the reproduction of inequality across generations" (p. 11). Instead of showing that schools advantage the economically privileged, research generally finds that "the link between social origins and schooling appears due to differences between families in the degree to which they provide a social environment that emphasizes schooling and inequalities among families in the resources that affect a child's performance on standardized tests" (p. 11). The educational advantage of the children of the wealthy is mainly due to the values their parents encourage, not their incomes.

Most recent research supports these findings. Sanford Dornbusch et. al (1996) replicated Coleman's findings that school funding has little to do with student performance. Erik Hanushek (1996) surveyed hundreds of

studies and found that most of them showed little or no relationship between student performance and per-pupil spending, teacher salaries, and
the like. Indeed, almost as many studies found the relationship to be negative as positive. Critics of this finding, like Wenglinsky (1997) and Hedges
and Greenwald (1996) find only small benefits from increased spending.
In a recent study of factors that affect the school performance of poor
children, Susan Mayer (1997) found that, contrary to her expectations, the
most important contributions parents make to learning, such as reading
to their children, visiting museums and libraries, and so on, have little to
do with wealth.

As indicated earlier, the structural emphasis on the role of power in inequality challenges the openness of capitalist economies, which has been
seen as one of its outstanding features. Joseph Schumpeter (1976) argued
that in contrast to traditional economies, "The process of 'Creative Destruction' is the essential fact about capitalism" (p. 83). In this view, relent-
less competition and innovation causes a constant churning in the economy
and society at large. The structural view of social inequality challenges this
emphasis on dynamism and instability by claiming that power entrenches
privilege. But studies of social mobility show that there is considerable
churning over time. This process takes place at the highest level of the economy. The Forbes 400, the wealthiest 400 Americans, are not immune: "The
fortunes of 45 percent of the listees were 'mostly inherited,' fourteen percent were built with the help of a significant inheritance, and the remaining
41 percent can be described as self-made" (Kahl & Gilbert, 1987, p. 220).
A study of top executives in large corporations found that only 10% came
from wealthy families, fewer than half had fathers who were managers or
professionals, and 23% came from lower-class backgrounds (Lipset, 1976,
p. 319). Schumpeter's understanding of capitalism is further confirmed by
evidence that "creative destruction" affects America's corporate giants and
at an accelerating rate:

> Of today's 100 largest public companies, only five ranked among the top 100 of
> 1917. Half of the firms in the top 100 are newcomers over just the past two de-
> cades. Although flux is a constant for the economy, the process seems to be tak-
> ing place faster. In the 60 years after 1917, it took an average of 30 years to re-
> place half of the companies in the top 100. Between 1977 and 1998, it took an
> average of 12 years. (Cox & Alm, 1999, p. 123)

As stated earlier, I do not mean to deny that groups collude to advantage their own members and exclude others. Rather, I have argued that this cannot be explained without introducing norms of solidarity or some other extra-rational motives. I have also argued that studies of social mobility show that exclusionary alliances are only partially and temporarily successful. The process of "creative destruction"—often aided by collective efforts on the part of the excluded—tends over time to erode structural barriers and limit the reproduction of social inequality. While "snapshot" studies provide evidence of exclusionary alliances, a dynamic view reveals that their success is more limited than structural theories allow.

CRIME AND OPPORTUNITY

Since the concept of structured opportunity has played a central role in sociological explanations of crime, it is worthwhile considering the strength of this relationship. This can be done conveniently by examining the correlation between unemployment, a rough measure of opportunity, and crime. Surprisingly, this relationship turns out to be slight. Charting homicide, probably the most accurately measured crime, reveals two peaks. The first came in 1933, representing the crest of a wave that began in 1905, continued through the prosperous 1920s, and then began to *decline* in 1934 as the Great Depression was deepening. Between 1933 and 1940, the murder rate dropped nearly 40%. Rates of property crimes reveal a similar pattern (Brantingham & Brantingham, 1984, pp. 189-190).

Between 1940 and 1960, the homicide rate remained relatively stable. In the mid-1960s, a sharp increase began that peaked in 1974 when the murder rate was double that of the late 1950s and far higher than it had been in the depths of the Great Depression (Brantingham & Brantingham, 1984, pp. 190, 122). Between 1963 and 1973, homicides in New York City tripled. Again, property thefts and most other forms of crime followed a similar pattern. Robbery in the United States increased from a rate of 60 per 100,000 in 1960 to 243 per 100,000 in 1980 (p. 124). The cause of this remarkable increase was not unemployment. In 1961, the unemployment rate was 6.6% and the Index crime rate was 1.9 per 1,000. By 1969 unemployment had dropped to 3.4% while the Index rate nearly doubled to 3.7 per 1,000 (Freeman, 1983, p. 96). The recession between 1980 and 1982 was accompanied by a small but clearly discernable drop in crime; as the economy revived, the crime rate increased (Himmelfarb, 1994, p. 63). Christopher Jencks (1992) arrays these relationships persuasively:

> Between 1962-1963 and 1968-1969 the black male teenage unemployment rate fell from 24.7 to 21.8%, and the white teenage male rate fell from 14.8 to 10.1%. Nevertheless, the murder rate rose by half. This pattern was reversed in the early 1980s. Between 1979 and 1983 teenage unemployment rose by almost half among both blacks and whites, but the murder rate fell by a sixth. (p. 117)

The recent decline in crime in New York City—homicide fell almost 75% between 1994 and 1999—far outstrips the decline in unemployment.

The weak relationship between crime and unemployment has been well documented. A review of several studies by Thomas Orsagh (1980) concluded that "unemployment may affect the crime rate, but even if it does, its general effect is too slight to be measured" (p. 183). Another survey by Richard Freeman (1983) concluded that the relationship is so weak that if unemployment were cut by 50%, the crime rate would drop by only 5% (p. 98).

These data show that the availability of opportunity, approximately measured by the rate of unemployment, has little to do with crime. There are other anomalies in opportunity theory. First, the place of crime in the life cycle is odd. It would be expected that limited job options would be more salient to a man approaching age 30 than for a teenager. But criminality declines sharply with maturity: conviction rates for men between the ages of 25 and 30 are about one-third the rates for boys between the ages of 14 and 16 (Brantingham & Brantingham, p. 140). Similarly, a man with a family faces more urgent economic imperatives than a single man, but single men are far more likely to turn to crime. It is noteworthy that women, despite various economic barriers, are invariably less prone to crime than men: "Men are 5 to 10 times more likely than women to commit almost every crime on which American society keeps records . . . [and] in all other societies that keep records" (Jencks, 1992, p. 97). Also, it is hard to see crimes such as rape, drug use, and most homicides and assaults as substitutes for employment.

It seems undeniable that cultural factors are central to crime. This is underlined by ethnic differences in crime rates that overwhelm the effect of economic circumstances. One example makes this point: "During the 1960s, one neighborhood in San Francisco had the lowest income, the highest unemployment rate, the highest proportion of families with incomes under $4000 a year. . . . That neighborhood was called Chinatown. Yet in 1965, there were only five persons of Chinese ancestry committed to prison in the entire state of California" (Wilson & Herrnstein, 1985, p. 473).

PART II

◆◆◆

ENGAGING CULTURE

4

Culture as a Structure

It was argued in Chapter 1 that structural theory goes off the rails at the start in the attempt to abstract structural factors from culture and to define rational action apart from values. It was also argued, in Chapter 3, that a core claim of structural sociology—that group power controls social inequality—*requires* norms of solidarity. The empirical weakness of structuralism further suggests the need to incorporate culture in explanation. But the *successes* of structural explanation—that is, the examples in Chapter 2 of culture being adapted to opportunity sets—require a way of treating it that avoids the cultural dope.

Culture has often been conceived as a sort of cognitive map that constrains behavior, a view expressed in Durkheim's (1950) definition of social facts as "ways of acting, thinking, and feeling, external to the individual, and endowed with a power of coercion, by reason of which they control him" (p. 3). The quasi-external and constraining aspect of culture leads Hays, Alexander, and others to consider it to be a kind of structure. It was argued in Chapter 1 that this conflates two rival forms of explanation insofar as the constraints of socialization and social expectations are very different than those of costs and benefits. But despite this difference, it is necessary to consider the conception of culture as "exterior" and determining. For if culture is so conceived, it is hard to account for the examples of norms and values withering in the face of practical exigencies.

Margaret Archer's (1988) critique of "The Myth of Cultural Integration" begins with the common anthropological description of primitive societies as controlled by homogeneous and enveloping belief systems. Representatively, Evans-Pritchard portrayed the Azande as caught in a seamless web of ideas: "A Zande cannot get out of its meshes because it is the only world he knows . . . he cannot think that his thought is wrong" (quoted in Archer, 1988, p. 7). In this view, "Primitive peoples are seen as inexorably trapped in a coherent cultural code which generates the behavioral uniformities observed" (p. 11). Cultural determinism is more deeply entrenched by the structuralism of Levi-Strauss in which behavior is constrained by universal cognitive patterns, "organizing mechanisms of the unconscious," that are unknown to social members (Archer, 1988, p. 41). An example of this "elimination of the subject" is Levi-Strauss's (1969) claim that individuals are conduits of myths rather than their producers: "Myths operate in men's minds without their being aware of the fact . . . as if the thinking process were taking place in the myths" (p. 12). Like Durkheim, Levi-Strauss—and Michael Foucault—"treat cultural systems as forces external to any individual" (Neitz & Hall, 1993, p. 16) that constrain thoughts and actions without our conscious understanding.

Norman Cohn's (1962) *The Pursuit of the Millennium* provides an illustration of the odd claim that myths can have, as it were, a life of their own. Cohn describes the apocalyptic prophecies of early Christianity that anticipated the return of Christ, an event that would be followed by a titanic struggle between good and evil resulting in a period of perfect human goodness and happiness: a new Eden. These visions sparked numerous violent outbursts in medieval and Reformation Europe as dispossessed peasants, often driven by disastrous plagues or famines, aimed to spark the revolution that would cleanse the world of evil.

Cohn's objective is to show the parallels between these early social movements and modern totalitarianism. Like the early movements, Communist and Nazi ideologies anticipated "a final, decisive struggle in which a world tyranny will be overthrown by a 'chosen people' [the vanguard of the proletariat or the Aryan race] and through which the world will be renewed and history brought to its consummation" (p. 309). They share a desire "to purify the world by destroying the agents of corruption" (p. 310). Indeed, the Jews and the bourgeoisie were often the main targets of medieval outbreaks of collective violence, the agents of the Antichrist that needed to be exterminated. The shared vision of medieval and modern revolutions was of "a state of total community, a society wholly unanimous in its beliefs and wholly free from inner conflicts" (p. 310).

Despite various surface differences, Cohn describes these movements as sharing a "peculiar subterranean fanaticism" (p. 319). He argues that "The old symbols and the old slogans have indeed disappeared, to be replaced by new ones; but the structure of the basic phantasies seems to have changed scarcely at all" (p. xiv). Lenin's declaration that "Ruthless war must be waged on the Kulaks! Death to them! . . . those bloodsuckers, vampires, plunderers of the people and profiteers, who fatten on famine" and Trotsky's promise that "we will create a true paradise for men on this earth" (p. 312) are near replicas of a rhetoric that antedate them by 500 years. The resilience of these myths, their power to move people dispersed in space and time, suggests that they may have, in some sense, a life of their own.

Archer (1988) traces cultural determinism in sociology from Durkheim and Sorokin through Parsons. Durkheim (1950) described individuals as "merely the indeterminate material that the social factor molds and transforms" (p. 106) and as governed by "social currents": "we can no more choose the style of our houses than of our clothing . . . both are equally obligatory" (p. 11). In this view, we engage the world through established forms of thought, a kind of inherited vocabulary, that shape our perceptions, thoughts, and actions: of course we wear what is normatively prescribed—alternatives are, in the strong version of this position, unthinkable.

Shifting to the issue of social order, Parsons rejected the contract theory of political society as a product of self-interested rational agreement because it cannot explain why we do not violate such contracts when cheating pays. Instead, Parsons believed that normative consensus is "the cornerstone making regular systems of action possible" (Archer, 1988, p. 35) Because he saw trained compliance as the foundation of order, Alvin Gouldner (1970) argued that Parsons reduced actors to "'eager tools,' willingly pursuing whatever goals have been 'internalized' in them" (p. 193). Similarly, Giddens (1976) charges that "there is no action in Parsons's 'action frame of reference,' only behavior which is propelled by need-dispositions or role-expectations. The stage is set, but the actors only perform according to scripts which have already been written out for them" (p. 16). While this interpretation will be criticized later, there is evidence in Parsons to support it, as well as Coleman's claim that normative compliance is, for Parsons, the theoretical equivalent of "maximizing utility in rational choice theory" (quoted in Wrong, 1994, p. 197) At one point, Parsons (1937) *defined* action as norm compliance: "In terms of the given conceptual scheme there is no such thing as action except as effort to conform with norms just as there is no such thing as motion except as change of location in space" (pp. 76-77).[1]

While his views are ambiguous and sometimes contradictory, Bourdieu has also portrayed actors as cultural dopes. In describing the "correspondence between social structures and mental structures" (Bourdieu & Wacquant, 1992, p. 12), he defined *habitus* as "systems of durable, transposable dispositions" that emerge out of and reproduce objective structures and conditions: "As an acquired system of generative schemes objectively adjusted to the particular conditions in which it is constituted, the habitus engenders *all the thoughts, all the perceptions,* and *all the actions* consistent with those conditions, and no others" (Bourdieu, 1977, p. 95, emphasis added).

Despite his economism Marx provides another source for the notion of culture as a kind of structure, relentlessly controlling conduct. His claim that "The ideas of the ruling class are in every epoch the ruling ideas" (quoted in Feuer, 1959, p. 26) has led to the so-called dominant ideology thesis. In this view, usually presented to explain the failure of the proletariat to act on its material interests by adopting socialism, the class that controls the means of material production also controls the means of "mental production": "The dominant ideology penetrates and infects the consciousness of the working class, because the working class comes to see and to experience reality through the conceptual categories of the dominant class" (Archer, 1988, p. 47). Ideological indoctrination causes even its victims to see capitalism as right and/or "natural" and hence unable to imagine alternatives.

Althusser's "abolition of the subject" moved beyond Marx by denying the ruling class authentic consciousness, portraying all persons as "caught by the constraints of a script and parts whose authors they cannot be, since it is in essence *an authorless theater*" (Althusser & Balibar, 1970, p. 193). Culture, in this view, is a product of the various "Ideological State Apparatuses" that inculcate individuals with the subjectivities suitable for their role in the productive system: "The structure of the relations of production determines the places and functions occupied and adopted by the agents of production, who are never anything more than the occupants of these places, insofar as they are the supports (trager) of these functions" (p. 180). Althusser's concept of the "problematic," roughly comparable to Thomas Kuhn's theory of paradigms, also denies autonomy by conceiving individuals as vehicles of intellectual schemas. Just as Levi-Strauss (1969) argued that individual minds are the unconscious vehicles of myths, Althusser, in Smith's (1985) description, contended that "it is no longer the individual subject who thinks and constructs theories, but the problematic that thinks in and through the subject" (p. 644). In Althusser's scheme, no one really understands the determinations of the "authorless theater" that is social order.

This emphasis on the constraining power of culture is central to other Marxist efforts to address the failure of socialism. Antonio Gramsci's concept of "hegemony" shifted the locus of class domination from material power to culture. In Perry Anderson's (1976-77) words, Gramsci argued that "it is the cultural ascendancy of the ruling class that essentially ensures the stability of the capitalist order" (p. 26). The Frankfurt School similarly portrayed workers as entirely dominated by mass culture. In this view, the modern proletariat can no more resist "the culture industry" than the Azande can have independent thoughts.

Despite the fundamental difference between emphasizing the power of culture and the constraints of costs and benefits, there is a parallel between the conception of culture as a structure and "materialist" notions of structure. In both, individual autonomy is considered to be illusory because power controls the economy and the culture. The political subtext of structural theories of inequality is to deny the freedom and hence the fairness of market societies by emphasizing the concentration of economic power. Similarly, the conception of culture as a structure challenges the liberal belief in intellectual autonomy by emphasizing the cultural power of dominant classes. The promise of autonomy in a regime of liberal capitalism is thus subverted by both economic and cultural domination. In its more pessimistic versions, structural thinking denies the possibility of individual freedom: economic and cultural hegemony is an inevitable feature of social order.

The idea of culture as a kind of structure has made its way into contemporary social science. Drawing on the work of Mary Douglas, Foucault, and others, Wuthnow et al. (1984) conceive of culture as an "autonomous entity" (p. 250) that has an existence "in some ways independent of [its] creators" (Wuthnow, 1987, p. 334). One of the advantages of this perspective, according to Wuthnow, is that it avoids the philosophical problem of knowledge of other minds in that we can "separate cultural analysis from considerations of individual subjectivity" (Wuthnow et al., 1984, p. 244) and focus on "patterns among symbols themselves" (Wuthnow, 1987, p. 341). As noted in Chapter 1, Hays (1994) includes culture as a type of structure because ideas: "compris[e] dynamic systems of meaning with a certain inner logic of their own" (p. 68). Just as the logic of an argument can force unwanted conclusions, cultural imperatives can compel conduct. In extreme versions, actors are portrayed as passive objects of supraindividual cultural forces. In George Kubler's (1962) Althusserian, or Parsonian[2] metaphor, culture is like a train moving down the tracks, and we are its passengers.

Some of the most rigorously "objectivist" structural theorists incorporate cultural factors in their lexicon. Mayhew (1980), for example, argues that "structuralists do not employ subjectivist concepts such as purpose or goals," and he aims to expunge all reference to "ghostly" or "subcranial" properties such as "values," "purpose," and "attitudes, emotions, sentiments, etc." (pp. 348, 363-364). But he includes "symbol systems organized into social ideologies" as a structural variable (p. 347). The apparent contradiction between excluding "values" and the like but including "ideologies" as structures is, purportedly, resolved by emphasizing the "exterior" and "coercive" nature of ideologies. While unable to deny ideas the power to affect action, terms such as *purpose* grant more agency than Mayhew will allow.

But the examples of culture being rejected or modified in light of practical exigencies cast doubt on the image of actors as normative drones. Such doubts easily find a foothold with the centrality of deviance, individual and collective, personal and political, in social life. The military is perhaps the most intensively structured, in all senses of the term, environment in modern societies. But defiance is ever present. Gerald Linderman (1997) describes various ways in which intensively trained and monitored soldiers resist orders through overly literal interpretation, delay, feigned miscommunication, falsification of records, and outright defiance (pp. 213-217). Even Durkheim (1961), while portraying actors as trager (supports) of "social currents" and defining morality as "rules [that are] fixed and specific" (p. 26), also emphasized the tentativeness of cultural control, illustrated by the ever-present threat of egoism and anomie. Not only does culture *not*, as Sahlins (1976) argued, constitute utility, the appeal of forbidden fruit suggests that social taboos can *stimulate* appetites.

Indeed, the dominant ideology theory implies that persons cannot be merely trager of culture. Susan James's (1985) critique of Althusser points out that the need to saturate a society with ideology suggests that actors "have a natural capacity to recognize and reflect on their interests . . . social practices only need legitimating if there is some chance that they may be rejected" (pp. 154-155). Archer (1988, p. 55) contends that, unlike his epigones, Marx denied both that the dominant culture is a seamless web of logical consistency and that it extinguishes rival ideas. In an argument directed both against misreadings of Marx and Parsonian sociology, Ambercrombie et al. (1980) similarly argue that subordinate classes have always maintained separate and often oppositional values and that Marx was well aware of this.

INTERPRETING CULTURE

Criticism of cultural determinism is no longer centered in structural sociology and economics. Alexander (1987a) describes ethnomethodology as showing "the methods by which actors make social norms their own . . . [and] binding rules were specified situationally and modified" (p. 28). Symbolic interactionism also emphasizes the situated, negotiated, and dynamic aspect of social norms. As Hans Joas (1987) describes this perspective, action is "not determined by a mere application of prescriptions or guidelines free of all intervention by the actor's self. Reflection and dialogue are required not just for the alteration of rules and norms, but also for their maintenance and reproduction" (p. 107). As Herbert Blumer (1969) put it, "It is the social process in group life that creates and upholds the rules, not the rules that create and uphold social life" (p. 66).

The recent revival of cultural theory, while insisting on its importance, has, for the most part, stressed the creativity of actors in interpreting culture. Several streams have contributed to this interpretive turn. Hermeneutics and phenomenology emphasize the variety of possible textual translations and the role of the reader in shaping meaning. The poststructural emphasis on the multiplicity of meanings denies the possibility of an "ideal reader" who faithfully mirrors a text. Challenging the Frankfurt conception of "mass culture" as turning persons into automatons, contemporary theorists of "popular culture" generally portray cultural receivers as "resistant readers"—that is, as "meaning makers" capable of "creating counter hegemonic cultural objects" and thereby "actively constructing subversive meanings" (Griswold, 1994, p. 90). In contrast to Kubler's metaphor of a train, John Fiske (1989) analogizes popular culture to a supermarket that actors can draw on to create their own meanings.

There are various grounds for doubting the cultural dope. Like the poststructuralists, Sewell (1992, p. 17) and Swidler (1986, p. 280) find autonomy in the *multiplicity* of cultural patterns, or "schemas" (rules), that are available in any society. Contrary to the "Myth of Cultural Integration," cultures are not devised by philosophers or jurists but evolve ad hoc, subject to various inputs. Archer (1988) points out that cultures unavoidably contain the residues of their own past and are subject to influences from frontiers. The result is a farrago of loosely connected—or disconnected and even contradictory—elements that allow room for choice (see also Emirbayer & Goodwin, 1994, p. 1441). For example, the culture of American masculinity, often simplistically caricatured, includes John Wayne and Jerry Lewis, Clint Eastwood and Woody Allen, Arnold Schwartzenegger and Jerry Seinfeld and countless other archetypes.

Redding's (1993) study of Chinese entrepreneurs provides some striking examples of the coexistence of seemingly contradictory values. For example, side by side with an emphasis on hard work, frugality, and other values commonly associated with their economic dynamism, the Chinese are ardent believers in luck. According to one Hong Kong business executive, "They believe that luck is very important actually. More important than anything else" (p. 201). Also, while Chinese employees seem dependent on and loyal to leaders and expect them to reciprocate with patriarchal concern (p. 130), they yearn for autonomy. A Hong Kong executive explained: "I don't like to work for others, be controlled by others. . . . It's the freedom that attracts me, not making more money" (p. 189). Such anomalies are not uncommon. Ladurie (1978) found a striking example of multiplicity in the fourteenth-century peasants of southern France who alternated between two quite different versions of Christianity.

In addition to providing choice for the actor, the multiplicity of cultural elements allows interpretive interplay between them, a process suggested by the postmodern concept of intertextuality. That is, a rule or a norm can be read in light of another rule or norm. Readers do not encounter cultural messages as blank slates but as encultured agents whose "horizons of expectations" (Griswold, 1994, p. 83) shape their receptions of cultural objects. Each cultural element is a lens through which the others are viewed. According to Gadamer, we can *only* interpret historical cultural objects through our own perspective. Thus, the study of history "does not consist in the restoration of the past, but in thoughtful mediation with contemporary life" (quoted in Outhwaite, 1985, p. 27).

This process is not confined to professional interpreters. Matza (1964) shows how mainstream notions of masculinity, found in heroic tales of frontier violence and so on, are appropriated by delinquents to support deviant values. Admonitions to nonviolence can thus be subverted in light of conventional values such as the defense of honor. While the (relative) homogeneity of traditionalist societies limits this process, modern society is, as postmodernists emphasize, a "pastiche" of disparate elements. Furthermore, globalization means that all contemporary societies are increasingly exposed to a variety of cultural inputs: with the emergence of electronic media, we all live on informational frontiers. The various combinations of intertextual play proliferate: the Chinese must now see Chairman Mao as, in some measure, an American icon. When Mohammed Ali became a world figure, this shifted his place in American culture. As Rosenau (1992) describes Bakhtin's view, "There is a global mixing, a simultaneous connection similar to the medieval carnival where every element refers to every other element" (p. 36).

The openness of cultural messages to alternate readings through different cultural lenses has been emphasized by critics of Ariel Dorfman and Armand Mattelart's (1975) *How to Read Donald Duck: Imperialist Ideology in the Disney Comic*. The thesis of this book is that Disney comics are an instrument of cultural domination, spreading values of consumerism, Western racial and cultural stereotypes, and so on. But critics have challenged this thesis. First, the text itself is open to alternate readings. Dorfman and Mattelart interpret Uncle Scrooge as a way of deflecting anticapitalist sentiments toward a comic parody "to leave intact the true mechanisms of domination" (p. 78). But Scrooge can also be seen as "a biting parody of the bourgeois entrepreneur" in "a closet critique of capitalism" (Tomlinson, 1991, p. 43). This ambiguity introduces "the relationship between text and audience" (p. 44) and "the individual's capacity for active selection and selective retention" (p. 45), which problematizes how other cultures interpret an American icon.

This issue is also addressed by Ien Ang's (1985) study, *Watching Dallas* which found divergent readings in different societies emerging from "a social process of viewing and discursive interpretation" (p. 48). That is, individuals in different societies typically viewed *Dallas* in groups, talked about it, and drew their own conclusions. Some of these readings resulted in an emphatic rejection of the consumerist values the program was alleged to impose. Some viewers saw it as testimony to the folly of greed.

Contrary to the claims of the dominant ideology thesis, "bourgeois" liberalism has proved to be especially protean. Liberal notions of equality have been particularly troublesome for their progenitors in that they are readily turned from the political realm to the economic. This ambiguity was exploited by Marx. In contrast to the dismissal of ideas as "ideological reflexes" or "phantoms" in *The German Ideology* (Marx, 1967b, p. 14), his critique of liberalism developed its radical implications. In *The Eighteenth Brumaire* (Marx, 1967a), he notes that

> the bourgeoisie had a true insight into the fact that all the weapons which it had forged against feudalism turned their points against itself. . . . It understood that all the so-called bourgeois liberties and organs of progress attacked and menaced its *class rule* at its social foundation and its political summit simultaneously. (p. 65)

Many contemporary political philosophers consider the association of liberal values and capitalism to be contingent, even contradictory, and shift the logic of liberalism toward radical egalitarianism. Kai Nielsen (1985) argues that "it is as evident as anything can be that there is a close correlation between wealth and power . . . if we prize liberty and autonomy, and if we prize democracy, we will also be egalitarians" (p. 8).

The reappropriation of ideology is part of everyday life. In his studies of oppositional working-class culture in schools, Paul Willis (1990) argued that dominant ideologies can be reinterpreted by those they are designed to dominate. Noting that "capitalist freedoms are potentially real freedoms" (p. 175), he argues that while "the counter-school culture and its processes arise from definite circumstances in a specific historical relation and are in no sense accidentally produced," its targets are far from helpless: "The recognition of determination does not, however, dismiss creativity" (p. 120).

The turning of belief systems in alternate directions is unavoidable because to be effective an ideology must be persuasive. This requires that ideologies make gestures toward universal validity, which allows them to be used in ways unforeseen by their creators. In studying the power of norms of fairness in collective bargaining, Elster (1989a) found that they are not trolley cars that bargainers can alight and leave at will: "if one party opens up a certain line of argument or invokes a certain social norm, it stays on the table forever" (p. 240). If, for example, management cites low profits to restrain wages, in times of prosperity, unions can deploy this argument to their advantage. Legitimating ideologies are two-edged swords that encourage counterideologies. This is why liberal doctrines of equal opportunity, equal rights, and equality before the law can lead to a radical egalitarianism: it is easily argued that none of these values are compatible with capitalist inequality. At the least, the dominated can demand that the dominant live up to their own rules. Hence a means of exclusion—"women aren't rational enough to . . ."—can become a means of inclusion—"Women are demonstrably rational enough to. . . ." Secondly, as will be argued, since the logic of a rule is ambiguous, it can be reinterpreted and deployed against its producer. So by either insisting on the logic of a rule or plausibly bending it, targets of indoctrination can turn rules against their producers.

The reappropriation of culture to new ends is described by Sewell (1992) as the actor's ability to "transpose" schemas: "To say that schemas are transposable . . . is to say that they can be applied to a wide and not fully predictable range of cases outside the context in which they are initially learned" (p. 17). Similarly, Swidler (1986), characterizes culture as a "tool kit of resources"—that is, assets that can be turned to various ends, and describes actors as "active, sometimes skilled users of culture" (p. 277). Like Sewell, Swidler emphasizes the ways in which "established cultural resources are reappropriated in new contexts" (p. 282). Two well-worked examples are the redeployment, under changed circumstances, of the traditional values of Jewish and Confucian scholarship to enable action originally disdained, such as secular and commercial endeavors.

The structural and economic emphasis on the sensitivity of actors to costs and benefits is another source of autonomy from culture. Weber, in Bourdieu and Wacquant's (1992) reading, argued that "social agents obey a rule only insofar as their interests in following it outweighs their interest in overlooking it" (p. 115). Insofar as Weber emphasized the inertia of tradition, and in other ways emphasized the autonomy of ideas from material circumstances, this may better reflect Bourdieu's view of culture. But material interests surely qualify the constraints of culture. Sewell's (1992) argument that "Knowledge of cultural schemas implies the ability to act creatively" (p. 20) is largely based on actor's ability to consider their instrumental value. In his view, schemas are "validated by the accumulation of resources that their enactment engenders. Schemas not empowered or regenerated by resources would eventually be abandoned and forgotten" (p. 13). By the "contexts" in which "established cultural resources are reappropriated," Swidler (1986) mainly means the "structural and historical opportunities [that] determine which strategies, and thus which cultural systems, succeed" (p. 284). Even Sahlins's (1981) emphasis on the autonomy of culture is qualified with a recognition of its sensitivity to practical need:

> People act upon circumstances according to their own cultural presuppositions. . . . [But] the worldly circumstances of human action are under no inevitable obligation to conform to [these] categories. . . . In the event they do not, the received categories are potentially revalued in practice. . . . At the extreme, what began as reproduction ends as transformation. (p. 72)

However, the conception of culture as entirely subject to cost-benefit calculations, or any approach that overemphasizes its malleability, can, if pushed too far, undercut its theoretical understanding. For what would be the point of creating ideologies if they can be turned any which way? As suggested earlier, if culture has the power to control actors, it cannot be *merely* a tool of opportunistic manipulation. An alternative to rendering the investment in culture inexplicable can be found in the softer versions of structural sociology that, in contrast to Sewell's claim that inefficacious schemas are "abandoned and forgotten," emphasize the interpretive process. This allows actors the qualified, but significant, autonomy demonstrated by Lin

(1985), Galliher and Cross (1983), and Matza (1964). In their analyses, although norms are manipulable, they are not infinitely so, and hence culture is seen to affect conduct even if its exact role cannot be foreseen. The radical structural argument that culture is powerless to control behavior is neither plausible nor theoretically coherent. Nor is it necessary to avoid the cultural dope. It is only necessary to show that culture is open to variable "readings" that are, in part, guided by the array of opportunities.

WITTGENSTEIN ON RULE FOLLOWING

The problem of recognizing the influence of culture without reducing actors to normative drones is tricky. But it is a necessary task, for although culture surely affects behavior, the structural examples of actors defying norms are compelling. The debate over the role of culture has been between those who dismiss its significance and those who consider it to be determinative, and both sides present compelling examples. What is needed is a way to recognize the significance of culture *and* its malleability.

Wittgenstein's (1953) theory of rule following provides a conception of culture that acknowledges its significance for behavior while avoiding the cultural dope. In a key example, he considers the instruction to continue a series of numbers, such as 1-2-3 . . . (para. 143, 185). But there are many ways the instruction could be followed: 4-5-6 . . . may seem obvious. But 1-2-3-1-2-3 . . . is a plausible response, as are others. Wittgenstein's point is that rules do not interpret themselves: they need to be interpreted by actors in order to be applied.

Wittgenstein (1953) emphasized the indeterminacy of rules throughout his work. He argued that linguistic usage is flexible: "the application of a word is not everywhere bounded by rules" (para. 84). For example, he asks, "Has the name Moses got a fixed and unequivocal use for me in all possible cases?" (para. 79). If we found evidence that a man with another name did some of what the Bible attributes to Moses we might say that this was Moses—or perhaps not. Hence, ordinary language users must make judgments about how to use words. If repairs were done to my house, I would say I live in the "same" building. But at some unclear point in a renovation project, I would want to say that I am now living in a new building.

The Revolutionary War ship, the U.S.S. Constitution, retains 10% to 15% of its original parts. Do we say that it is the "same" boat?

The flexibility of linguistic usage is central to Wittgenstein's discussions of criteria and symptoms. In science, for example, we must *decide* if a trait is to be treated as a symptom (a characteristic accompaniment) or a criterion (a necessary condition) of a phenomenon. And this can change: "Nothing is commoner than for the meaning of an expression to oscillate, for a phenomenon to be regarded sometimes as a symptom, sometimes as a criterion, of a state of affairs" (Wittgenstein, 1970, para. 438). For example, we might use eight-leggedness as a criterion of an insect. But if a ten-legged animal was found that in other respects resembled insects, we might decided that eight legs are a symptom rather than a criterion.

Instead of fast rules, Wittgenstein (1953) describes the use of words as sharing a "family resemblance" (p. 32): that is, there is no unifying thread of similarity that runs through the various uses of, for example, the word *game*. Chess, baseball, solitaire, Russian Roulette, the game of love, and a war game have no one thing in common. Because there is no fixed criterion for using a word, language is open in that new uses are always possible. This means that using language, like following a rule, requires judgment: a competent language user *cannot* be a cultural dope. One of Wittgenstein's (1953) key remarks on language—"the meaning of a word is its use in the language" (p. 20)—suggests both the heterogeneity and the dynamics of linguistic practices. Indeed, if the meaning of a word *is* its use, a rule, a sign, and so on have *no* meaning apart from an application. In the spirit of Wittgenstein, Charles Taylor (1993) describes the application of a rule as "a continual 'interpretation' and reinterpretation of what the rule really means" (p. 57). However, the phrase "really means" can mislead if it suggests that there is an *essential* meaning that the actor "finds." But if "[an] arrow points *only* in the application that a living being makes of it" (Wittgenstein, 1953, para. 454, emphasis added), we cannot speak of its meaning apart from use. Similarly, we cannot define "authentic" liberalism apart from its various articulations. There is, as it were, no god's eye perspective on the "real" meaning of a doctrine, which is why dissension among the orthodox is common. This view evokes Kant's belief that the noumenal world cannot be conceived apart from the categories of perception. There is, as it were, no cultural "ding an sich" (thing in itself).

As Taylor (1993) concludes, "The "rule" lies essentially *in* the practice" (p. 45).

The problematic nature of enacting a rule requires a capacity for agency that is beyond the normative drone of cultural determinism. Amartya Sen (1997) describes a dilemma presented by the Confucian principle of filial devotion to the state. When told by a provincial governor that "among my people, there is a man of unbending integrity: when his father stole a sheep, he denounced him," Confucius replied: "Among my people, men of integrity do things differently: a father covers up for his son, a son covers up for his father" (p. 36). Rules are not substitutes for agency: their application *requires* it. Puzzlement about how to apply a doctrine is unavoidable even in carefully designed cultural products, such as law and philosophy. The debate about the meaning of "the greatest good for the greatest number" or "compelling state interest" is endless. Durkheim's (1961) belief that morality required "fixed and specific" rules expressed a hope for determinacy that cannot be realized. And Wuthnow's aim to "separate cultural analysis from considerations of individual subjectivity" (Wuthnow et al., 1984, p. 244) reveals a misplaced belief in the "objective" nature of culture. To some degree, the Azande cannot help but think their own thoughts.

There are different themes in Wittgenstein on *how* rules are interpreted. In large measure, he saw rule following as a function of cultural training: "Following a rule is analogous to obeying an order. We are trained to do so; we react to an order in a particular way" (1953, para. 206). At one point he describes rule following as a kind of trained reflex that has no "reason": "This is simply what I do. . . . This is how it strikes me. . . . I obey the rule *blindly*" (para. 219). In these comments, agency seems to be evaporating.

But as the variability of language use implies, training in customs cannot fully explain rule following. The above comments are meant to deny the "subterranean" mental processes some philosophers attributed to meaningful action, not to reduce rule followers to automata.[3] Wittgenstein maintains agency by implicating *practical* considerations, as well as custom and training, in human activities. This theme has been masked by interpreters who attribute a radical conventionalism to Wittgenstein. Peter Winch (1964) interprets Wittgenstein as portraying cultural conventions as floating more or less free of "material" reality. In this view, discourse about the world is so culture-bound that questions of truth and falsity cannot be asked across different ways of life. Considering Azande witchcraft, Winch argues that because "the concepts used by primitive peoples can only be interpreted in the context of the way of life of those peoples" (p. 315), using science "as a paradigm against which to measure the intellectual respectability of other modes of discourse" (p. 308) is a kind of ethnocentrism.

But Wittgenstein's conventionalism is qualified by emphasis on engagement with practical exigencies. He says, "It is a fact of experience that human beings alter their concepts, exchange them for others, when they learn new facts: when in this way what was formerly important to them becomes unimportant, and vice versa" (1970, para. 352). This innocuous remark suggests that rule following is not entirely a matter of custom. In a discussion of the use of criteria and symptoms in medical diagnosis, he seems to imply conventionalism: "In practice, if you were asked which phenomenon is the defining criterion and which is a symptom, you would in most cases be unable to answer this question except by making an arbitrary decision *ad hoc*." But this does not mean that we make such judgments willy-nilly. Wittgenstein continues: "It may be *practical* to define a word by taking one phenomenon as the defining criterion, but we shall easily be persuaded to define the word by means of what, according to our first use, was a symptom" (Wittgenstein, 1958, p. 25. emphasis added). In constructing scientific definitions, he illustrates what he means by "practical": "It is usual to make phenomena that allow of exact measurement into defining criteria" (Wittgenstein, 1970, para. 438). These comments portray actors as deploying language variably, but not arbitrarily, in that usages are tied to their practical interests, such as the scientist's need for exact measurement: "A natural foundation for the way [a] concept is formed is the complex nature and the variety of human contingencies" (para. 439). But Wittgenstein's notion of practicality should not be interpreted narrowly; it can encompass, the "human contingencies" of, for example, religious activities.

These comments suggest that there is an instrumental component in rule following. Sometimes we follow rules "blindly," but difficult cases that require judgment are common. For example, while ordinarily we have little trouble using the word *human,* determining the status of a fetus requires examination of our concept of a person, which turns out to be far from clear.

Determining what we mean—or choose to mean—by the word will involve not just consulting a convention but an array of considerations, including various costs—such as the cost of medicating a sickly fetus or the cost to a rape victim of carrying it to term. As is evident in this example, the process may involve political dispute and the role of power. Moreover, definitions are unstable. In vitro fertilization has sparked debates about whether the mother of a child is the woman who supplies the egg, the uterus, or the one who contracted the enterprise: perhaps they are all its mother. New medical technology, which can, for example, keep the "brain dead" alive in some sense, has made the definition of *dead* highly problematic.

Wittgenstein's (1953) emphasis on practicality is highlighted in his comparison of language to a toolbox (para. 11)—that is, a set of instruments to be used in practical tasks. Indeed, much of his work is an attempt to resolve what he considered to be the senseless philosophical puzzles that emerge when language "goes on holiday" (para. 38)—that is, when it is removed from a context of activities. His central example of this is Descartes's claim that he was able to doubt that he had a body, or that the external world exists. But claiming to doubt apart from any practical context of usage is a *misuse* of language: "What we can ask is whether it can make sense to doubt it" (1969, para. 2). Wittgenstein derided the artificial problems of philosophy that emerge when language is taken out of its natural context. In ordinary language, doubt emerges in practical situations. We must, for example, cite grounds for doubt and describe ways of resolving it. Most important, we expect that doubts affect conduct. But none of these features appear in the philosopher's profession of doubt: "Couldn't we peacefully leave him to doubt it, since it makes no difference at all" (para. 120). He was equally unimpressed with G. E. Moore's response to Descartes: "I know that I have two hands" (1970 para. 405). Both Descartes's doubt and Moore's answer were examples of "philosopher's nonsense" (1953, p. 221) in that ordinary expressions were torn from any real context of practical activity: "I feel as if these words were like 'Good morning' said to someone in the middle of a conversation" (1969, para. 464). I can *say* that I doubt that I have never been on the moon. But such an utterance would be "idle": "Nothing would follow from it, nothing be explained by it. It would not tie in with anything in my life" (para. 117). Wittgenstein's emphasis on the embeddedness of speech in practice undercuts the skepticism alleged by postmodern and other relativisms, which are unavoidably contradicted by the lives of their advocates: "My life shews that I know or am certain that there is a chair over there, or a door, and so on" (para. 7).

Wittgenstein's implication of language and rules in systems of practical conduct introduces an aspect of meaning that is often ignored by various schools of interpretive social science. In determining the meaning of a word or a rule, we must understand the context of activities in which it is embedded: "Only in the stream of thought *and life* do words have meaning" (1970, para. 173. emphasis added). Meaning is thus not simply textual. Classical hermeneutics was a kind of *Kulturphilosophie* that defined the interpretive ground as a cultural ethos, or *Geist*. This approach persists in contemporary interpretive approaches. But understanding, for Wittgenstein, is only partly like reading a text, for the interpretive context is not confined to culture:

> How could human behavior be described? Surely only by sketching the actions of a variety of humans, as they are all mixed up together. What determines our judgement, our concepts, and reactions, is not what *one* man is doing *now*, an individual action, but the whole hurly-burly of human actions, the background against which we see any action. (para. 567)

This comment bears not only on the interpretive efforts of external observers; social actors must also interpret their culture, not just by "reading" its "texts" but by understanding, for example, how a social rule is used in "the whole hurly-burly" of social practices. In considering the problem of translation, Wittgenstein (1958) says, "Whether a word of the language of our tribe is rightly translated into a word of the English language depends on the role it plays in the whole life of the tribe" (p. 103). To understand a word, a rule, or any cultural item, observers and social actors must understand the role it plays in an entire system of social practices, for "the speaking of language is part of an activity, or of a form of life" (1953, para. 23). This point can be emphasized by considering words and phrases that are freighted with implications, such as "affirmative action," "family values," or *jihad*. Even a seemingly innocuous word such as *merit* is considered by some to be a means of excluding those who do not meet the (arguably arbitrary) standards defined by dominant groups. To understand *what* is being said when these terms are used requires understanding an array of social factors. The complexities of the interpretive process for ordinary language users enhances both the need for agency and its scope. Meanings are often contradictory and contestable and interpretations of, for example, "being filial" are, as Lin's analysis shows, subject to strategic considerations.

Wittgenstein's conception of the openness of rules is nicely illustrated in Galliher and Cross's (1983) account of how Mormons reconcile gambling with their religious beliefs. Their accommodation may seem to be sheer opportunism, and surely this plays a role. But the claim that because the house nearly always wins, they aren't "really" gambling is plausible. Like any word, *gambling* has no fixed criteria of application. While a cheat appears to gamble, he is only miming gambling, even if, due to imperfect control, he runs risks. Also, much legitimate business, like "playing" the market, cannot be easily distinguished from gambling. Our commonsense concept of gambling is unclear enough to allow considerable flexibility in its use.

Because of this emphasis on agency, there are suggestions of existentialism in Wittgenstein. One parallel is a shared understanding of how persons engage culture. In his critique of determinism, Jean-Paul Sartre (1957) also stressed agency in interpreting rules. Discussing application of the Kantian injunction to never treat people as means he contends that "values are vague . . . always too broad for the concrete and specific case that we are considering" (p. 26). Ultimately, individuals must choose a course of action because "no general ethics can show you what is to be done; there are no omens in the world. The Catholics will reply 'But there are.' Granted—but, in any [specific] case, I myself choose the meaning they have" (p. 28). The individual who claims to be acting on a sign from God, or an ethical injunction, is still acting freely in that "he alone decided what the sign meant . . . he is fully responsible for the interpretation" (p. 29). An important difference between Wittgenstein and Sartre is that, in contrast to the latter's individualism—"he alone"—the former emphasizes collective activities or language games as giving meaning to rules.

While not often philosophically elaborated, many sociologists have recognized the role of actors in interpreting and applying rules. Even during the heyday of Parsons, there were significant challenges to the view that actors reflexively obey cultural imperatives. This is especially evident in the work of theorists of deviance who have found, like Matza, that conventional norms are opportunistically adapted. For example, Lee Rainwater's (1967) study of ghetto dwellers uses Hyman Rodman's (1963) concept of "value stretch" to argue that deviant lifestyles often represent "adaptations of societal values to their constraining situation" (Kornhauser, 1978, p. 133). Ruth Kornhauser surveys various studies that show that "in the slum societal values are retained but attenuated" (p. 134). For example, the belief in marriage and fidelity is, she argues, maintained but relaxed in light of situational exigencies such as the lack of stable employment. This view of culture as subject to opportunistic manipulation has become increasingly common with the fading of Parsons's influence. Although his exact meaning is unclear, Alexander (1990) argues that "we cannot understand culture without reference to social structural constraints" (p. 26). More explicitly recognizing the impact of "material" factors on rules, Hays (1994) contends that "cultural transformations occur in the context of structurally provided possibilities and structurally maintained constraints" (p. 69).

Indeed, there are problems in attributing cultural determinism to Parsons. Parsons's cultural dope is generally portrayed along two dimensions. First, culture is thought to follow its own vectors more or less independently of "material" influences. Second, individuals are seen as conforming faithfully to cultural imperatives. As John Heritage (1987) describes Parsons's view, "If moral values are to be an effective prophylactic against Hobbesian chaos, the members of a social order will not be capable of an instrumental orientation toward the normative elements which they have internalized" (p. 229). While Parsons provides footholds for the charge of cultural determinism, there are points where a different conception of culture is suggested. First, Parsons and Shils (1951) point out that "the recalcitrance of events, particularly the foci of man's organic nature and the scarcity of means or resources, imposes certain functional imperatives on action" (p. 173). Action is not independent of the "material" world or free to follow the logic of culture alone. Also, while Parsons speaks of the personality system as saturated with cultural training, it is not a monad of culture: "the integration of a personality as a concrete empirical action system can never be a simple "reflection" or "realization" of a value system. It must involve the adjustment of such a value system to the exigencies of the object situation and to the exigencies of organic needs" (Parsons & Shils, 1951, p. 145). Personality and action are thus not strictly cultural products, autonomous of material reality. Practical needs emerging from our organic nature require a critical engagement with culture.

A second aspect of agency in Parson's theory of culture appears in the ability of actors to interpret culture and select among cultural alternatives in light of their own needs. Driven by "need-dispositions and their consequent potentiality for resisting the pressure of expectations" actors can find "a creative variant of an available cultural pattern" (Parsons & Shils, 1951, p. 182). In recognizing this process, it is important that, contrary to Archer and other critics, Parsons did not portray culture as a seamless whole. He described even "a highly integrated society" as "heterogeneous" (p. 219) and spoke of "Inconsistencies within the value system" (p. 175). All of this allows a degree of autonomy from culture insufficiently recognized by critics.

To be sure, in various ways, Parsons was inclined to privilege culture. Values are described as largely governing both personality and the social system (Parsons & Shils, 1951, p. 203). While acknowledging that persons can act in a calculating rather than norm-driven way, he maintained that "instrumental actions are subsidiary in the sense that the desirability of the goal is given by patterns of value-orientation, as is the assessment of cost" (p. 165). Parsons's greatest vulnerability to the "oversocialized" charge is his portrayal of persons as primarily motivated to conform to expectations: "Human society, we may say, is only possible at all because, within the limits of plasticity and sensitivity, sufficient basic human gratifications come to be bound up with conformity with role-expectations and with eliciting the favorable attitudes of others" (p. 149). He recognized "limits" to this need to conform but also believed that "what people want most is to be responded to, loved, approved, and esteemed" (p. 150).

Hence, while Parsons (1966), confessed at one point that he was "a cultural determinist" (p. 113), he provided grounds for autonomy from cultural imperatives and disavowed the " 'emanationist' fallacy" in which "culture as a system is treated as closed and either conceptually or empirically independent of social structure and personality" (Parsons & Shils, 1951, p. 240). Parsons declared the three systems to be "analytically co-equal" and criticized the tendency of "proponents of each of the three disciplines concerned to attempt to close their own systems, and to declare their theoretical independence of the others" (p. 239). Hence, Parsons's cultural determinism does not mean that he saw actors as merely cultural dopes.

While it is first among equals, the individual is not reduced to a "trager" of culture. In these comments, Parsons's conception of culture is not incompatible with Marx's critique of the Hegelian conception of ideas as autonomous of material practice.

5

The Limits of Interpretation

INVESTING IN CULTURE

Rejecting the view of culture as inert and relentlessly controlling conduct is an important advance. Indeed, to be useful, a rule must allow interpretive variation because not all possible situations of its application can be anticipated. Generally, a culture can endure only if it is flexible enough to engage changing circumstances. But this view has, in some versions, gone too far. Theoretical schools ranging from materialist Marxism to contemporary network theory have argued that culture is virtually irrelevant to conduct. This view is common among sociologists who see behavior as entirely controlled by structures of opportunity. Blau (1977) seeks a sociology in which "formal properties of social positions and relations are abstracted from their substantive contents, notably from cultural and psychological contents" (p. 28). But this claim fails because, as was argued in Chapter 1, many structures are constituted by culture. Furthermore, it is unable to explain why persons *have* culture. Douglass North (1984) argues that the dismissal of the role of ideology in economic thought is theoretically incoherent: "If ideology is not important, then economists must explain the enormous amount of resources that political units and other principals in political and economic activity devote to attempting to convince participants of the justice or injustice of contractual arrangements" (p. 39). It is impossible to explain why actors alleged to be exclusively interest driven would invest in norms unless such investments serve their interests. But this implies that norms *do* condition behavior—which means that behavior *cannot* be exclusively instrumental. Radical instrumentalism is nicely hoist on this

often-mentioned but underappreciated contradiction. Similarly, the claim
that ideology legitimates interests, argued by Blau, Collins (see Chapter 3)
and many others, implies a sensitivity to moral logic. Ideology has instrumental value only if it can affect behavior—which reveals the significance
of the "moral sense." A pretense of morality has legitimating power only
if morality matters. As Elster (1989a) puts it, "If some people successfully
exploit norms for self-interested purposes, it can only be because others
are willing to let norms take precedence over self-interest" (p. 128). Perhaps Lenin and Trotsky (see Chapter 4) were using the apocalyptic themes
of early Christianity instrumentally: to mobilize revolutionary passion. But
this could work only if their targets took such ideas seriously.

It is more plausible, as in the softer forms of structuralism, to argue the
flexibility—not the irrelevance—of culture. But even this position needs to
be qualified. This can be shown by considering its most radicalized version.
A key claim of postmodernism is that there are no grounds for distinguishing between an "authentic" and a "distorted" interpretation of a text. In this
view, the reader displaces the authority of both author and text. In Barthes's
(1977) aphorism, "The birth of the reader must be at the cost of the death of
the Author" (p. 148). In its extreme version, the postmodern reader can
"make anyone else's speech mean anything we choose to make it"
(Schwartz, 1990, p. 30). Meaning is, in this view, radically indeterminate.
For Foucault (1980), interpretations are power and interest driven: "Truth
isn't outside power, or lacking in power . . . it is produced only by virtue of
multiple forms of constraint" (p. 131). There is a vast intellectual gulf between structural sociology and postmodernism. But both challenge the constraining power of culture by emphasizing the interest-driven ways in which
it is interpreted.

It is often pointed out that the claim of reader autonomy stumbles over
the so-called Mannheim problem—that is, the reflexive implications of relativism. For what is the point of publishing a text about reader autonomy, or
anything else, that can be interpreted any which way? If this is a sophomoric
point, it is warranted by the naive relativism of postmodernism, which, like
the denial of objective reality, is hard to take seriously. Wittgenstein undercut provocative philosophical assertions, like Descartes's claim to doubt the
existence of his body, with the argument that while one can utter the words,
one cannot *show* this doubt in conduct. One wants to ask, Can a post-

modernist *live* her theoretical professions? Could she interpret a stop sign to mean go? This philosophical posturing evokes C. S. Pierce's (1934) anticipation of Wittgenstein's critique: "[Descartes] skepticism will be a mere self-deception, and not a real doubt. . . . Let us not pretend to doubt in philosophy what we do not doubt in our hearts" (p. 156). The fact that the structural sociologist, or the economist, bothers to write or speak suggests a belief in the power of ideas that is theoretically denied.

Another problem with radical interpretivism is that, like other forms of skepticism, it has no stopping point. A rule can be variously interpreted. But if *the interpretation* can also be variously interpreted, we have entered a regress in which the very idea of rule-governed action is lost. If texts are infinitely malleable, the idea of a text is subverted, and each of us is locked into an irremediable solipsism of private interpretations. Indeed, the foundation of social order—that is, coordinated action, is undermined.

In allowing a role for interpretation, it is not necessary to accept the eccentric claim that texts, rules, and so on have *no* intrinsic meaning. *Moby Dick* cannot be "read" however the "empowered reader" chooses—for example, as a motorcycle repair manual: the machine won't run. Wittgenstein (1953) argues that the instruction "Complete this series: 1 . . . 2 . . . 3 . . ." can be variously interpreted, and he considers the possibility that "every course of action can be made out to accord with the rule" (para. 201). But it would be senseless to complete the series as "do . . . re . . . me" or "Vini, Vidi, Vici." One might imagine a game in which the challenge is to come up with odd responses. But this would be a game *because* it defies common sense. Without implied limits on responses, it would have no point. Furthermore, Wittgenstein's emphasis on practicality, and his arguments that meanings cannot be private, sets limits: interpretations and meanings must make sense in the context of a system of social practices. The doctrine of meaning and use (1953, para. 202) does not preclude the possibility of misuse, which is a major theme in Wittgenstein's critique of philosophy.

These points bear on the actual manipulation of rules in society. The exculpatory logic of Matza's delinquents (see Chapter 2) must be plausible. Their aim is to stretch the law, not entirely reject it. In this effort they show both a need for moral justification in terms of dominant values and some understanding of what the laws mean: no offender cites bankruptcy law to justify a mugging. Similarly, Sartre's (1957) emphasis on the interpretation of ethical rules can be exaggerated: while there are difficulties in interpreting Kant's injunction to treat all persons "never simply as a means, but always at the same time as an end," it could not plausibly be read to mean "kill all strangers." John Locke's liberalism has implications that challenged his intent. For example, his belief that persons "should be equal one amongst another without subordination or subjection" (Locke, 1952, p. 4) can be pulled to the left and turned against his commitment to capitalist accumulation, which leads to subordination and subjection. But Lockean liberation cannot be stretched to support fascism. Lockeans, such as Thomas Jefferson, owned slaves, and Locke himself held shares in the slave trade. But the contradiction between their beliefs and their practices were easily visible, and as DeTocqueville anticipated, they ultimately could not be explained away: "The most formidable of all the ills which threaten the future existence of the Union arises from the presence of a black population upon its territory" (DeTocqueville, 1961, p. 424). The frequency of social conflict about what rules are adopted shows that they make a difference in conduct and that they are not infinitely flexible: although the rules of chess allow players considerable latitude, changing them has consequences for how the game will be played.

Steve Derne (1994) illustrates both the creativity of actors *and* the limits imposed by culture. He finds that contemporary Indian men who defy the tradition of arranged marriage typically justify love matches from within their culture by "manipulat[ing] existing cultural stories" (p. 276). In one case, a respondent defended his choice of a bride, not by citing her personal characteristics or by reference to his own happiness, but drawing on traditional values, by emphasizing that she was of the same caste (p. 276). But Derne points out that while cultural norms are subject to opportunistic deployment, they nevertheless set limits on conduct: "Even as Hindu men act on their individual desires by breaking with social norms, they are constrained to use the rich, legitimate vocabulary that deemphasizes individual volition." As a result, "While the collectivist framework for understanding action does not keep men from innovating, it does constrain them by limiting the strategies they can use" (p. 279). Culture can be analogized to a chess set. While a player can display considerable ingenuity in moving the pieces, they must be moved according to the rules.

Radical skepticism about the meaning of texts calls to mind Wittgenstein's warning that philosophical errors emerge from a one-sided diet of examples (1953, para. 593). Disputes about the interpretation of literary works, the domain that inspired much poststructuralist thinking, cannot be taken as paradigmatic: textual ambiguity, as Wittgenstein (1953) pointed out, is a *variable:* a signpost "sometimes leaves room for doubt and sometimes not" (para. 85). At an airport I once found myself unsure about whether an arrow—↑—meant that my destination was straight ahead or a level up. But ordinarily such a sign leaves little room for real doubt. Moreover, even in the domains most subject to interpretive dispute there is usually consensus about basic meanings. Neitz and Hall (1993) sketch the critical controversy about the meaning of the movie *Mildred Pierce.* But they point out that "not one of the critics doubts that *Mildred Pierce* is about gender relations" (p. 203). In his grand jury testimony, President Clinton drew laughs by professing to be uncertain about the meaning of *is, alone,* and *sexual relations.*

The limits on interpretation mean that the content of a culture has consequences for action that endure interpretative innovation. The growth of capitalism in the Meiji restoration shows the durable influence of culture amidst changing interpretations. Japanese capitalism did not, as in the European case, develop through the emergence of a new class carrying a new ideology. Instead, entrepreneurs were mainly samurai. This example illustrates the *adaptability* of culture insofar as business had been traditionally disdained by the samurai. But it also illustrates the *enduring influence* of culture. According to Kamekichi Takahashi (1969), "A special Japanese entrepreneurial mentality developed from the leaven of the traditional samurai consciousness among the leading businessmen of the Meiji era" (p. 34). Specific themes in the samurai code, like the ideal of service to his lord, provided the dedicated government administrators that enhanced modernization. Also, while traditional samurai held money making in contempt, parts of their code, like submission to organizational discipline and service to the nation, could be reappropriated to support business enterprise. The concepts of "samurai in spirit but businessmen in talent" and "service to the nation through industry" provided bridges between the feudal and the modern orders. Indeed, "the resurrection in a new garb of the traditional samurai spirit" (p. 28) created an entrepreneurial class that was more adept at modern business than the traditional merchant class. But the traditional values did not evaporate leaving no trace: differences between Japanese and American capitalism, such as the reciprocal loyalties of firm and employee, suggest their enduring influence.

The durability of cultural training is stressed in Albert Cohen's (1955) theory of delinquency. When lower-class youths find that they lack the cultural skills for conventional success, they sometimes turn to nonutilitarian forms of crime, such as vandalism and violence. But conventional values are not extinguished. Cohen sees a compulsive and irrational quality in much juvenile crime that he interprets as reaction-formation—that is, a struggle against deeply internalized values that cannot be achieved.

The limited adaptability of culture suggests that a cultural legacy can fail, under any interpretation, to offer resources for certain situations: it is unlikely that samurai ideals could be used to support, say, peasant labor. Many societies cannot replicate the success of Japan because their cultures cannot be adjusted to the modern context. The New Zealand movie *Once Were Warriors* depicts the difficulties the Maori encounter in facing a modern society for which their warrior legacy offers scant resources. When successful reappropriations occur, the culture must be examined to identify the features that lend themselves to new courses of action.[1]

This conception of culture as, within limits, adaptable, can shed light on the enduring controversy over its bearing on economic development. In recent years, a focal point of this debate has been the role of Confucianism in the growth of Asian economies. Critics of the Asian version of the Weberian thesis, such as J. Bhagwati (1998, p. 34), cite the long-term stagnation of economies enveloped in Confucian values and describe the themes that discourage entrepreneurialism, such as contempt for material greed, disdain for manual labor, the emphasis on aesthetic cultivation, and so on.

But these anticapitalist values do not preclude the mobilization of Confucian values to support economic development. Analyzing the cultural roots of Chinese capitalism, Redding (1993) describes the Confucian conception of the family as "the central pivot of life" and argues that "the ideological base for the work ethic lies in the deep sense of obligation to family" (p. 39). A virtual "cult of family" (p. 52), inspiring a powerful sense of duty even to past and future generations, plays a role comparable to the doctrine of predestination in Calvinism by encouraging an extra-rational obsession with work.[2] Also, the Confucian ideal of self-cultivation encouraged a discipline useful to a variety of tasks.

While Confucianism was explicitly hostile to money making, it nevertheless provided values that, in changed circumstances, supported capitalist enterprise. Those who emphasize the incompatibilities of Confucianism and capitalism, and conclude that culture is irrelevant to development, read cultures too literally and fail to apply the creative imagination its bearers often display. Bhagwati (1998) quotes an early nineteenth-century observer of Japan on the lack of a work ethic: "To see your men at work made me feel that you are a very satisfied easy-going race who reckon time is no object." His conclusion that "growth seems to be compatible with all kinds of values and cultures" (p. 34) underestimates the paradox of the flexibility *and* the enduring influence of culture. This is captured in Redding's (1993) description of the cultural roots of Chinese entrepreneurs: "The Overseas Chinese have created social systems where the businessman can escape from the dead weight of Chinese tradition. His immense flourishing in these circumstances, although in part a tribute to what he brought from his cultural heritage, is at the same time an acknowledgement that parts of the Confucian tradition were abandoned as useless" (p. 197).

Redding's portrayal of a value system leading its carriers to goals that were not originally intended evokes Weber's (1958) thesis that "the cultural consequences of the Reformation were to a great extent . . . unforeseen and even unwished for results of the labours of the reformers. They were often far removed from or even in contradiction to all that they themselves sought to attain" (p. 90). The phrase "unforeseen and even unwished for" could describe Marx's portrayal of the internal dynamics of liberalism.

CULTURAL DOPES

The (partial) autonomy of culture—that is, its power to control behavior and to resist opportunistic interpretation—can be emphasized with examples that reveal that culture is not *merely* adaptive to opportunities. A warrant to take culture seriously as a force in its own right can be found in cases that structural sociology—and economics—cannot explain: actors slavishly following beliefs that subvert their practical needs. The Yanomami Indians of the Amazon believe that bad magic is the cause of even accidental and natural deaths and that vengeance must be taken. Consequently, the tribe is riven with revenge killings: 30% of the deaths of adult males are homicides (Elster, 1989a, p. 136).

Examples like this are not rare. Robert Edgarton (1992) in *Sick Societies* presents a variety of foolish and self-destructive practices that hold actors in their grip. For example, for all their technological ingenuity, the Inuit of the Arctic Circle sustained many emphatically *mal*adaptive practices:

> They avoided lakes that they admitted offered superior fishing and hunting because they were thought to be inhabited by monstrous man-eating fish, and they avoided excellent campsites in order to avoid malevolent ghosts and spirits. Good hunting and fishing areas could not be visited at night for fear of "wild babies"—creatures resembling human infants—that were thought to devour people like wolves or, more remarkable still, tickle them to death. (p. 60)

The belief that illness is caused by witchcraft and that witches must be killed led the Gebusi of Papua New Guinea to replicate the Yanomami in rates of murder (p. 172). On the advice of an eighteen-year-old prophet, the Xhosa, in 1850, killed all their dun- and yellow-colored cattle to break a drought thought to be the work of witches (p. 173).

Edgarton's purpose is to challenge the common view in anthropology that culture is invariably adaptive. This sentiment, particularly when applied to primitive societies, is fueled by ethical and epistemological relativism and romanticism. It reached an apex in Malinowski's functionalist claim that "in every type of civilization, every custom, material object, idea and belief fulfills some vital function, has some task to accomplish, represents an indispensable part within a working whole" (quoted in Edgarton, p. 31). Routinely underreported by anthropologists was abundant evidence of "senseless cruelty, needless suffering, and monumental folly" (p. 15). The Ijaw of Nigeria, despite valuing children above all else, killed twins: a practice they could not explain (p. 58). Tasmanians, suffering intense hunger, refused to eat fish (p. 49) etc. etc.

To combat the "functionalist fallacy," Jon Elster (1989a) cites numerous examples of the "reality, importance and autonomy" (p. 107) of norms that cannot be rationalized as adaptive. Even the use of money is bound by norms. For example, we hesitate to offer a neighbor money to mow our lawn because "it isn't done." No one would be harmed by selling a place in a movie line—and two people would be better off—but this too "isn't done" (p. 111). Medical practice is replete with norms that subvert instrumental calculation, including a reluctance "to conserve resources by withdrawing care from acutely ill patients even when the anticipated benefit of that care was vanishingly small" (p. 115). Elster quotes DeTocqueville on the appeals of egalitarianism in democratic societies: "The passion for equality seeps into every corner of the human heart, expands and fills the whole. It is no use telling them that by this blind surrender to an exclusive passion they are compromising their dearest interests; they are deaf" (p. 123). Norms of vengeance and retribution can be especially destructive. Recent Balkan history has confirmed Djilas's emphasis on the obsession with vengeance in his Montenegran childhood: "Revenge is an overpowering and consuming fire. It flares upon and burns away every other thought and emotion" (quoted in Elster, 1989a, p. 120).[3]

There are many noninstrumental dimensions to culture. The literature of socioeconomics is rich with examples of the power of moral rules to override practical interests. There is an extensive experimental literature showing that considerations of justice play a prominent role in economic transactions and can frequently override self-interest. For example, in the name of fairness, experimental subjects commonly allocate higher rewards to teammates, and hence less to themselves, than is required. Often, payments deemed less than fair are rejected altogether (see Kahneman et al., 1987).

Attempts at synthesis of cultural and structural explanation often falter because of a failure to recognize the autonomy of culture. For example, Sewell (1992) undercuts the theoretical role of culture by ultimately subordinating it to instrumental purposes: "If schemas [cultural rules] are to be sustained or reproduced over time . . . they must be validated by the accumulation of resources that their enactment engenders" (p. 13). But in making this point with the claim that a successful military operation will inspire a transformation of military tactics (p. 18), Sewell has chosen a particularly inappropriate domain. Arguing against Clausewitz's rationalist dictum, that "war is *not* the continuation of policy by other means" (emphasis added), John Keegan (1993, p. 3) provides numerous examples of military practice that defy practical sense. He argues that warfare is a deeply cultural and emotional endeavor that "reaches into the most secret places of the human heart, places where self dissolves rational purpose, where pride reigns, where emotion is paramount, where instinct is king" (p. 3).

Indeed, Sewell (1992) could hardly have chosen a less appropriate venue to demonstrate the priority of instrumental logic. Perhaps anticipating the problem of collective action, G. K. Chesterton warned that "the rational soldier will not fight," a fact that commanders know and make provisions for. While examples of self-interested defiance of authority (described in Chapter 4) are common, the military also illustrates the power of norms to bind men to circumstances of horrific danger. A character in James Jones's (1962) novel *The Thin Red Line,* having discovered that he is a coward, is astonished by his inability to take the coward's way out: "And here he lay, as bound and tied by his own mental processes and social indoctrination as if they were ropes, simply because while he could admit to himself privately that he was a coward, he did not have the guts to admit it publicly." Private Fife contemplates with astonishment the constraints of a brick wall that "was really no wall at all" (p. 216). There would be few medals awarded in combat if such norms could not overwhelm self-interest.

Introducing another nonrational aspect of combat, Noel Perrin's (1979) *Giving Up the Gun* describes the power of aesthetic preferences to overwhelm practical reason. In the sixteenth century, the Japanese firearms industry was among the most sophisticated in the world. Through government decree, there were hardly any firearms in Japan one hundred years later. There were plausibly instrumental reasons for this. Samurai dominance, based on swordsmanship, was threatened by the relative ease of gaining skill with firearms. But a contributory, perhaps even primary, reason for banning the manufacture of guns was that the samurai loved their swords: they were thought to embody "the soul of the samurai" (p. 36). Also, guns were disdained as vulgar, and gunfights were seen as crudely violent while swordplay could be appreciated as "a kind of danger-laden ballet" (p. 42). The bodily positions of a shooter were considered clumsy in comparison to the dancer's grace of the swordsman. These views rested on a unique aesthetic cum metaphysic: "The samurai of Japan were never willing to make a distinction between what was beautiful and what was useful" (p. 41). Also, battle for the samurai was a ritualized event that must conform to moral and aesthetic values. Paralleling the refusal of medieval European knights to use bows in combat, although they hunted with them, the samurai hunted with guns, but would not fight with them: Killing from a distance was thought to be cowardly (p. 102). Because firearms, more easily monopolized than edged weapons, do not in fact destabilize the elite, it seems likely that these aesthetic and moral values were not just a smokescreen for instrumental advantage. In the Satsuma Rebellion of 1876, a group of samurai quixotically, and suicidally, deployed their swords against firearms. And while many samurai businessmen used their traditional culture instrumentally, the kamikaze followed its imperatives to their deaths.

The social science commitment to "rationalizing the irrational" (Elster, 1984, p. 135) is especially evident in the conception of culture as adaptive. But culture is not merely a convenience, instrumentally interpreted to serve practical interests. Rules destructive to human well-being can rule. Kornhauser (1978) points out, approvingly, that all versions of functionalism "agree that human beings are so constituted that they do not knowingly construct cultural values from experiences that are obviously destructive of self or society" (p. 15). Criticizing culturally based theories of crime, she contends that "delinquent activities cannot be collectively endowed with value by human beings whose fate it is to live with one another" (p. 229). Her conclusion is that crime represents the loss of cultural constraints, not the grip of perverse values. But Steven Holmes (1990) has assembled a list of motivations subversive of self-interest and social order (pride, anger, fear, grief, hatred, etc.) that figure prominently in the writings of Adam Smith, David Hume, and others typically portrayed as seeing "calculating self-interest" as dominant. These motives include the foundation of the cultural dope: "the obsessive desire to follow rules" (p. 279). Many of these motivations have found their way into cultural systems. In contrast to the functionalist belief that the purpose of social rules is to curb unruly individuals, John Locke (1954), although a rationalist and a utilitarian, believed that destructive impulses are often institutionalized:

> There is almost no vice, no infringement of natural law, no moral wrong, which anyone who consults the history of the world and observes the affairs of men will not readily perceive to have been not only privately committed somewhere on earth, but also approved by public authority and custom. Nor has there been anything so shameful in its nature that it has not been either sanctified somewhere by religion, or put in the place of virtue and abundantly rewarded with praise. (Essay V, p. 167)

It was argued earlier that contemporary cultural theory has provided a necessary antidote to the conception of actors as cultural dopes. But emphasizing "the creative, resistant subject as cultural receiver" (Press, 1994, p. 229) underestimates the authority of rules. Similarly, the ethnomethodological portrayal of norms "as elastic and revisable resources which are adjusted and altered over the course of their application to concrete contexts" (Heritage, 1987, p. 247) portrays actors as too artful, too knowing, to account for the cases in which actors serve culture, often at great cost to their "material" and other interests.

Swidler's (1986) concept of culture as a "tool kit" raises the same problem. Arguing that culture shapes action, not by setting goals, but by providing competencies that govern the choice of goals, she claims that "people will come to value ends for which their cultural equipment is well suited" (p. 277). In this view, actors evaluate their culturally derived competencies and then choose suitable goals. Culture thus becomes a convenience that actors can instrumentally manage, rejecting goals that are out of reach. But Cohen's (1955) theory of delinquency suggests that ingrained goals are not so easily jettisoned. Surely much human anguish comes from resistance to adapting our goals to our circumstances.

Also, while Swidler offers some compelling examples of actors following their skills—or habitus—rather than their goals, other examples show that ends can compel action and even inspire development of a new habitus. A familiar example of the turning of cultural skills to new ends is the redeployment by modern Jews of traditional religious scholarship to secular purposes. But Zionism suggests a different process. For some, this movement aimed at cultivating a new habitus. In *Tough Jews,* Paul Breines (1990) describes a significant Zionist motivation as the belief that statelessness created unmanly Jews: nonviolent, timid, ingratiating, and so on. The desire to remediate these traits helped motivate the Zionist project. For many of its advocates, a Jewish homeland was necessary to create "healthy" Jews. Max Nordau, one of Zionist founder Theodor Herzl's acolytes, advocated the creation of "Muskeljudentum"—muscle Jews—through the founding of gymnastic clubs in order to reproduce the Hebrews of ancient times: "Let us take up our oldest traditions: let us once again become deep-chested, sturdy, sharp-eyed men" (Breines, 1990, p. 143). Vladmir

Jabotinsky was the most aggressive advocate of the effort to remake the ghetto Jew:

> Our starting point is to take the typical Yid of today and to imagine his diametrical opposite. . . . Because the Yid is ugly, sickly, and lacks decorum, we shall endow the ideal image of the Hebrew with masculine beauty. The Yid is trodden upon and easily frightened and, therefore, the Hebrew ought to be proud and independent. The Yid is despised by all and, therefore, the Hebrew ought to charm all. The Yid has accepted submission and, therefore, the Hebrew ought to learn to command. The Yid wants to conceal his identity from strangers and, therefore, the Hebrew should look the world straight in the eye and declare: "I am a Hebrew" (Breines, 1990, p. 165).[4]

The goal, or end, of Zionism was, for some, chosen to create persons with a different sort of "cultural equipment." What Swidler (1986) considers largely fixed—habitus—is here precisely the object of transformation. A goal *incompatible* with an ingrained habitus was chosen in order to engender a new habitus. Many studies of social mobility have described the process through which members of excluded groups cultivate a new habitus to attain higher status.[5]

Arguing that "established cultural ends are jettisoned with apparent ease" (p. 278), Swidler (1986) argues that cultural skills have more to do with behavior than do goals. She draws on Michael Walzer's *The Revolution of the Saints* to show that Calvin "repeatedly adjusted the logic of this theology to stimulate the discipline he saw as necessary for fallen man" (p. 280). In this example, ends are chosen, or rejected, in terms of their compatibility with cultural competencies: "What people want [their ends] . . . is of little help in explaining their action" (p. 274). But Swidler is too hasty in dismissing the importance of ends. Calvin's need to articulate the goal of salvation in order to inspire a disciplined way of life actually shows their importance for conduct.

A further problem emerges in the problem of distinguishing between means and ends. The restraint Calvin sought to redeem "fallen man" is, arguably, an end—an ideal of behavior. Similarly, it is not clear that the samurai who turned to business was adapting an established habitus to a new end or sought stable goals through a new habitus. If the conduct of the samurai is seen to be directed to an abstract end—such as service to society—the shift from warfare to business can be seen as a shift in venue rather than goal. The pursuit of business success can thus be interpreted, not as a new goal that matches a fixed habitus, but as a way to achieve a fixed goal by adopting a new habitus.

A surprising contrast to the concept of culture as adaptive is provided by Marx who, at least in his early work, acknowledged that culture has a grip that can override practical need and an emotional appeal that is at least partly independent of its instrumental value: "Ideas, which have conquered our intelligence and our minds, ideas that reason has forged in our conscience, are chains from which we cannot tear ourselves away without breaking our hearts" (quoted in Alexander, 1988a, p. 261). His characterization of "The tradition of all the dead generations" as weighing like "a nightmare the brain of the living" (Marx, 1967a, p. 15) suggests a similar view. And Engels, more the economic determinist than Marx, considered futile efforts to find a "material" explanation for every social practice. Commenting on primitive myths, he says, "Surely it would be pedantic to try and find economic causes for all this primitive nonsense" (quoted in Feuer, 1959, p. 25). While culture is often manipulated to maximize instrumental needs, this is not all that culture does. Sahlins's (1976) argument that culture *defines* utility implies that it cannot only *serve* utility.

PART III

---◆◆◆---

TOWARD A MULTIDIMENSIONAL SOCIOLOGY

6

Understanding Opportunity: Three Cases

◆◆◆ ─────────────────────────────────────

Having seen, in Chapter 5, that culture is (partially) autonomous—that is, that it does not always serve material interests and that it is not infinitely malleable, an important step toward a multidimensional sociology can be taken by showing its role in *constituting* opportunity. The need for this is suggested by the arguments in Chapter 3 that structural variables, especially blocked opportunity, cannot account for some key social phenomena, such as crime and status attainment. In the view to be developed, opportunity cannot be conceptualized as "external" and "objective" because it is constituted by the cultural resources of actors. The method will be to reexamine three empirical studies in which the causal priority of opportunity structures is theoretically affirmed but that provide sufficient ethnographic detail to allow a rival interpretation. Despite the authors' stubborn commitment to structural explanation, their data contain the seeds of a very different understanding of the process of status attainment—one in which culturally ingrained dispositions are deeply implicated in the fates of their subjects. The aim, however, is to go beyond the familiar plea for a multidimensional sociology in which culture affects choices within boundaries set by structures of opportunity. Rather, it is to show that opportunity cannot be conceptualized apart from the cultural resources of actors.

AIN'T NO MAKIN' IT, BY JAY MACLEOD

This ethnography of two groups of young men living in the same public housing project finds that, despite facing similar circumstances, their outlooks, values, and ways of life are radically different. This is intriguing to MacLeod (1987) because he approached the project committed to Bourdieu's concept of structural determination: "Objective structures tend to produce structured subjective dispositions that produce structured actions which, in turn, tend to reproduce objective structure" (quoted in MacLeod, 1987, p. 14). The main mechanism of this process of reproduction is "the regulation of aspirations" (p. 21). But MacLeod found that there is considerable play between objective structures and subjective dispositions and, specifically, between aspirations and opportunities.

The Hallway Hangers incarnate all the vices ever attributed to the underclass. Fighting is the main source of status, and one of their local heroes is a man in prison for shooting two police officers: "He's golden, he's there. That's the best you can fucking do" (p. 27). They have numerous arrests for theft, violence, and so on, and they consume and sell a pharmacopoeia of intoxicants. They hate schools and teachers and disdain academic achievement: "Good grades in school can lead to ostracism" (p. 26). Women are objects of scorn and exploitation, and racial hatred (the Hallway Hangers are white) is one of the dominant motifs of their conversation.

The (black) Brothers are described in sharp contrast. While facing essentially the same opportunities, they do well in school and are persuaded that this will ensure their futures. The violence, drugs, and thieving that occupy the Hallway Hangers are eschewed by the Brothers as pointless and self-destructive.

Perhaps the main difference in the habitus of these groups is that the Brothers have accepted the ideology of achievement. This appears in their basic understandings of social order. While the Hallway Hangers are bitter about the lack of social fairness—they "look to outside forces" (p. 69) to explain successes and failure—the Brothers believe that society is open to effort: "If you work hard, really put your mind to it, you can do it. You can make it" (p. 79). The Brothers voice an ethic of personal responsibility and "attribute lack of success on the job market exclusively to personal inadequacy" (p. 78). In contrast, the Hallway Hangers believe that success is mostly a matter of pull. Of those who succeed, "Their fucking parents know people" (p. 72). And they are cynical. Successful businessmen are seen as "legally ripping everyone off" (p. 32).

There is a sharp contrast in each group's sense of personal efficacy. The Hallway Hangers feel that they have little control over their futures: "I don't fucking know. Twenty years. I may be fucking dead. I live a day at a time. I'll probably be in the fucking pen" (p. 61). But a Brother expresses confidence about his future: "I'll have a regular house, y'know, with a yard and everything. I'll have a steady job, a good job" (p. 5). The Brothers mull over the sorts of lives they want and consider what must be done to attain them: "I might have a wife, some kids. I might be holding a regular business job, like an old guy. I hope I'll be able to do a lot of skiing and stuff like that when I'm old" (p. 74). The Hallway Hangers refuse to think about their futures: "Around here you gotta take life day by day" (p. 61), and true to the culture of poverty, they insist on immediate gratification: "All of us down here, we just don't wanna make a buck, we wanna make a fast buck. We want it *now*" (p. 106). MacLeod finds that while the Brothers "have hopes for the future" (p. 77), "the concept of an aspiration is essentially alien to the Hallway Hangers" (p. 68). This is related to their belief that the system is closed to them: "Out here, there's not the opportunity to make money" (p. 5). In contrast, the Brothers believe that "If you work hard, it'll pay off in the end" (p. 79).

The Hallway Hangers' conception of masculinity is especially disabling. It underlies their hostility toward school. Academic work is not the sort of thing a real man does: "If you're a straight A student, you get razzed" (p. 26). While the Brothers "show no evidence of disrespect for teachers or other school officials, and their disciplinary records are for the most part clean" (p. 91), the Hallway Hangers resist subordination, considering it to be an affront to their autonomy: "I hate the fucking teachers. I don't like someone always telling me what the fuck to do" (p. 107). The only teacher they respect has a black belt in karate and earns a lot of money as a real estate broker.

One—arguably structural—factor that helps explain the differences between these two groups is that, while most live in single-parent households, the Brothers are more likely to have a male authority in the home. Also, all of the Brothers' fathers work (p. 55). While high school diplomas are rare in the families of the Hallway Hangers, nearly half the parents of the Brothers have graduated high school. Most important, parents of the Brothers exercise authority over their children. The contrast in parenting between the groups was evident to one of the Brothers:

> I guess our parents are a lot tighter than their parents. . . . From the very beginning, ever since we were born they'd be telling us, "Do this; do that." Always disciplining us. As far as their parents go, I can't really say their parents are bad, but their parents aren't helping any. (p. 57)

This evaluation is confirmed by one of the Hallway Hanger's description of his mother: "She don't fucking care. I mean, I'm sure she cares, but she don't push nothing on me" (p. 56). Parental training seems to have more impact on dispositions than do opportunities.[1]

MacLeod draws a theoretical baseline from Bourdieu that emphasizes the control of opportunity over outlook and conduct: "The structure of the objective chances of social upgrading . . . conditions agent's dispositions towards upgrading through education—dispositions which in turn play a determining role in defining the likelihood of entering education, adhering to its norms and succeeding in it" (Bourdieu & Passeron, 1977, p. 156). But his data show that there is considerable play between habitus and opportunity insofar as two groups facing approximately equivalent "objective chances" have developed entirely different dispositions that strongly affect their life chances. While the Brothers' "objective life chances are probably lower than those of the Hallway Hangers" (MacLeod, 1987, p. 80), "none seems to feel that nurturing an aspiration is a futile exercise" (p. 74). Moreover, there are signs that the Brothers' futures will approximate their hopes. They are doing fairly well in school and seem bound for solid working-class or even middle-class status. The futures of the Hallway Hangers are bleak and they know it.

These findings tempt MacLeod to abandon belief in the controlling power of social structure: "What the Hallway Hangers and the Brothers demonstrate quite clearly . . . is that the way in which individuals and groups respond to structures of domination is open-ended" (p. 138). Rather than seeing persons as controlled by opportunity structures, he acknowledges that "individuals, with their distinctive assets and character traits, have a good deal of autonomy" (p. 148). In opposition to a one-way determinism, he avers the "interpenetration of human consciousness and structural determinants" and argues "for a balance between theories that emphasize structural determinants and those that give prominence to the cultural sphere" (p. 148).

But despite abundant contrary evidence, MacLeod ultimately argues that there is "no escape" from "structural forms of class domination" (p. 152). Having acknowledged "the relative autonomy of the cultural level" (p. 139) and the "autonomy" of individuals from the "structure of domination" (p. 149), he then claims that

> cultural practices operate within the limits defined by class, gender, and racial barriers ... it matters little how lower-class teenagers respond to the vicissitudes of their situation. No matter how clearly they understand their lives, no matter what cultural innovations they produce, no matter how diligently they devote themselves to school, they cannot escape the constraints of social class. (p. 149)

After showing that the Brothers are well along in escaping their class origins, the text—remarkably—ends with, "The tragedy is that the Brothers are more likely to find fault with themselves than with the economic system" (p. 162).

THE MISSISSIPPI CHINESE, BY JAMES LOEWEN

In the closing years of the nineteenth century, landowners in the Mississippi Delta radically changed the demography of their district and inadvertently initiated a fascinating social experiment. They imported a few hundred Chinese laborers, mainly from California, to employ as sharecroppers. But within a few years, there were *no* Chinese sharecroppers working in the Delta. Nearly all of them earned their living by operating retail groceries serving blacks. This transition from sharecropping to small business was the first step in an extraordinary tale of social mobility, economic and cultural. When they first arrived, the Chinese were defined as virtual blacks. But over time, they were more or less officially upgraded to the status of white people. This might seem to be testimony to the structural nature of opportunity. For the key to Chinese mobility was a market niche that provided the means for their social ascent. But important cultural factors were implicated in the existence of this opportunity and in the capacity of the Chinese to exploit it.

First, the niche existed because of unwillingness of whites to engage in retail trade with black customers. In the status system of the South, waiting on blacks was seen as degrading, and the few whites who ran grocery stores in black areas were shunned. Altogether, the Delta maintained certain "pre-capitalist, almost feudal" (Loewen, 1988, p. 51) notions of status, and retail trade, as well as manual labor, was not considered to be honorable work: "Mississippi whites have been neither attracted toward nor particularly successful in retail business" (p. 49). But because they were not part of the local status system, the Chinese saw no degradation in this, nor were they considered by whites to be stigmatized by contact with blacks. As strangers, they were "relatively impervious to the status attacks against businessmen in black neighborhoods which kept whites from competing with them effectively" (p. 50).

This market niche remained unfilled by blacks. Loewen's explanation of this emphasizes features of Mississippi blacks and the peculiarities of the Southern caste system. First, in contrast to the Chinese, blacks had no business tradition. Several of Loewen's black informants "pointed to a timidity about risk-taking in general as a prime source of black business failures and of their smallness" (p. 44). Also, as participants in Southern culture, Mississippi blacks absorbed values inimical to business enterprise: "They have taken over from Delta whites the notion that neither hard work in business nor 'waiting on' or catering to the customer are 'honorable' tasks" (p. 41).[2] Delta blacks were further disadvantaged by the pulls of solidarity with potential customers: black customers demanded credit from black merchants that was not expected from the Chinese. The Chinese benefited from "the lack of close personal ties between the Chinese merchant and his prospective black clientele," whereas for the black merchant, "personal ties mean personal claims" (p. 39).

Intense jealousy further disabled black entrepreneurs. While the Chinese honored those who sought advancement, blacks were resentful of upward mobility: "There is a marked pattern of jealousy in Delta Negro society" (p. 45). This attitude was especially intense among middle-class blacks who were reluctant to patronize black storekeepers: "The middle-class Negroes hate to see another Negro get ahead" (p. 47).[3] Also, peculiarities of the Southern caste system advantaged Chinese merchants. Blacks took pleasure in being waited on by white clerks. This gratification could not be provided by a black businessman but could be approximated by a Chinese. This status enhancement was amplified if merchants denied respect to lower-class blacks, and so "some Chinese merchants feel that they must be nasty to the lower-class black in order to get business from the middle class. Being rude to 'niggers' sets the Chinese up as a surrogate white, so that it is an achievement to gain his courtesy" (p. 47). And finally, black merchants faced "a lack of trust in their competence and honesty" (p. 47). Black customers believed, often contrary to fact, that they got better deals from white or Chinese merchants.

The portrait of Chinese success in the Mississippi Delta can be completed by an understanding of other features of Chinese culture. In addition to having an established business tradition, the Chinese received help from family and friends. They loaned money to one another and vouched for the integrity of newcomers. Retail groceries could be started with little capital because, with this support, wholesalers were willing to front them stock. In contrast to the jealousy among blacks, and their weak family ties (p. 41), Chinese provided crucial support for one another's business activities.

The upshot of this system was that the Mississippi Chinese were able, in a few generations, to approximate white status. At the time of Loewen's study, Chinese grocers, which included nearly all Chinese in the area, earned "perhaps twice as much, on the average, as the white median income in the Delta" (p. 53). The Chinese were eventually able to attain near parity with whites in social status despite difficulties of language, a lack of political power, little informal influence, slight knowledge of the legal system, and so on. Originally treated as virtual blacks, the Mississippi Chinese, by the 1960s, had become virtual whites: living in the same neighborhoods, belonging to the same churches and clubs, and, increasingly, intermarrying with white people. In 1965, a Chinese was elected mayor of a Delta town, and in a final irony, Chinese merchants were recruited by the (white) citizens councils (p. 96).

Loewen's theoretical understanding of his findings is curious. In a remark oddly discontinuous with much of his book, Loewen warns that the success of Chinese in Mississippi "is not . . . to be explained by imagined or real cultural traits of the entering sojourners, for the same people journeyed elsewhere with very different results" (p. 36). He argues that "pulls from the American social structure far outweigh possible pushes from the value system brought over by the immigrant" (p. 56). Loewen's discomfort with the role of culture is particularly apparent in comments written twenty years after the original research. Denying that the dominant image of Chinese immigrants as a "model minority" reflects "some innate or even some basic cultural characteristic of the group," Loewen suggests that these traits are an adaptive response to their situation: "Immigrant groups construct, negotiate, and change their ethnic identities in relation to their aspirations and values, the views and behavior of other groups they must deal with, and the social and economic realities they face" (p. 201). This is an ambiguous, or confused, statement insofar as "aspirations and values" are separated from "ethnic identities." But it reveals an attempt to shift emphasis from the cultural traits of Chinese to "social and economic realities."[4]

However, the heart of Loewen's book clearly indicates that various traits of the Chinese essential to their success antedated their experience of American society. Also, his portrayal of Delta society shows that the opportunities available to Chinese immigrants emerge out of a complex cultural system. It might be argued that in some sense the Chinese had access to an "objective" opportunity. But this "social and economic reality" cannot be separated from various features of Southern culture, and the ability of the Chinese to exploit it is culturally rooted. Early Chinese arrivals encouraged relatives to join them because "the economic situation in Mississippi was so promising" (p. 34). This perception of an area widely considered to be economically stagnant, and providing so few opportunities for indigenes, vividly illustrates the interpenetration of structural opportunities with culture and psychology.

HARD CHOICES, BY KATHLEEN GERSON

Kathleen Gerson's (1985) study of women's career choices was cited in Chapter 2 to illustrate how opportunity modifies cultural training. But it also illustrates the limitations of opportunity theory. Gerson's thesis is that the balance between the availability of jobs and good options for homemaking is more important than early socialization in determining the course of her subject's lives. Her main evidence is the finding that women who were traditionally oriented early in their lives frequently developed career commitments later on and vice versa. Indeed, "Change was more common than stability" (p. 67). Women who encountered good domestic situations—well-employed husbands supportive of child bearing—were drawn to homemaking, while the pull of good job opportunities, or the push of financial or domestic stress, channeled women into paid careers, largely independently of how they were brought up and even of their early adult values: "An unanticipated encounter with the structure of opportunities either at home or at work almost always triggered the change in these women's life direction" (p. 70).

Cultural and psychological dispositions are seen by Gerson as having little weight. Closely following Kanter's (1977) argument, she portrays women's beliefs and values as optimizing adaptations rather than as the expressions of "a distinct feminine personality" (Gerson, 1985, p. 200) or "deep-seated gender differences in motivation" (p. 201). Preferences are seen as adaptive. Even those women who choose traditional lives are, Gerson believes, driven more by the structure of opportunities than by their values: "Domestically oriented women faced an opportunity structure that motivated them to reproduce both a traditional sexual division of labor and an ideology to justify that arrangement" (p. 132). Expressed preferences for domesticity are interpreted as reflecting situational constraints rather than internalized values: "Given the limited opportunities these women encountered in the paid labor force, such a stance is hardly surprising" (p. 130). Neither values nor personality traits but "the structuring of options open to women" (p. 201) explains their choices: "Their action did not result from a psychological handicap peculiar to the female sex" (p. 96).

However, Gerson's data often contradict her theoretical model. Her interviews show that the women's opportunities cannot be disentangled from cultural values, their own and others'. For example, when offered a chance to move from secretarial to sales work, one woman deferred to her husband's wish that she remain a secretary (p. 96). Another relinquished a desire to join the police force when her husband objected. Gerson explains these choices as responses to "structural circumstances that forced them to choose between love and work" (p. 96). But just as opportunity structures in Mississippi emerged out of a system of cultural values, women's "structural" circumstances are importantly formed by the culturally based preferences of their husbands: "Patriarchal authority prevailed" (p. 97). In another case, a woman claiming to be 'sort of starstruck' with her husband

(p. 102) chose early pregnancy over a career. Gerson explains this in terms of "the structure of traditional (or patriarchal) marriage and the maintenance of a committed relationship within such a marriage" (p. 102). She describes another woman who gave up hopes of a career in law or business in deference to the traditionalist values of her family: "It was pretty much put down by the family, who felt that was ridiculous" (p. 104). By including the preferences of husbands and families as structural constraints, Gerson, like Loewen, has incorporated cultural values into her concept of social structure. Surely the women Gerson interviewed faced what can appropriately be called constraints, which they sought to make the best of. As noted in Chapter 1, many theorists include culture as a kind of structure. But these constraints and women's reactions to them cannot be purged of the cultural and psychological elements that Gerson purports to supersede by emphasizing the dominating influence of structures of opportunity. While using the rhetoric of "objective" opportunity to explain conduct, which she contrasts with cultural explanations, she has conflated the two.

THE SOCIAL CONSTRUCTION OF OPPORTUNITY

Each of the studies surveyed here employs a theoretical model in which opportunity is seen as controlling, not just unequal outcomes, but conduct, culture, and personality. But the data resist the authors' program of superseding cultural with structural analysis. The key barriers to mobility in these studies are cultural values, such as attitudes about retail trade, women's proper place, and schooling.

As discussed in Chapter 5, many theorists include culture as a kind of structural barrier. But while culture can be theorized, in some extended sense, as an "external/objective" factor, it was argued that actors are not trager of culture. Perhaps most tellingly, Wittgenstein has shown that even a resolve to follow rules requires an interpretive process that loosens their constraining power. Most important for these cases, portraying actors as prisoners of their training contradicts the author's theoretical project. Gerson's women, and Mississippi whites and blacks, were blocked, not primarily by the "objective" availability of alternatives, but by values that made them sensitive to the disapproval of husbands and the stigma of retail trade. This does not show a slavish obedience to culture. But it does show that social disapproval mattered because the subjects of these studies held values that overwhelmed their economic interests.

In Gerson's study, the cultural attitudes that block women's opportunities barely approximate the "thinglike" quality of structural barriers. To be effective, they require *compliance*. Gerson uses an objectivist rhetoric, speaking of women as "forced," "consigned," and "blocked." In this, she replicates the self-interpretations of her subjects: "I didn't have much choice" (p. 97). "There were no other options for me at that time" (p. 104). But this is a misleading way to describe deference to familial preferences—and a prime example of what Sartre called "bad faith": the masking of choice with the rhetoric of constraint. This can be highlighted by imagining the likelihood of a man becoming a househusband in deference to comparable pressures. Denise and William Bielby (1988) found that women are indeed more responsive than men to incentives in the labor market, moving in and out of paid labor as remuneration rises and falls. But they conclude that this means that women's normative commitment to work is weaker than men's for whom, as Friedland and Robertson (1990) put it, "working fulfills strong normative expectations formed early in a man's life about what a male does" (p. 26). It is worth noting that Gerson (1985) interviewed women who were young adults in the 1970s, a period in which, because traditional barriers had begun to break down, the rhetoric of "forcing" had become less appropriate. The newly emergent feminism provided cultural resources that many women drew on to support the pursuit of careers, as the data on women's mobility cited in Chapter 4 show. Gerson would be on stronger ground if the barriers were the attitudes of employers because their power to hire and fire does not rest on the compliance of women.

Importantly, Loewen (1988) does not explain why retail trade is disdained in the South nor does Gerson explain why husbands prefer their wives in domestic roles. A full structural analysis cannot stop at including normative sanctions in the calculations of those they govern: it must provide a parallel account of the *origins* of those sanctions—that is, such norms must be shown to be in their advocate's self-interest. But the stigma of retail work and hostility to women doing "men's" work are left hanging. Indeed, because the first narrowed the options of Mississippi whites and the second lowered family incomes, these values were, arguably, maladaptive.[5]

The Hallway Hangers (MacLeod, 1987) present the strongest challenge to the theoretical program of structural sociology. Given their prolific deviance, their portrayal as slaves to rules is implausible. But while they were not normative drones, they were disabled by their own values and habitus, which, outside of their peer group, cost them dearly. It is doubtful that the disdain for retail trade in Mississippi or the exclusion of women from men's work can be interpreted as maximizing responses. It is certain that the Hallway Hangers inflicted substantial damage on themselves. In light of Edgarton's (1992) examples of dysfunctional cultures (Chapter 5), this should come as no surprise.

The concept of opportunity has been underconceptualized by structural sociology—and by neoclassical economics. Opportunities are conceived of as "external" and "objective": such as doors that can be open or closed. Cultural values backed by social power—such as the refusal of an employer to hire—can indeed constitute external barriers. But in each of these studies, barriers are not "thinglike." Various traits of actors are implicated. This suggests that actors and their cultural values do not merely react to or reflect opportunities: they importantly *constitute* them. Rather than being free-standing and determining, opportunity exists in a dialectical relationship with cultural and other traits of actors. This relationship goes beyond Alexander's (1984) conception of "interpretive norms" mediating "impinging conditions." Alexander approximately describes Gerson's subjects, who are culturally equipped for careers in paid labor. In their case, social norms blocked their opportunities, but the other cases suggest a more intimate relationship between traits of actors and opportunities. They reveal that opportunities are both expanded and constricted by the values, skills, perceptions, and other features of actors. The Brothers' values and habitus allowed them to see school differently than did the Hallway Hangers, who suffered numerous disabling habits of thought. The Mississippi Chinese, because of an entrepreneurial tradition, found lucrative possibilities in a landscape others found barren.

MacLeod (1987) approaches a conception of opportunity that reveals its dependence on actors and culture when he speaks of "the interpenetration of human consciousness and structural determinants" (p. 148). In this, he echoes Paul Willis's (1977) description of "the couplet structure/culture" as "part of a necessary circle in which neither term is thinkable alone" (p. 174). But despite finding that the boundary between "objective" structures and "subjective" orientations is vanishingly small, MacLeod retreats to "the primacy of the opportunity structure in determining the aspirations of the Hallway Hangers" (p. 62). Like many others dissatisfied with a "unidimensional" approach, MacLeod affirms—but then abandons—a dialectic. In this, he replicates Bourdieu's equivocal conception of habitus as sometimes determining and sometimes amenable to strategic deployment.

HOW CULTURE MATTERS

The role of cultural resources in constituting opportunity has often been noted. It is implied by Swidler's (1986) argument that "action and values are organized to take advantage of cultural competencies" (275). Although Swidler was criticized in Chapter 5 for excessive instrumentalism and for understressing the enduring power of goals, she offers the important insight that the "objective" availability of opportunities is of little use for those who lack the suitable "cultural equipment" (p. 275).

Swidler is vague about the cultural competencies that enable opportunity, speaking of the " 'tool kit' of symbols, stories, rituals, and world views" (p. 273), "a style or a set of skills and habits" (p. 275), and "a specific ethos, a style of regulating action" (p. 280). This vagueness is understandable: it is unlikely that there can be a systematic or comprehensive account of the ways in which cultural skills constitute opportunity. But certain aspects of this process stand out. A particularly important component is the way *identities* or self-concepts mediate opportunities. As shown in Chapter 3, to emphasize situational variables, structural sociology, like neoclassical economics, sees actors as essentially featureless. As Spiro Latsis (1972) puts it, "The neoclassical view stresses the situation and turns the decision making agent into a cypher" (p. 233). If we have selves at all, they are akin to investments, always responsive to the main chance. Friedland and Robertson (1990) describe Gary Becker's approach as reducing "the self to a form of human capital" by arguing that "we choose our preferences to maximize utilities" (p. 25). This view is paralleled by Gerson's emphasis on the adaptability of preferences to opportunities and by Swidler's argument that ends are chosen in light of cultural skills.

But these studies reveal durable identities that control conduct largely by defining interests. Southern views of retail trade and race stigmatized an identity for indigenes that was valued by the Chinese. The Hallway Hangers are committed to identities that narrow their opportunities. To them, school is a place of constriction and degradation. Jackson Toby (1989) captures this perception of schools by describing chronic troublemakers as "students who experience classroom instruction not as an opportunity but as imprisonment" (p. 27). In contrast, the Brothers, because they define themselves differently, see the school as a path to upward mobility. Various factors are implicated in the identities these two groups brought to school. Their attitudes about masculinity are crucial. To be a diligent and obedient student was emasculating to the Hallway Hangers, but not to the Brothers. Gerson contends that women pursue their best options, having no durable commitment to either homemaking or careers. But her data show that while some women react to shifting opportunities, others have ingrained identities—such as being a dutiful wife and daughter—that define their interests and hence determine what, for them, a rational choice is. Insofar as her subjects were found to easily change their strategies in response to shifting opportunities, their identities are unstable. But this is not an invariant trait: it is an artifact of what Swidler (1986) calls "unsettled lives" (p. 278), a period in which women were caught between traditional values and the new alternatives opened by the feminist movement.

The importance of identity has often turned up in sociological research. Willis (1990) emphasizes "the mythology of masculine reputation" (p. 186) as an adaptation to prospects of low mobility but also a durable commitment that *reproduces* that circumstance: working class youths' disdain for education as unmanly ensured their restriction to manual labor. Similarly, Herbert Gans's study (1962) of *The Urban Villagers* found that Italians, unlike Jews, saw doing well in school as a threat to the masculine identities of boys. Numerous recent studies have found that for some groups, school success is seen to undermine a preferred identity. The fear of some black students that doing well in school is "acting white" is cited by Ogbu and Fordham (1986) as an obstacle to educational attainment.

In *The Seductions of Crime*, Jack Katz (1988) presents an alternative to economistic explanations of crime that emphasizes the role of identity. His critique of economic explanations is based on the many anomalies this approach cannot account for. A chapter called "Righteous Slaughter" describes homicides that defy rational calculation: the plain-view murder of a neighbor who refuses to move his truck from the killer's driveway, killing a child who soils itself, many spousal murders, and so on. Similarly, "Sneaky Thrills" describes the attractions of shoplifting to middle-class youth who steal what they can easily buy or do not need. More generally, Katz points out that many criminal careers "start early in adolescence, long before job opportunities could . . . become meaningful considerations" (p. 314) and most criminals go straight with maturity: just as blocked opportunities become visible and begin to matter.

Developing a conception of crime meant to challenge anomie theory, Katz emphasizes "the irrelevance of utilitarian calculations" (p. 114) and analyzes various nonrational motivations of crime. Among these are "the obsessive desire to break rules. . . . Primordial restlessness or the desire to do something, anything—to be where the action is . . . the will to exercise dominance over victims . . . a positive relish, even to the point of self-destruction" in generating violence (p. 138), and "the thrill of confrontation with an armed victim" (p. 167). Katz also cites one of the nonutilitarian motives described by Steven Holmes (1990, p. 279) as "the love of uncertainty": "I like to do stick-up. I like to take the risk" (p. 206). For these men, crime is not just a job: it's an adventure.

Katz sees the construction and defense of identities as a central motivation. Righteous murder is often provoked by "the experience of public degradation" (p. 24) as a victim "teases, dares, or defies" (p. 20) the killer (Holmes: "extreme touchiness about social slights.") resulting in "killing in defense of the Good" (p. 15). Even the killing of a disobedient child can be spurred by an attempt "to honor parental authority" (p. 13).[6] Unsurprisingly, "the construction of maleness" (p. 238) is a keystone of many crimes. For example, "Doing Stickup" resists economic explanation because "burglary and robbery, the most lucrative of non-drug crimes, average only about $80" (p. 164). The risk of injury from a resisting victim and the near certainty of prison for the many robberies needed merely to match the returns of minimum-wage work leads Katz to ask a fundamental question glossed over with the presumption of economic motives: "What are they trying to do?" (p. 165). The answer, in large measure, is "the project of being a badass": a tough, violent man who can terrorize and control others while staying cool in a volatile situation (p. 225). Examining the project of armed street robbery up close uncovers anomalies that suggest something other than an alternative path to success. For example, economics cannot explain the common refusal of "the rational course": "Running off when victims resist to find other, easier, equally promising victims" (p. 193). Running off undermines what the robber really seeks: to be "reconfirmed as triumphant hardman" (p. 225).

The use of moral rhetoric to mask instrumental motives is often noted in social science. Representatively, Blau claims that "by assuming a moral obligation to be charitable to the poor, the upper class establishes a claim to moral righteousness and superiority, which ideologically justifies and fortifies its superior social status and power" (quoted in Wolfe, 1989, p. 195). Showing how moral claims serve as smokescreens for mainly material interests is a central theme in conflict theory, postmodern thought, and so on. But this practice of "unmasking" moral claims, a legacy of Marx's theory of ideology, needs to be supplemented by the reverse: that is, unmasking the *nonmaterial* goals often hidden beneath an instrumentalist rhetoric. Katz contends that economic rhetoric is often used to provide a rational gloss to noneconomic impulses. For example, the thrill of gratuitous violence is masked in a project of material acquisitiveness in a society that certifies the latter as "normal" but not the former. To make this point, Katz (1988) quotes Nietzsche: "He robbed when he murdered. He did not want to be ashamed of his madness" (p. 274).[7] This explains the eruptions of excessive, often outrageous violence in what seem to be economic crimes: those who take pleasure in violence are reluctant to reveal this perverse impulse. In a reversal of the use of noneconomic motives to mask instrumental actions, Katz's criminals (mirroring the theoretical aim of structural sociology and economics) rationalize their conduct in a way acceptable to a utilitarian culture. This effort is facilitated by the availability of social science explanations of crime as driven by constricted opportunity.[8]

Katz does not entirely discount the relevance of blocked opportunity to the choice of criminal careers. Speaking of violent urban gangs, he allows that "perhaps, somewhere lurking behind the violence of street elites, there are pathetic, negative conditions: an anticipatory fear of failure in adult careers, resentment over social or racial injustice." (p. 138). In this, Katz credits Merton's claim that blocked opportunity can lie behind noneconomic criminality, such as the "retreatism" of drug users. But because there are multiple ways to respond to blocked opportunity, such explanations are, at best, incomplete. And while identities can begin as adaptive responses, they tend to become autonomous sources of motivation. Most important, blocked opportunity does not acknowledge or explain "the delight in violence." (p. 138). That is, even if restricted opportunities make criminal violence more attractive, this presumes that the latter provides intrinsic satisfaction.

Katz explains the preponderance of blacks in armed street robbery partly in terms of the lack of more lucrative criminal opportunities because of the lack of black businesses, black labor unions, and similar institutions that can offer "employment opportunities to black hardmen" (p. 259). But he contends that "the realities of ghetto crime are literally too 'bad' to be confined to the role of 'innovative means' for conventional ends" (p. 317). Rather, "for some urban, black ghetto-located young men, the stickup is particularly attractive as a distinctive way of being black" (p. 239).[9] Katz quotes a street hustler to correct the theoretically imposed assumption that violent criminals want what we all want and differ only in their opportunity set: "Straight people don't understand. I mean, they think dudes is after the things straight people got. It ain't that at all. People in the life ain't looking for no home and grass in the yard and shit like that. We the show people. The glamour people" (p. 315). Indeed, a life of utilitarian calculation is precisely what those who surrender to the seductions of crime disdain: "The hardman triumphs, after all, by inducing others to calculate the costs and benefits" (p. 235).

This understanding of the subsidiary role of economics in crime parallels Geertz's (1973) interpretation of Balinese cockfighting. While betting is involved, money is not the point. Cockfighting is a means for the pursuit of "esteem, honor, dignity, respect" (p. 433). In a sense, cockfighting is less instrumental, and more purely expressive, than the pursuit of status implies. It is, Geertz believes, a form of art: "a story they tell themselves about themselves" (p. 448).[10]

The "show people" remark suggests another aspect of crime as a project of identity construction. Todd Bucholtz (1989), an economist, scoffs at novelist Evelyn Waugh's eccentric comment that almost "all crime is due to the repressed desire for aesthetic expression" (p. 192). But the utility of much criminal activity is questionable, unless the notion of utility is stretched to tautology. And even if there is a thread of economic rationality in mugging, for example, it is far from the only "rational" response to poverty or unemployment. Counting the multiple costs of a life of crime, it is unlikely to be the maximizing response. The aesthetic thrill that movie audiences take in the spectacle of crime suggests that the criminal can find similar delight in his own deeds. This logic does not apply only to criminals. Crime novelist Elmore Leonard (1981) suggests that opportunities for violence is one of the attractions of policing: "Whatever the reason," Bryan said, "yeah, there're people who like to shoot people. There're cops who look for an excuse. There're guys who get into armed robbery, I'm pretty sure, hoping they'll have to use their gun" (p. 147).

The structuralist argument that blocked opportunity is a factor in making crime, even its noninstrumental forms, a more attractive option is plausible, as Katz (1988) acknowledges. But structures of opportunity do not create a "single-exit" situation in which crime is *compelled*. There are, almost always, alternatives. Hence, such explanations are, at best, incomplete. At their worst, they are pseudoexplanations.

Merton's (1938) understanding of crime is more nuanced than some of his epigones. While he saw blocked opportunity as criminogenic, he allowed for a variety of responses, such as the retreatism of drug abusers and the ritualism of those stuck in dead-end jobs. Finestone similarly describes the "cat" searching for drug-induced "kicks" as a response to blocked opportunity. In contrast, Wacquant (1993) credits a ghetto resident's claim that "you *got* to burglarize your own people" (p. 18, emphasis added)—just as Gerson (1985) accepts her respondent's language of constraint and Wallerstein (1974) (see Chapter 2) describes Portugal as having "no choice" in its economic destiny.

This insistence on finding economic logic in conduct that defies instrumental rationality calls to mind Wittgenstein's critique of Sir James Frazer's efforts in *The Golden Bough* to rationalize the conduct of aboriginal societies: "What narrowness of life we find in Frazer. And as a result: how impossible for him to understand a different way of life from the English one of his time" (quoted in Monk, 1990, p. 310). This comment nicely describes Wacquant's (1993) argument—replicating Gary Becker's (1979) homogenization of preferences—that "ghetto dwellers are not a distinctive breed of men and women: they are ordinary people trying to make a living and improve their lot as best they can under the unusually oppressive circumstance imposed upon them" (p. 15).

This denial of differentness, the conception of the criminal as a frustrated bourgeois, is common in social science. Ruth Kornhauser (1978) also narrows the motivational gap between criminals and conformists: "Human beings are so constituted that they do not knowingly construct cultural values from experiences that are obviously destructive of self or society" (p. 15). Arguing that "parents of all strata prefer and attempt to inculcate conventional values," she contends that the breakdown of cultural controls, rather than deviant culture, is the source of deviant behavior: "Lower-class *culture* is a generating milieu for conformity, not deviance" (p. 208). But John Locke's (1954) belief that "shameful" vices and "moral wrongs" have often gained public support (see Chapter 5) has been abundantly documented by the ethnographic studies cited by Edgarton (1992).

In a critique of the neoclassical view of objective interests, Martin Hollis (1979) emphasizes the role of identity in conduct. He contends that rather than being homogeneously motivated, individuals approach situations with their own "projects, desires, and beliefs" (p. 3). Arguing that culture and reason cannot be disentangled, Hollis contends that because actors seek to express and confirm their identities in their conduct, "rational action is no longer action which yields an individual more for less but action which lets a man be himself" (p. 9). Denying that interests can be specified apart from self-concepts, he contends that "real interests are bound up not with what we want but with what we are" (p. 12) and hence action is "a way of being and becoming, of expressing and developing the self" (p. 13). The Hallway Hangers may want to *have* much of what the Brothers want. But they do not want to *be* what the Brothers are.[11]

To show how commitment to identities can subvert economic rationality, Jon Elster (1989c) considers the example of a man who would pay $10, but no more, to have his lawn mowed but who would refuse to mow his neighbor's identical lawn for $20. Because he would mow his own lawn rather than pay $11 but then refuse more than he has judged the task to be worth, his conduct makes no economic sense. It reveals that "he doesn't think of himself as the kind of person who would mow other people's lawns for money" (p. 110). Some classical puzzles of rational choice theory, such as tipping in a restaurant to which one will not return, anonymous donations to charities, and clapping in a mass audience, can be resolved by recognizing the expressive dimension of action.

The emphasis on identity in action evokes Hegel's challenge to the "possessive individualism" of utilitarianism with a conception of the human good as a project of self-expression. The force of this goal of articulating the self, rather than possessing things, comes from Hegel's notion of action as a process in which the self is created, not merely revealed. As John Gray (1987) describes this view,

> A great deal of human behavior is not purposeful or calculational at all, but rather self-expressive or self-disclosing. We vote, or go to church, sing, pray or make love, meet our friends or go on long voyages, not always in order to achieve any further end or to implement any rational plan of life, but simply to express our sense of ourselves as being the kind of people we are. (p. 46)

As suggested, the problem of identity bears on the issue of "objective" interests. Challenging this notion, Barry Hindess (1988) argues that

> interests have consequences only in so far as they enter actor's deliberations and contribute towards providing them with reasons for action. Interests in this sense have to be formulated or capable of formulation by those who act on them—which is to say that the existence of interests depends on forms of thought. (p. 110)

In contrast, while conceding that "ideological position is not just a 'reflex' of material conditions" (p. 208) and that forms of thought play a role in defining interests (p. 173), Terry Eagleton (1991) argues that it is perfectly reasonable to say, for example, that it is in the objective interests of a galley slave that he work less hard or get more to eat and that a slave who fails to see this can be rightfully said to suffer false consciousness (p. 206). Similarly, Porpora (1987, p. 112) believes that an observer can rightfully say which move is in the interests of a chess player.

But these examples fail to engage the hard cases. Agreement that a starving man needs food hardly bears on the more nuanced issues that trouble the concept of interests—for example, determining if an individual's interests lie with class, gender, religion, or race. An array of possible interests is unavoidable insofar as persons always have multiple identities: Workers are also consumers, and when considering, say, free trade they must decide between cheaper goods and greater pressure on wages. Also, once we have determined that an actor is a "chess player," her identity has been established and the issue of what she wants has been settled. The assumptions that politicians want to maximize votes, that prisoners would rather serve less time, or that investors seek to maximize their returns does not help resolve more troubling cases sociologists routinely encounter.

In interesting cases, what has to be determined is the interest-defining game being played, and this determination must incorporate the actor's ideas of her identity and interests. Eagleton's example sounds right because it seems "natural" that a slave would want more food and less work. But even here, culture and belief systems, as Parsons and others point out, define costs and benefits. Medieval Christian hermits sought lives of material deprivation for spiritual reasons, and it would be presumptuous and poor social science to insist that such choices are irrational. Choice is implicated in more ordinary cases such as a worker deciding between overtime and family duties. As Weber and others imply, pursuing economic interests is itself choosing an identity, a path of self-expression. As James Rule (1989) has put it, "We need to consider processes by which the *specific* interests fueling a particular action are selected from the array of potential interests latent in the personalities of the actors" (p. 152). Analogously, a nation must *determine* what its interests are in light of values and ideologies. Despite his economism, Bourdieu argues that "far from being an anthropological invariant, interest is a *historical arbitrary,* a historical construction that can be known only through historical analysis" (quoted in Calhoun, 1993, p. 71). The power of identities to confound universal notions of interests is illustrated by Goffman's (1963) account of the adoption of stigmas as valued identities: "objective" disabilities can become a source of self-esteem.[12]

The importance of identity in constituting opportunity does not gainsay Loewen's (1988) structural claim that "immigrant groups construct, negotiate, and change their ethnic identities in relation to . . . the social and economic realities they face" (p. 201). It is to emphasize that, like other elements of culture, identities are "sticky" and hence are partly autonomous of "economic realities." Perhaps most important, Loewen's study, like the others described, shows that economic realities cannot be conceptualized autonomously of their dialectical relation to actor's identities.

A related aspect of the social construction of opportunity is how actors define their situations. Hindess (1984) denies that "rational choices are given in the logic of the actor's situation"—that is, "incentives, costs and opportunities" (p. 269), and contends that "the cultural and educational diversity of most societies ensures that there will be considerable variation in the forms of thought employed by or available to actors" (Hindess, 1988, p. 110). Because "actors have several forms of assessment available to them" (1984, p. 270), situations, such as identities, can be variously defined. The two often occur together: "Racist and sexist discourses are available to many British workers which make it possible for them to formulate objectives that contradict those of worker solidarity" (p. 270). Racial or gender identities commonly outweigh class interests.

Contradicting the portrayals of Parsons as an advocate of a uniform, dominant value system that constrains action, Parson and Shils (1951) also allowed that actors must choose among multiple modes of assessment: "Even in a simple society, the cultural pattern presented as a situational object will be richer in content, more varied in scope, and of course, more contradictory than a single personality" (p. 181). As argued in Chapter 4, Parsons allowed more room for agency than is generally recognized: "The personality system will therefore tend to select particular elements from the available cultural pattern which will then become parts of the orientation system of the actor" (p. 181). Some diversity of forms of assessment is inevitable in any society, but this can vary and expands in modern society as cultural diversity multiplies.

The constitution of the context of action by actors' modes of assessment is emphasized by Herbert Simons' (1987) critique of what he terms the "one world" assumption of neoclassical economics—that is, the stipulation that "actors share the same perceptions" (White, 1988, p. 230). Simons emphasizes the "definition of the situation" or "frame" to show that different actors highlight different aspects of the world. An example is presidential voting. Because a candidate represents various standpoints, inquiry is required to know *what* is being voted for. ("A vote for Clinton is a vote for ...?"). This means that actors cannot be seen as situationally driven because the context of action can be variously defined: "Selected aspects of reality are noticed as the 'givens' (factual bases) for reasoning about action" (Simons, 1987, p. 26). We must *discover* what about the situation motivates action. This is nicely illustrated in the silent movie *Gold Rush* when Charlie Chaplin's starving character experiences a paradigm shift and suddenly "sees" his companion as food.

Oddly, Simons' emphasis on the actor's constitution of the environment matches an aspect of Sartre's (1957) affirmation of freedom. "Renouncing all mechanical causation" (p. 78), Sartre describes an existential psychoanalysis:

> It abandons the supposition that the environment acts mechanically on the subject under consideration. The environment can act on the subject only to the exact extent that he comprehends it: that is, transforms it into a situation. Hence no objective description of this environment could be of any use to us. (p. 77)

Paralleling his denial, sketched in Chapter 4, of the determinative power of rules, Sartre's commitment to autonomy precludes the controlling power of "objective" situations. Again, his views can be faulted as too individualistic. The assessment of situations usually emerges from a collective process. Also, Sartre's declaration of freedom needs to be qualified. Situations are not entirely constructs, and just as there are limits on how rules can be interpreted, freedom in assessing situations is limited by the availability of forms of thought. This can leave actors incapable of dealing with unique situations or lead them to apply inappropriate assessments to unprecedented circumstances.[13]

The definition of situations is, like the determination of interests, related to self-assessments. The Mississippi Chinese saw their environment differently than did blacks and whites in large part because they saw *themselves* differently: catering to customers was not a threat to their self-esteem.[14] The Hallway Hangers' perception of schools as demeaning of masculinity was mediated through their identities and derived interests.

There are many additional components implicated in the assessments of self and situation. Jon Elster (1979) speaks of "values which determine the visibility of alternatives" (p. 67). For example, just as a rope is a means of escape from a burning building only for the agile, an unattended cash register is an economic opportunity only for a certain sort of person: a thief. Values determine whether, for example, transplantable organs, illegal drugs, or children are treated as economic resources. Sexual services are economic resources and human flesh is a nutritional resource—for some but not for others. The "feasible set"—that is, the range of actions open to an individual—is thus expanded and limited by values. It is not just that values allow or disallow opportunities to be exploited. Their relationship is more intimate. As Little (1989) puts it, "Cultural values influence action by shaping individual *perceptions* of the social world and of available options for action" (p. 56, emphasis added).

Folk theories about social process are importantly implicated in the constitution of opportunity. This is illustrated in the contrast between the Brothers' perception of the world as rewarding effort and the Hallway Hangers' claim that "out here, there's not the opportunity to make money" (p. 19). The Hallway Hangers saw the social order as controlled by "pull," whereas the Brothers saw society as open to and rewarding of effort. The former view encouraged, and the latter discouraged, effort.

Drawing on the work of Mary Douglas, Thompson et al. (1990) describe the ways in which cultural perceptions—folk theories of society, nature, human nature, and so on—affect conduct. For example, if nature is seen as "benign"—fundamentally stable—experimentation is encouraged. In contrast, if nature is seen as "ephemeral"—"a terrifying unforgiving place and the least jolt may trigger its complete collapse" (p. 26)—innovation is discouraged: "Whereas Nature Benign encourages bold experimentation in the face of uncertainty. . . . Nature Ephemeral encourages timorous forbearance" (p. 27). Because these myths describe what the world is like, they help define what an opportunity is. What one culture sees as a chance for innovation, another will see as a reckless flirtation with disaster: "Each define as rational behavior what the others define as irrational" (p. 31). The most basic forms of conduct are embedded in cultural systems:

> "Objective reality" does not determine how people try to make ends meet; on the contrary, adherents of each way of life define needs and resources—human nature and physical nature—in such a way that the strategy they use to make ends meet supports their cultural bias and hence sustains their way of life. (p. 38)

A wide range of interacting ideas mediate the perceptions that bear on economic conduct. For example, an egalitarian ideology sees material abundance as a spur to greed and envy and so encourages ideas of nature that discourage acquisitiveness: such as "fragile ecosystems," "overloaded arks," and "global villages" (p. 44). Rather than refute economic thinking, Douglas aims to place rationality in its cultural context: "Our theory is not a rejection of rational choice; rather we contend that rational choice explanations are deficient unless they are united with ways of life" (Thompson et al., p. 42).

The idea that opportunity is culturally constructed parallels Sewell's (1992) claim that cultural schemas are implicated in constituting "resources." By resources, Sewell, drawing on Giddens, means "anything that can serve as a source of power in social interactions" (p. 11). Resources can be material objects and human capacities: "physical strength, dexterity, knowledge, and emotional commitments that can be used to enhance or maintain power" (p. 11). While resources are not exactly opportunities, they play a comparable role in Sewell's thought in that they *provide* opportunities. Hence, Sewell's claim that resources are "a consequence of the schemas that inform their use" (p. 11)—a computer, for example, is useful only to those who know how to use it—resembles my argument that opportunity requires a suitable cultural endowment: "The activation of material things as resources, the determination of their value and social power, is dependent on the cultural schemas that inform their social use" (p. 12). Not just material things but institutions, such as schools and the like, are "activated" by schemas.

Sewell's conflation of schemas and resources parallels Marx. In contrast to an occasional technological determinism, Marx (1963b) was emphatic—at times—that productive resources are constituted by the social practices that envelop them:

> Machinery is no more an economic category than the ox which draws the plough. The application of machinery in the present day is one of the relations of our present economic system, but the way in which machinery is utilized is totally distinct from the machinery itself. Powder remains the same whether it is used to wound a man or dress his wound" (p. 156).

These comments affirm an "organic union" between elements that Marx sometimes treats as discrete and anticipate Sewell's argument that material means are culturally constituted. Marx's position is more encompassing than Sewell's in that entire forms of social organization—a way of life—rather than schemas, are implicated in the constitution of resources. Barry Hindess (1977) finds a similar conflation of culture and material factors in Weber. To make his point that "objective economic conditions do not enforce or facilitate the correct subjective meanings; they themselves can only exist if they are recognized by these subjective attitudes," Hindess quotes Weber: "A machine can be understood only in terms of the meaning which its production and use have had or were intended to have. . . . Without reference to this meaning such an object remains wholly unintelligible" (p. 48).

The various ways in which situations can be assessed, and commensurate actions chosen, can be illustrated in the multiple "modes of economic calculation" (Hindess, 1984, p. 263) available to a white male worker laid off from a California manufacturing plant. He might blame (a) immigrants—and advocate restrictive laws, (b) affirmative action—and vote for the California Civil Rights Initiative, (c) capitalism—and join a socialist movement, (d) his lack of skills—and take training, or (e) globalization—and vote for Pat Buchanan. Each of these courses of actions, and many others—perhaps prayer—are plausible and arguably rational. Indeed, experts differ on which is the most appropriate assessment of this situation.

In sum, "rational" action is commonly *underdetermined* by "objective" situations and emerges through a mobilization of values, self-concepts, theories of nature and society, and so on. The variety of possible responses to situations stands in sharp contrast to structuralist emphasis on the constraining nature of situations. A striking example of this is Wacquant's (1993) claim that the conduct of life in the ghetto is structurally mandated. He considers ghetto lifestyles to "obey a social rationality" that "is well adapted to their immediate socioeconomic context" (p. 15). Circumstances of economic deprivation and social exclusion result in a motivational situation in which "intense competition for, and conflict over, scarce resources" (p. 16) leaves ghetto residents with "little choice" (p. 22) but criminal careers. Wacquant quotes a resident as accurately describing how "unemployment and underemployment *compel* ghetto residents (emphasis added)" (p. 21) to " 'Steal, knock old ladies down and take their pension checks.' " (p. 23). Because drug dealers cannot turn to the police to enforce contracts, the "culture of terror" that surrounds this enterprise is described as "a business requirement" (p. 24).

But ghetto life hardly constitutes a "single exit" situation in which crime is the only rational response. In light of the variety of plausible, and arguably superior, responses—which, in fact, most ghetto residents choose—Wacquant's interpretation is a *pseudo*explanation in that it fails to show that the behaviors he analyzes are compelled by the circumstances he describes.[15] Paralleling MacLeod's (1987) argument that "the way in which individuals and groups respond to structures of domination is open-ended" (p. 138), Christopher Jencks (1992) emphasizes the variety of responses to ghettoization:

> If discrimination spurs its victims to greater effort ("we have to be twice as good as they in order to do equally well"), it may actually help them economically. If discrimination convinces its victims that effort is never rewarded, or if it makes them so angry or resentful that they are unable to work with their oppressors, it can have catastrophic economic consequences. (p. 26)

The variety of responses to racism is vividly illustrated by the history of the Japanese-American Regiment 442. Recruited largely from internment camps, it became one of the most decorated American units in World War II. As Sahlins (1976) puts it, "Individuals and social groups, in struggling against one another, transforming nature, organizing their life in common, bring into play a system of concepts which is never the only possible one" (p. 20). Material conditions are engaged by encultured actors who deploy various "systems of concepts": indeed, we can hardly speak of the "objective economic conditions" of action apart from actors' modes of assessment. In contrast to Wacquant's (1993) implication that the "rationality" of ghetto culture is situationally mandated, Sahlins argues that "the 'rational' and 'objective' scheme of any given human group is never the only possible one" (p. 168).

Herbert Simons' (1987) critique of situational determinism in economics and his assertion of the need to understand actors' modes of thinking also highlights the importance of actors' assessments:

> To understand the processes that the economic actor employs in making decisions calls for observing these processes directly while they are going on, either in real world situations or in the laboratory and/or interrogating the decision maker about beliefs, expectations, and methods of calculation and reasoning. (p. 27)

Although arguing for a rational choice approach, Wippler and Lindenberg (1987) also recognize that the structure of opportunities is not determinative in that individuals are capable of "discovering opportunities created by the structural constraints; that is, they are endowed with the ability to enlarge the set of structurally given feasible alternatives. For example, certain entrepreneurs perceive the potential of a technological invention for increasing their profit" (p. 146). The capacity of "discovering opportunities created by the structural constraints" exactly describes the Mississippi Chinese.

The implication of culture in opportunity does not gainsay that actors often face obstacles of various sorts that are as solid as walls. Even when there is a will, there may not be a way. But with the maximizing assumption, structural sociology, like economics, presumes that where there is a way, there is a will. This is how Ronald Burt (1992) can echo Ricardo's claim (see Chapter 3) that "The will is seldom wanting when the power exists" with the claim that "the network is its own explanation of motivation" (p. 36). These studies show that the will is not an artifact of opportunity: the *way* requires a certain sort of *will*.

However, the role of culture in constituting opportunity must be qualified by recalling that, while subject to interpretation, culture does set limits to action and is not infinitely malleable. Sometimes actors lack the cultural resources that can provide appropriate lines of action.

SCIENCE AND CULTURE

The adoption of homo economicus by structural sociology is motivated by a certain model of science. If the environment can be conceptualized as a set of "objective" costs and benefits and if the subjectivity of the actor can be reduced to self-interested maximizing, the feasibility of predicting behavior is enhanced. As Kahneman et al. (1987) describe this program,

> The model of the agents [in elementary microeconomics] is so simple that their decisions become predictable from an objective description of the environment . . . [which] can be completely described in terms of specific opportunities to maximize the objective functions, and it is assumed that all such opportunities are exploited. (p. 114)

This is why Gary Becker (1979) makes the claim, so jarring to common sense, that "preferences are assumed not to change substantially over time, nor to be very different between wealthy and poor persons, or even between persons in different societies and cultures" (p. 9).

But if actors are not homogeneous, if the assumption that tastes do not "differ importantly between people" (Becker & Stigler, 1977, p. 76) fails, the task of explanation and prediction is complicated—especially if the environment of costs and benefits must also be defined in culturally idiosyncratic terms. For now, situational determinism is lost and a "thick" interpretive understanding of action and its environment is required. Rather than assuming that preferences are uniform, we must find out what specific actors want, and instead of assuming that they engage an "objective" environment of costs and benefits, we must find out how actors see their situation. To avoid these interpretive complexities, rational choice theory replaces culture with "a core set of human interests and beliefs that constitutes the basis for much behavior, around which cultural variations rotate" (Little, 1991, p. 148).

Many rational choice theorists have retreated from the effort to confine explanation to the environment of costs and benefits. Hechter and Friedman (1988) argue that "institutions [including norms] affect outcomes not by virtue of custom or of hallowed tradition, but only to the degree that they carry with them the capacity to reward or punish" (p. 210). But they concede that "normative expectations of others" (p. 206) also affect behavior. But cultural variation cannot be tacked on to rational choice theories. Daniel Little (1991b) argues that "once we require that rational choice take normative constraints and commitments into account as well as interests, it is much more difficult to provide formal rational choice models" (p. 153). Hollis (1983) worries that "widening the grounds of rational judgement" to include factors such as the agent's identity, results in explanatory "chaos" (p. 259). The problem Little and Hollis suggest is that culture erodes the determinacy of situations. If (variable) cultural factors such as identities, norms, definitions of situations, and so on mediate between actors and their situations, "rational" conduct can take various forms: the Brothers and the Hallway Hangers thus respond differently to a similar situation. And since cultural rules of conduct are subject to interpretation, a second layer of unpredictability emerges. This is why most economists have preferred the assumption of self-interest over norms and have emphasized constraints over preferences. In Vanberg's (1988) words, "Becker's approach is based on the premise that no interpersonal differences or intrapersonal changes in preferences exist and, therefore, differences and changes in behavior are to be explained exclusively in terms of [income and price] constraints" (p. 9). But the studies surveyed here show that the environment of action and the actor's reaction to that environment are saturated with culture.

The vulnerability of rational choice theory to deviation from the assumption of rationality is suggested by the impact of Simons' (1987) introduction of the concept of "satisficing." Merely relaxing the assumption of maximizing, by allowing that actors only seek "good enough" outcomes, compromises the project of rational choice explanation. Not just satisficing, but anything, such as norms, that erodes the narrow set of traits attributed to homo economicus raises problems. As Hutchison (1984) puts it, the logic of "single-exit" explanations requires a series of strong assumptions: "With fully adequate knowledge, correct expectations, and virtually unbounded rationality . . . only one set of decisions will be possible. But with inadequate knowledge, erroneous expectations, or bounded rationality, there may be a wide range of possibilities" (p. 27). Adam Prezworski (1985) similarly notes the theoretical significance of actor heterogeneity: "Insofar as competition, with fully adequate knowledge and rationality, dominates, then single-exit situations are set up which permit the deduction of 'laws' of economic science." But "a realistic description of society in which selfish, altruistic and ideological individuals coexist at any time may make any deductive analysis next to impossible" (p. 386). Hutchison (1984) also cites multiple threats to the assumption of actor homogeneity: "Insofar as customs, habits, or 'institutions' shape decisions, these may change and vary at different times and places" (pp. 25, 27).

Many theorists have tried to incorporate more realistic conceptions about action. Even Gary Becker (1979) allows a role for "psychic costs" (p. 11). Thompson et al. (1990, p. 177) aim to supplement, not repudiate, rational choice theory by incorporating the variable "ways of life." But with these adjustments, the theoretical logic of rational choice is severely compromised. Emirbayer and Goodwin's (1994) critique of network theory recognizes many of the problems of rational choice, and they argue that identities, values, and the like must be incorporated. But like Hechter and others, they underestimate the implications of this adjustment. The promise that network connections alone offer great explanatory power and that the problems of interpretive analysis can thereby be avoided, would be negated. Thick cultural interpretation cannot simply be grafted on to structural explanation, leaving everything else intact. To save network theory from its unrealistic assumptions, Emirbayer and Goodwin have cut out its theoretical heart.

Contrary to their theoretical claims, the three studies examined here show that the assumption of maximization must be replaced with what Simons (1987) implies: an ethnography—rather than a demography—of status attainment that reveals how the orientations of actors—identities, defined interests, values, folk theories, and so on—constitute opportunities and motivate action. Because these studies are ethnographically rich, the deficiencies of the assumption of situational determinism is visible. It is likely that comparable information would reveal similar inadequacies in the rationality assumption that underpins structural sociology.

7

The Dialectic of Structure and Culture

OPPORTUNITIES AS AFFORDANCES

Chapters 5 and 6 emphasized the autonomy of culture in two ways. The former showed that it can overwhelm instrumental needs: indeed, its imperatives can destroy individuals and cause great harm to societies. The latter chapter emphasized the force of culture in another way by showing how opportunity is constituted by the appropriate cultural resources: the Mississippi Chinese "found" opportunities by viewing their circumstances in light of their entrepreneurial legacy. But earlier chapters pulled in another direction by demonstrating the malleability of culture in relation to structural factors, especially opportunity. Lin (1985), Matza (1964), and others are persuasive that rules and values are strategically modified by opportunistic actors, and Wittgenstein provides a philosophical foundation for this view by arguing that we cannot say what a rule means apart from its articulation by practical actors.

This relationship of culture and social structure is puzzling, even contradictory. On one hand, culture is shown to adapt to opportunity. On the other, it not only resists opportunistic interpretation but also constitutes opportunities. Most treatments of culture and structure seek to resolve this contradiction by giving the whip hand to one or the other—that is, to show that "in the final analysis" one "ultimately" controls behavior and the other is the epiphenomenal or dependent variable. Instead, I have tried to demonstrate a (dialectical) commingling of the two.

This elusive relationship can be clarified with James Gibson's (1979) concept of affordances. By an affordance, Gibson meant features of the environment that create possibilities for organisms: "The *affordances* of the environment are what it *offers* the animal, what it *provides* or *furnishes,* either for good or ill" (p. 127). Gibson emphasized that environmental affordances exist *in relation* to traits of animals. In Harry Heft's (1989) formulation, affordances "emerge out of the interaction of the animal and the environment . . . they are relational in nature" (p. 4). For example, grass is a nutritional resource for animals with the capacity to digest it.

Most basically, the physical properties of persons and objects determine affordances. A cardboard box may be strong enough to afford sitting for a child, but not for an adult. But various other traits of actors are implicated. A knob of rock affords a handhold for the skilled climber. A clinic for acrophobics might be liable for reckless endangerment if only conventional fire escapes were provided because they do not afford a path to safety for the psychologically disabled. Gibson also allows the "extension of affordances to the culturally based meaning of objects" (Heft, 1989, p. 10): "Which particular affordances are utilized in a given environmental setting will depend on intentional processes of the perceiver" (p. 10). For example, a mailbox affords communication for those who have the concept "mailing." This implies that affordances can be "specific to a particular culture" and are "constrained by values" (p. 19) as well as by physical traits and skills.

The concept of affordances, particularly when extended to the cultural sphere, parallels the argument presented in Chapter 6 on the relation between actors and opportunities. Because of various traits of the Brothers— their understandings of the larger society, their skills, values, self-concepts, and so on—school affords them opportunities that are unavailable to the Hallway Hangers. The school, like the cardboard box is, of course, there. But what the school *affords* depends on traits of the actor. In this sense, an opportunity, like an affordance, is "neither in the object nor in the mind of the beholder . . . it emerges from their relationship" (Heft, 1989, p. 14). Affordances "cut across the dichotomy of subjective-objective. . . . It is equally a fact of the environment and a fact of behavior. It is both physical and psychical, yet neither" (Gibson, 1979, p. 129).

The specifically social dimension of affordances must be emphasized, for they are not just constructions of individuals. Collective practices, such as respect for good grades and obedient behavior, are key to constituting school as an opportunity. In Wittgenstein's terms, affordances emerge within a "form of life." Various collective beliefs and practices established affordances for the Mississippi Chinese: an entrepreneurial tradition, communal provision of start-up funds, willingness to vouch for newcomers, and so on.[1]

The concept of affordances can be extended to culture as well. That is, culture does not only create environmental affordances: it is *itself* an affordance. As argued in Chapter 4, culture is open to alternate interpretations. For example, a spoon conventionally affords eating. But for a prisoner planning escape, it can be a digging tool. A cultural object can thus have multiple affordances depending on how it is defined. This example suggests that the actor's practical interests and opportunities are implicated in finding affordances in culture.

Conceiving of culture in this way highlights an important aspect of the role of culture in action. As described in Chapter 6, Bourdieu and Wacquant (1992) see opportunity as mediated by habitus, speaking of "the minimum economic and cultural capital necessary to perceive and seize the 'potential opportunities' formally offered to all" (p. 124). This comment anticipates what MacLeod and others have found: it is not possible to speak of opportunity absent appropriate cultural "equipment." But it does not allow *agency* in relation to culture in the manner suggested by Lin's (1985) study of filial piety and Matza's (1984) analysis of delinquents and the law. That is, the "other half" of the dialectic whereby opportunities construct culture is underplayed. Robin Leidner's (1993) study of work, *Fast Talk and Fast Food*, shows how actors can strategically deploy their cultural resources. In contrast to Willis's (1990) account of how masculine identities restrict options, she describes how they can be adapted to enhance opportunities. For example, male insurance agents interpreted their work as "honorable and fitting for a man" (Leidner, 1993, p. 203) by seeing the overcoming of customer resistance as a display of will and determination. Selling was seen as a kind of joust, a venue to achieve domination. Similarly, male workers at MacDonalds saw the ability to absorb rude treatment from customers, not as an affront to manly pride, but as a sign of superior self-control. Just as samurai ideals were flexible enough to support business activities, work that would seem to undermine masculine values can be interpreted in a way that affirms them.

Leidner's findings introduce an important aspect of the relation between culture and opportunity. Because Bourdieu sees habitus as an adaptation to opportunity and determining conduct, he affirms the ultimate controlling power of opportunity. Bourdieu has been ambiguous, and sometimes contradictory, on this issue. At times he finds agency in habitus: "I wished to put forward the 'creative,' active, and inventive capacities of habitus and of agent (which the word usually does not convey)" (quoted in Alexander, 1995, p. 136). But elsewhere, he describes habitus as merely "reflective" of objective circumstances: "dispositions . . . are the product of economic and social processes that are more or less completely reducible to these constraints" (p. 137). Confusion about this issue is common. While Calhoun (1993, p. 78) believes that the term suggests flexibility, Alexander (1995) argues that, in the end, Bourdieu sees habitus as reproducing systems of domination (p. 173). Emirbayer and Mische (1998) find in Bourdieu the belief that "there may be much ingenuity and resourcefulness to the selection of responses from practical repertoires" (p. 980), while Sewell (1992) describes habitus as "agent-proof" (p. 15). George Ritzer (1992), understandably, seems puzzled: "While habitus is an internalized structure that constrains thought and choice of action, it does *not* determine them" (p. 579)—"Bourdieu's agents seem to be dominated by their habitus" (p. 588).

Whatever Bourdieu's view might be, Leidner's (1993) finding that actors deploy culture creatively means that it does not merely reproduce "economic and social processes." Cultural capital is not something that one *has* or *lacks:* it is a resource that can be used by actors to engage their circumstances. Bourdieu might contend that Leidner's subjects are actually reproducing their domination: merely rationalizing their degraded status. But there are examples of agents drawing on habitus that cannot be dismissed as reproduction: the samurai redeployed their cultural resources to become leaders in Japan's emerging capitalist society.

DIALECTICS

Gibson's (1979) concept of affordances illustrates a way of thinking that has historically been known as "dialectical." This notoriously murky concept has been introduced earlier without sufficient explication. Having presented some illustrations, its meaning can now be clarified by examining its use by its most famous advocate. Marx's aim was to show the inter-penetration, or "organic union," of factors that are conventionally considered to be independent.[2] Applying this logic, Marx contended that physical objects must be understood in their relations with one another. For example, he claimed that "The sun is the object of the plant—an indispensable object to it confirming its life—just as the plant is an object of the sun, being an expression of the life awakening power of the sun" (quoted in Ollman, 1971, p. 29). In this view, a property of the sun, its capacity to induce organic growth, appears in relation to a plant. At the same time, the plant's potential for growth appears in relation to the sun.

The dialectical perspective is central to Marx's understanding of persons. For example, he challenged "reflective" materialism, by emphasizing the constitution of the natural world by human perception. In this view, humans do not simply mirror nature: our perceptual faculties—"practical, human sense activity" (Marx, 1964, p. 68)—organize experience. Because they make experience coherent, Marx (1963b) described the senses as "theoreticians in practice" (p. 160). For example, the vision of animals blind-folded at birth remains poor when the restrictions are removed because their eyes have not learned to organize the visual world. This also illustrates the reciprocal process whereby the senses that organize the world are formed in interchange with it: the eye is trained by the process of seeing. Generalizing this process, Marx claimed that "Nature is the inorganic body of man" (p. 126) because "the cultivation of the five senses is the work of all previous history" (p. 161). These odd claims suggest that the material world and the perceiver are mutually constituted. The eye that constructs nature emerged out of the experience of nature.

Marx's conception of sense perception resembles Kant's critique of empiricism. Kant's aphorism "intuitions [sensations] without concepts are blind" suggests that perceptual faculties give form to the natural world. But more like Hegel, and more dialectically, Marx saw the perceptual constitution of the world as historically variable insofar as our perceptions are culturally conditioned. Criticizing Feuerbach, he claimed, "He does not see how the sensuous world around him is not a thing given direct from all eternity, ever the same, but the product of industry and of the state of society" (Marx, 1967b, p. 35). Variability in perceptual skill is illustrated in the ability of experts to see features in X-ray images that are invisible to the untrained eye. Our experience in the world shapes the ways we experience it.

Of more direct relevance here is Marx's dialectic of persons and social resources. Gibson's (1979) concept of affordances matches Marx's (1963a) description of the role of actors in constituting cultural objects: "The most beautiful music has no meaning for the nonmusical ear." At the same time, the traits of actors are created by social objects: "Man's musical sense is only awakened by music" (p. 161). Music and a musical sense thus form "an organic union." In Gibson's terms, what objects afford, and hence their character as objects, depends on the traits and conduct of users, which, in turn, emerge in relation to these objects.

THE DIALECTIC OF STRUCTURE AND CULTURE

In Chapter 6 it was argued that opportunity cannot be conceptualized apart from the cultural resources of actors. But these arguments were intended to challenge the conception of culture as epiphenomenal or otiose, not to gainsay the process, sketched in Chapter 4, through which culture is adapted to structural exigencies. The relationship can be illustrated in this way:

Culture ← (opportunity) ——— Actor ——— (culture) → Opportunity

Actors articulate, or "read," culture in light of the array of opportunities. At the same time, opportunities are "read" or constituted in light of cultural resources. This is a dynamic process in that the culture that constructs opportunity is at the same time opportunistically interpreted. They form "an organic union" in that the character of each is established in its relations with the other. Just as affordances are "neither in the object nor in the mind," a school is an opportunity only for those with the cultural resources that are the academic equivalent of a "musical sense." At the same time, those cultural resources evolve and are articulated in light of the actor's array of opportunities. Before reverting to his emphasis on the controlling power of opportunity, MacLeod (1987) echoes Willis as accurately describing "the couplet structure/culture" as "part of a necessary circle in which neither term is thinkable alone" (Willis, 1977, p. 174).

In Chapter 1, Alexander's multidimensional approach was criticized as "additive" rather than dialectical. His argument that "specific religious and cultural factors" determine the orientations of social classes seems to mean that, for example, a Buddhist worker might react differently than a Christian to the same economic situation. While this is a worthwhile step beyond a "unidimensional" or "materialist" understanding of class orientation, the *interaction* of class position and "religious and cultural factors" is left out. Religious doctrines are not static. They are read in light of class position and various other, often practical, factors. A fully dialectical approach, captured in Wittgenstein's (1953, para. 43) doctrine of meaning as use and illustrated in the Galliher and Cross (1983) study of the malleability of Mormon theology, suggests the futility of defining a doctrine apart from its expression in practical life. Marx's (1967b) materialism, often read as dismissing the role of ideas, can be better interpreted as an argument for their embeddedness in practical life: "Men are the producers of their conceptions, ideas, etc.—real active men as they are conditioned by a definite development of their productive forces and of the intercourse corresponding to these" (p. 14).

As described in Chapter 6, Sewell (1992) defines structure "as composed simultaneously of schemas [rules] . . . and of resources" (p. 13) and portrays these elements of structure as interrelated: "If resources are effects of schemas, it is also true that schemas are effects of resources . . . they mutually imply and sustain each other" (p. 13). It is not clear if Sewell means that the interchange between schemas and resources is propelled by the affordance-seeking agent. But his claim that "If schemas are to be sustained or reproduced . . . they must be validated by the accumulation of resources" (p. 13) seems to suggest that cultural elements are evaluated in terms of practical concerns. This would match my portrayal of culture as adaptive to opportunity, for it implies that the schemas/cultures that construct resources/opportunities are opportunistically constructed and reconstructed. At the risk of redundancy: cultural legacies (schemas) mediate/constitute opportunities (resources) while opportunities mediate/constitute cultural legacies. This occurs via affordance-seeking agents who read their culture in light of their opportunities and vice versa. This process takes place synchronically and diachronically. That is, at a given point in time the actor reads each in light of the other. But both have a history: cultural legacies and opportunities have evolved through this ongoing dialectic.

As suggested above, numerous theorists have sought to establish a dialectic between structure and culture. MacLeod (1987) speaks of "the interpenetration of human consciousness and structural determinants" (p. 148). But his theoretical commitment is to "the primacy of the opportunity structure" (p. 62). A dialectical perspective is often lost to the temptation to prioritize a preferred variable—that is, to assert its autonomy from and causal dominance over the other. As noted earlier, Alexander (1990) says that "we cannot understand culture without reference to social structural constraints" (p. 26). This formulation suggests a full dialectic if Alexander means that to *understand* culture we must examine its practical expression. But if this is his meaning, it is not sustained. The gap between Alexander's (1995) additive multidimensionality and a fully synthetic approach is revealed in *Fin de Siecle Social Theory* where he affirms the independence of culture from material factors. In an earlier essay, Alexander (1988b) claimed that "rather than dichotomizing culture and material life, [Parsonian theory] argues for the simultaneous independence and interpenetration of personality, social system, and culture" (p. 190). But this dialectical approach is contradicted in an affirmation of the *autonomy* of norms from rational calculation: "Internalized, normative order and rational action are like oil and water; they can be placed beside one another but they cannot mix" (Alexander, 1995, p. 155).

In making this argument, Alexander (1995) criticizes the extreme claim that norms are "*merely* objects of calculation" and argues that norms cannot be subject to "an *exclusively* rational calculation" (p. 155, emphasis added). But short of this extreme—and rare—position, authentic normative commitment does not preclude instrumental calculation. It is not necessary to argue that norms are entirely insulated from rational calculation—"like oil and water"—to recognize their "grip on the mind" (Elster, 1989a, p. 128). One can, for example, take the injunction "Thou Shalt Not Steal" seriously, feeling "embarrassment, anxiety, guilt and shame" (p. 99) at its violation, and still be responsive to its "cost." Alexander (1995) claims that "norms which are merely objects of calculation can only be the norms of others, not of the actor herself" (p. 155). But to cite the standard counter to this Kantian absolutism, considering the practical consequences of telling the truth to a killer seeking his victim does not gainsay a genuine commitment to truth telling. Moses himself, if not Kant, would, according to standard Jewish doctrine, permit violation of the kosher laws to avoid a worse evil, such as starvation. The elements Alexander analogizes to oil and water are routinely mixed by practical actors: a law-abiding man may steal food to save his starving child without repudiating his commitment to laws against theft. Suggesting a dialectical relation between norms and practical reason, Wittgenstein argues that rules *must* be articulated by practical actors and hence their "contamination" by instrumental considerations is unavoidable. Similarly, rather than dismissing ideas as "reflections" of "material practice," Marx (1967b) sought to "explain the formation of ideas from material practice" (p. 28).

Despite his sustained effort to theorize an "interpenetration" of cultural and structural dimensions of action and admonitions about "false prioritizing," in the end Alexander (1988b, p. 220; see also 1987a, p. 26), replicates Parsons's failure to maintain a conception of the components of action as "analytically coequal" by describing culture as "the cybernetically highest element in patterning action systems" (Parsons, 1966, p. 113). Alexander's effort to insulate norms from "materialism" and/or utilitarianism echoes Parsons's eventual admission that he is "a cultural determinist rather than a social determinist" (Parsons, 1966, p. 113).[3] As mentioned in Chapter 1, Alexander has noted that "every major theoretical tradition" has both aimed for a multidimensional approach "as its primary theoretical goal" and rejected this project. In the end, he replicates this contradiction.

Sewell (1992) comes closer to a sustained dialectic. But insofar as schemas "must be *validated* by the accumulation of resources," he ultimately mirrors Alexander by subordinating culture to instrumental reason. The collapse of Sewell's dialectic is foreshadowed by his use of the term "abandoned," which fails to capture the way in which rules are *adapted* by opportunistic actors while remaining relevant to action—a process the studies cited here have demonstrated and which Wittgenstein considers to be essential to rule following.[4] Swidler (1986) also subordinates culture to instrumental reason: "It is . . . the concrete situations in which . . . cultural models are enacted that determine which take root and thrive, and which wither and die" (p. 1442). Paradoxically, this underestimates both the durability *and* the adaptability of cultural models. By reducing culture to a handmaiden of practical reason, Sewell and Swidler cannot explain the examples of culture subverting practical needs.

Emirbayer and Goodwin (1994) seek a fully dialectical approach: "Culture and social relations [defined as networks] empirically interpenetrate with and mutually condition one another so thoroughly that it is well-nigh impossible to conceive of the one without the other" (p. 1438). But while arguing that these interpenetrations are not "adequately conceptualized" and aiming to show their "concrete social interrelationship" (p. 1442), their description of *how* "Culture and social relations empirically interpenetrate" is vague.

One problem is that they do not theorize culture in a way that reveals its constitution by practical actors. This is partly remediated in a later article where Emirbayer and Mische (1998) cite Charles Taylor's (Wittgensteinian) argument that "A rule doesn't [just] apply itself; it has to be applied, and this may involve difficult, finely tuned judgements" (p. 994). They concretize the interpretive process by arguing that it is guided by actors' efforts to engage "situational contingencies" (p. 999).

But while gaining ground in the synthetic project with this concept of culture, Emirbayer and Mische (1998) lose vital ground in their concept of social structure. Emirbayer and Goodwin (1994) defined social structure as "networks of social ties" and allowed actors the ability to "reconfigure" (p. 1445) structures, as well as culture: "Human agency, as we conceptualize it, entails the capacity of socially embedded actors to appropriate, reproduce, and potentially, to innovate upon received cultural categories and conditions of action in accordance with their personal and collective ideals, interests, and commitments" (p. 1443). They conclude with a dialectical conception of actors and the "conditions of action": "if cultural and societal (network) structures shape actors, then it is equally true that actors shape these structures in turn" (p. 1445). My argument that actors constitute culture and social structures *in light of one another* aims at greater specificity about how this happens. This is implied by Emirbayer and Goodwin, but it is worth the risk of fussiness to reveal *how* action is constrained by and shapes cultural and societal structures. Under the assumption that to theorize agency we must appropriately theorize the constraints in relation to which it occurs, I have reconceived culture and social structure in a way that makes agency central.

However, Emirbayer and Goodwin's (1994) dialectic of structure and culture is obscured in the later article where Emirbayer and Mische (1998) adopt a *generic* concept of structure as "contexts of action" (p. 964) or "situational contexts/structuring environments" (p. 1004). The authors allude to the earlier "disaggregation" of the concept of structure into "the cultural context" and the "social-structural context"—that is, "network patterns of social ties" (p. 970, n. 5). But they adopt the more diffuse "structuring contexts" (p. 1012).[5] With this move, they reintroduce the vagueness that has so often confounded efforts to turn structure from a *perspective* to an *analytical concept*. Most important, conflating the two elements of structure—culture and the array of opportunities—into "situational contingencies" or "life circumstances" (p. 999) loses the theoretical leverage gained in the earlier article where the disaggregated concept of structure leads to an understanding of *how* they interpenetrate—that is, the ways in which each is constituted by the actor in light of the other. If agency emerges in the *dialectic* of culture and social structure, their derivation of agency is also obscured by merging these two elements.

There is a practical cost in conflating culture and social structure. Even though appropriate values are needed for school to afford opportunity—and values are in turn constituted in light of opportunities—it is in fact possible "to conceive of one without the other." For example, it makes sense to ask if changing values or rewards is the best way to enhance school performance or deter crime. The advantage of a dialectical perspective is that while the interdependence of culture and structure is stressed, they are not merged to the point where their analytic distinction is masked. This is why Archer (1988) warns of the danger of conflation. Hence, we can say that students need to be taught the value of learning or, alternately, that providing material benefits will motivate better performance. While Marx saw the sun and the plant as interdependent, he maintained their distinction. To extend the analogy with school, while plants are dialectically related to the sun, we can enhance yields by genetic manipulation.

CULTURE, STRUCTURE, AND AGENCY

The issue of agency has been broached in the portrayal of culture and social structure as constituted by social actors. It is worth being more specific about this because integrating voluntarism and determinism has been a central theme in social science, often overlapping the debate over cultural and structural determination. Alexander (1988c) claims that many contemporary theorists agree that "action and structure must now be intertwined" (p. 77).[6]

Alexander (1987b) finds voluntarism in culture (p. 14; see also 1982, chap. 3). This view is derived from Parsons who, as Wrong (1994) puts it, asserted "the autonomy of human ends or purposes," meaning by this "the impossibility of reducing them to the dictates of biology or the directly imposed constraints of the external nonhuman environment. The freedom to choose or create goals and affirm values was primary to Parsons, hence his choice of the 'voluntaristic theory of action' to designate his conception of the basic subject matter of social science" (p. 38). This position is motivated by the belief that a utilitarian model of action leaves persons in thrall to their appetites and/or "material" conditions.

Rooting freedom in the control of appetites through moral training has been the dominant view in philosophy. While mainly associated with Kant, it can be found in a range of philosophical schools, including the utilitarians. John Locke (1902) believed that "the principle of all virtue and excellency lies in a power of denying ourselves the satisfaction of our own desires, where reason does not authorize them" (p. 187). Arguing that appetites must be shaped by values, John Stuart Mill (1895) believed that "none but a person of confirmed virtue is free" (p. 551). Despite doubting that social order could be based on moral training, Adam Smith (1976b) defined virtue as self-command "over the most ungovernable passions of human nature" (p. 25). This view of autonomy also appears in emphatically nonutilitarian thinkers. Edmund Burke said that "men are qualified for civil liberty in exact proportion to their disposition to put moral chains upon their own appetites" (quoted in Vanberg, 1988, p. 1). Durkheim (1961) also believed that "liberty is the fruit of regulation. Through the practice of morals we develop the capacity to govern and regulate ourselves, which is the whole reality of liberty" (p. 54).

But rationalists consider instrumental reason, rather than moral training, to be the source of agency. According to Descartes, liberation required the overthrow of tradition which he saw as a repository of ignorance and hence an impediment to freedom: "The chief cause of errors is to be found in the prejudices of our childhood" (quoted in Gellner, 1992, p. 46). His project of radical doubt was, in large part, aimed at liberation from culture:

"We must take care scrupulously to withhold our assent from the opinions we have formerly admitted" (p. 8). This view also runs a wide gamut. Insofar as Marx (1967a) portrayed "the history of all past generations" as an "alp that weighs on the mind of the living" (p. 15) and saw freedom as throwing off "false consciousness" and acting on "interests," he also regarded instrumental reason as the path to liberation.

Unsurprisingly, this is the preferred view of economists who, a la Descartes, tend to see culture as a kind of "noise"—that is, a threat to clear thought. According to Alan Wolfe (1989), "the University of Chicago tradition in economics is hostile to culture, viewing it as an obstacle to the ability of people to make their decisions as rationally as possible. From its point of view, culture is an impediment to freedom" (p. 46). Michael Hechter and Debra Friedman (1988) believe that one of the advantages of rational choice theory is that it offers the actor "more respect" (p. 216; see also Coleman, 1990, p. 4). In contrast to the postmodernist's "oversocialized" view of persons as entirely products of culture, James Hanley (1999) argues that "rational choice recognizes that humans do make choices, that they have the option of making intelligent decisions based on their own self-interests" (p. 40). Sewell's (1992) view of freedom is also instrumentalist. Challenging Bourdieu's emphasis on the power of habitus (p. 15), he cites the Kybele's anticolonial revolution as an example of agency, which he defines as "enhancing power and resources" (p. 20): "To be an agent means to be capable of some degree of control over the social relations in which one is enmeshed" (p. 20).

Both cultural and instrumental conceptions of agency are problematic. Alexander (1982, chap. 3) and others rightly doubt that the rational-instrumental view of action can underwrite freedom. This is evident in David Hume's (1978) description of reason as "the slave of the passions" (p. 493) and in Jeremy Bentham's (1973) description of mankind as "under the governance of two sovereign masters, *pain and pleasure*. It is for them alone to point out what we ought to do as well as to determine what we shall do" (p. 17). In this view, reason enhances our ability to satisfy desire but is helpless to *restrain* desire. Nor did Hobbes allow agency. In his view, appetites rule intellect: "The Thoughts are to the Desires, as Scouts and Spies, to range abroad and find the way to the Things Desired" (quoted in Berne, 1981, p. 372). Because choice is (merely) "the last appetite in deliberating"

(Hobbes, 1985, p. 49), he concluded that "neither is the freedom of willing or not willing greater in man than in other living creatures" (Hobbes, 1966, p. 409). The conception of agency as nothing more than the ability to calculate the ratio of pain to pleasure can lead to "the behaviorism towards which some of orthodox Chicago [economic] positivists leans" (Barry, 1987, p. 50).[7]

Sewell's conception of agency also rests on a constricted concept of freedom: there are many arenas of authentic action—such as caring for a child or writing a poem—that have nothing to do with "enhancing power and resources." Indeed, Sewell (1992) echoes Hobbes's portrait of persons as driven by "a perpetual and restless striving of power after power, that ceaseth only in death" (Hobbes, 1985, p. 161). Hobbesian man may be free of cultural restraints, but he remains in thrall to the shifting winds of opportunity and desire.

But while normative regulation can liberate actors from the tyranny of desire, it's potential for agency is also problematic. Dennis Wrong (1994) points out that by "voluntarism" Parsons "did not mean 'free will' exercised by individuals but the collective choice and institutionalization of goals and norms undetermined by biology or the natural environment. His position therefore does not exclude a cultural or social determinism" (p. 39).[8] Alexander (1982) acknowledges that his sense of voluntarism is eccentric: "Orthodox religious action . . . is voluntary in this sense" (p. 109). But the portrait drawn by Edgarton (1992) (see Chapter 5) of individuals controlled by their cultures shows that persons can be slaves to rules as much as to appetites. Durkheim's (1961) conception of moral training as the base of freedom does not comport well with his portrait of persons as cultural dopes.

A dialectical understanding of culture and opportunity creates grounds for agency not available in either instrumentalism or normative regulation. The actor is modeled as engaging both cultural imperatives and opportunities, but is a trager of neither. While both forms of determination are acknowledged, agency is preserved in the ability of the actor to critically engage each in light of the other. The grip of culture can be loosened by the ability to "price" its consequences. A second dimension of agency appears in the ability of actors to opportunistically "read" rules. But this does not mean that agency emerges only in slipping the leash of culture: culture can be a resource for agency by controlling the unrestrained pursuit of self-interest that subjects the structural dope to Bentham's "two sovereign masters."

As suggested in Chapter 1, the problems of agency and synthesis can be solved together. Insofar as rules must be interpreted by practical actors and opportunities are constructed by encultured actors, both are *fundamentally* agential. And because each is implicated in the actor's constitution of the other, they are *essentially* interpenetrating.

THE LIMITS OF AGENCY

The problem of agency is tricky in that *too much* undermines the project of social explanation—and violates common sense—by denying the determinations that constrain action. This problem appears—unexpectedly—in Bourdieu. In contrast to his claim that habitus "engenders all the thoughts, all the perceptions, and all the actions" (1977, p. 95), he allows that actors can "consciously master the relation they entertain with their dispositions. They can deliberately let them 'act' or they can on the contrary inhibit them by virtue of consciousness" (Bourdieu & Wacquant, 1992, p. 137). This abrupt turn to agency is amplified in a striking claim: "Social agents will *actively* determine, on the basis of the[ir] socially and historically constituted categories of perception and appreciation, the situation that determines. One can even say that *social agents are determined only to the extent that they determine themselves*" (p. 136). Here it seems that "the situation that determines," which can be read as encompassing culture and structure, is in some measure a product of the actor. Bourdieu's vacillation between structuralism and voluntarism is resolved here with evocation of Sartre's impassioned denial, in *Saint Genet,* of determinism: "We are not lumps of clay, and what is important is not what people make of us but what we ourselves make of what they have made of us" (p. 528).

The first problem in this is that it appears *deux ex machina.* The source of freedom from structural determinations that are elsewhere presented as inexorable is not explained. Also, Bourdieu has not reconceived culture and structure in a way that allows agency.[9]

Most important, this extravagant voluntarism is unsustainable. Opportunities are not entirely constituted by the cultural resources of actors.

South Africa under apartheid presented obstacles that were as solid as locked doors, as does, in one way or another, any social order. Similarly, actors are endowed with specific cultural resources that, while subject to variable readings, are not endlessly malleable. The postmodern claim that "the recipient of a cultural object can make meanings virtually independent of the cultural object itself" (Griswold, p. 85) subverts the very idea of culture. Indeed, social order itself becomes inexplicable. And as argued in Chapter 5, if rules can be interpreted idiosyncratically, the social investment in culture—and the postmodernists' investment in her own work—makes no sense. The efforts of Matza's (1964) boys to neutralize the grip of legal rules and of Mormons to bend religious proscriptions shows the creativity of actors and the flexibility of norms. But these examples also demonstrate the importance of gaining legitimacy vis-à-vis established norms and the limited degrees of freedom they allow. It is hard to improve on Marx's (1967a) recognition of constraint and agency: "Men make their own history, but they do not make it just as they please: they do not make it under circumstances chosen by themselves, but under circumstances directly encountered, given, and transmitted from the past" (p. 15).

In view of the persistence of instrumentalism in social science, it is worth reiterating that the frequency of practices that drive individuals and societies to destitution and death shows that the cultural dope is not a social science invention. Rules can rule. The recalcitrance of culture is not captured by Swidler's (1986) characterization of culture as a tool kit or by the ethnomethodological reduction of rules to "practices" and hence, as Alexander (1988a, p. 241) put it, the conception of social structure as "completely emergent from practices." Nor can the symbolic interactionist emphasis on the negotiated nature of norms account for their often-demonstrated power to thwart self-interest.

Similarly, Sewell's (1992) claim that schemas "must be validated by the accumulation of resources" underestimates their power to *subvert* practical needs. Keegan's (1993) argument that military practices often defy instrumental logic is illustrated in John Ellis's (1987) *The Social History of the Machine Gun*. Ellis describes the reluctance of tradition-steeped European, and especially British, officer corps to employ machine guns. Taking too seriously the aphorism that the battle of Waterloo was won on the playing fields of Eton, they saw war as a kind of sport in which victory ought to be determined by individual bravery and will and whose ethical and aesthetic dimensions must be respected. The thought of "the glorious cavalry charge" (p. 55) being swept away by weaponry run by machine operators was offensive enough that the British Army entered World War I with scanty numbers of this devastating weapon. Their romanticism had disastrous results: "The essential tragedy of the First World War was that the British commanders did not grasp . . . that three men and a machine gun can stop a battalion of heroes" (p. 123). It is noteworthy that the British were pleased to use machine guns against native rebellions, a venue where glory was not an issue.

While the adaptability of Chinese culture has often been emphasized, some practices endure even when they subvert goals. For example, mistrust of nonfamily, an adaptive response to a system in which the legal system was unreliable, becomes an encumbrance when it results in a preference for incompetent relatives over professional managers. Indeed, failure can sometimes lead to a redoubled commitment to the "old ways," illustrated by resurgent Russian and Islamic traditionalism.

Emirbayer and Mische's (1998) theory of agency also suffers from an exaggerated instrumentalism. They find agency in the ability of actors "to reconfigure received schemas by generating alternative possible responses to the problematic situations they confront in their lives" (p. 984). Drawing on the phenomenology of Schutz and Husserl, they emphasize the reconfiguration of "routines, dispositions, preconceptions, competencies, schemas, patterns, typifications, and traditions" (p. 975) as actors engage "situational contingencies" (p. 999). They conclude, quoting Sewell, "Agency . . . consists primarily in the capacity of resource-equipped actors to act creatively through the transposition of existing schemas into new contexts" (p. 1005).

But schemas do not just provide responses to problematic situations, and they are not infinitely malleable. Again, there is a gap between Emirbayer and Goodwin and Emirbayer and Mische. The later claim that "schemas can be challenged, reconsidered, and reformulated" (Emirbayer & Mische, 1998, p. 983) does not maintain the earlier argument that "cultural structures are both constraining and enabling of social action" (Emirbayer & Goodwin, 1994, p. 1441) because they have "their own autonomous inner logic" (p. 1440). Emirbayer and Mische (1998) concede that "there is no hypothetical moment in which agency actually gets "free" of structure" (p. 1004). But the "independent causal significance" (p. 1431) of "ideals, beliefs, and values" (p. 1446) emphasized by Emirbayer and Goodwin (1994) is scanted in the later article. As a result, while Emirbayer and Mische (1998) allow for variability in agency (pp. 964, 1004), they are unable to account for the cultural dopes described in Chapter 5.

A second problem with this view is a constricted conception of agency. Boudon and Bourricauld (1992) (see Chapter 2) are right to stress the resilience of utilitarianism in sociological theory because Emirbayer and Mische, like Swidler, Sewell, and others, imply an instrumentalist view of agency insofar as cultural training is conceived as an encumbrance—unless it can be reconfigured to facilitate adaptation to problematic situations. Practical adaptation is the *criterion* of agency, and the cultural dope of Durkheim and Parsons is its main obstacle. But as argued above, while the ability to reconfigure schemas avoids the cultural dope, it risks the behavioral dope—controlled by "two sovereign masters"—by subordinating schemas to practical goals.

Recognizing the role of culture in agency requires understanding its dual role. While cultural training can subvert agency, it can also enhance agency by insulating actors from the pursuit of instrumental advantage. As mentioned above, Kant found autonomy in devotion to rational (i.e., universalizable) moral principles, not the satisfaction of desire through instrumental reason. His rejection of the utilitarian conflation of the good and the useful, embodied in his slogan: "Let justice prevail though the world perish for it" was derived from Rousseau's (1950) conception of "moral liberty" as obedience to moral laws, even when they subvert our practical interests: "the mere impulse of appetite is slavery, while obedience to a law which we prescribe to ourselves is liberty" (p. 19). In this view, authentic agency emerges in *not* bending moral rules to suit practical needs—in doing the right thing even if it hurts. This is lost if schemas are reduced to the service of practical need. Paradoxically, while cultural training can *restrict* freedom, the grip of values can also *enable* moral autonomy, which, for Rousseau and Kant, is the only real autonomy. It might be difficult to decide in a given case whether values are inspiring the obedience of a cultural dope or facilitating moral autonomy, and because Alexander and Parsons tie agency to moral culture, they cannot explore these alternatives. But both possibilities are masked by the reduction of schemas to adaptive tools. Paradoxically, the power of schemas to both restrict agency and to facilitate it by insulating actors from instrumentalism is lost when they are subordinated to practical reason.

The partial autonomy of culture and structure bears on the debate over causal priority. As indicated in Chapter 1, most theorists have insisted on subsuming rival approaches. Becker (1976) argues the universality of maximizing behavior: "The heart of my argument is that human behavior is not compartmentalized, sometimes based on maximizing, sometimes not, sometimes motivated by stable preferences, sometimes by volatile ones, sometimes resulting in an optimal accumulation, sometimes not" (p. 14). In contrast, Gellner (1992), like Sahlins, reduces instrumental reason to a cultural schema and describes its dominance as "one highly distinctive and indeed unique culture" (p. 52). Similarly, Paul DiMaggio (1990) speaks of reason as a form of ritual (p. 122).

Rather than challenging examples that seem to show the priority of ideal or material factors "in the final analysis," or the dominance of different institutional sectors, such as the economy or religion, it is best to allow *variations* in their influence. DiMaggio (1990) addresses this issue by describing "four axes of variation in economic orientation" (p. 117). First, there are variations between individuals: "Some people are more likely than others to approach exchanges with scripts drawn from market ideology as opposed to other available cultural resources" (p. 117). Some feminists challenge the universality of "rational economic man" and portray women as motivated by more communitarian values, such as Carol Gilligan's (1982) "ethic of care." There may also be class differences. Steven Holmes (1990) notes that the sixteenth-century theologian Richard Hooker "summarized traditional thinking with his claim that the common people are motivated by self-interest, while religious and political elites are motivated by virtue and devotion to the common good" (p. 284). A modern version of this view appears in theories of the culture of poverty. Edward Banfield (1970) contends that the lower classes are driven by self-interest and are incapable of the community-spiritedness of the elite. This claim is reiterated, but with a reversed political valence, by structural theories that model the dominated as more rational than the dominant groups who exclude them because of race, class, or gender bias.

A second source of variation noted by DiMaggio (1990) is the nature of role relations: Strangers are more likely to be treated instrumentally than acquaintances. Third, there is variation among goods or services: "We expect exchanges involving soybeans, screwdrivers, or Saran wrap to more readily evoke the orientation typical of homo economicus than exchanges involving land or labor, which in turn may more broadly trigger market scripts than those in which babies, body organs, or emotional or physical intimacy are exchanged" (p. 118). Fourth, different settings, such as the church or the family versus the market, inspire different types of conduct.

DiMaggio does not mention the possibility that there is historical variation in orientation. Harold Schneider (1974) outlines the debate in anthropology between the "formalists" who believe that the neoclassical model applies universally and the "substantivists" who argue that this model is specific to Western capitalism. Illustrating the latter view, Weber described the historical displacement of tradition by rationality and argued that the same system can shift its motivational base. In *The Protestant Ethic and the Spirit of Capitalism,* he argued that modern capitalism is "emancipated from its old [religious] supports" (Weber, 1958, p. 72) and is sustained by market competition that "forces the individual . . . to conform to capitalistic rules of action" (p. 54). Contrary to the claims of his epigones, Marx (1964) also recognized historical variation in motivation: "The [feudal] lord does not try to extract the maximum profit from his estate. He rather consumes what is there, and tranquilly leaves the care of producing it to the serfs and tenant farmers. That is the *aristocratic* condition of landownership which reflects a romantic *glory* upon its lords" (p. 123).

In light of these variations, Richard Zeckhauser (1987) describes the debate between "behavioral" and "rational" economics as mainly a "turf battle" in which each side has secure territory. Behavior in markets usually confirms the latter perspective, while other venues, such as religion, provide counterexamples. Hence, "Each side is triumphant in the landscape it views" (p. 256). This debate is best resolved by rejecting the imperial claims of instrumentalist or normative approaches and allowing each side its domain.

Flexibility about the *degree,* as well as the type, of determination can also avoid irresolvable debates. Opportunities can be more or less structured: crowded city traffic allows fewer options and hence a smaller role for ability and motivation than, say, Stanley's efforts to find Dr. Livingstone. A bureaucrat is more constrained than an entrepreneur. Similarly, rules vary in the degree of agency allowed. While room for interpretation remains, "Thou shalt not steal" imposes sharper constraints than "Thou shalt honor thy father and mother." Because "The environments of action can be more or less open" (Alexander, 1988a, p. 327), explanation should sometimes focus on the "cows"—that is, agents—and sometimes on the "fences"—the constraints on action.

8

The Dialectic of Desire

THE DISAPPEARING SELF

The actor thus far has been modeled as a rational cipher—that is, an entity without distinctive traits, engaging culture and opportunity. This reflects the sociological perspective in which the self is viewed as a point of intersection of social forces—the array of costs and benefits or cultural rules. This view is especially evident in structural sociology. Indifference to personality leads Charles Warriner (1981) to replicate Mayhew's (1980) claim that "from the point of view of social organization all individuals are interchangeable": "It is not only easier but also more consistent with the data to argue that all regular actors in organizations are alike (in other words, that personal biography makes little difference in what they do)" (p. 187). Network theorists conceive of persons as "nodes"—that is, points of intersecting social ties—and explain behavior as a function of social location. As argued earlier, this view is central to the rational choice claim that actors "could be picked at random from their groups, because it made no difference *who* they were" (Hindess, 1988, p. 29).

The erasure of personality is implicit in less radical versions of structural sociology: eliminating culture as a factor in behavior is tantamount to eliminating the self. This is expressed in the tendency to downplay the *history* of actors. Kanter (1977) says, "My view, then, sees behavior as the result of a sense making process involving *present* experiencing rather than of psychological conditioning in which the dim past is a controlling force" (p. 252). Gerson (1985) also elides the actor's history by explaining action in light of the "constraints and opportunities in the *immediate* social environment" (p. 192). Wacquant (1993) stresses the controlling force of "the *immediate* socioeconomic context" (p. 15), and Granovetter (1985) aims to explain conduct in terms of the actor's "*present* situation" (p. 506) (all emphasis added).

Radical situationism is not confined to structural sociology. By emphasizing the adaptability of norms, symbolic interactionism explains action in terms of "situational relevance, not previous socialization" (Alexander, 1987a, p. 27). Ethnomethodology similarly argues that "binding rules are specified situationally and modified" (p. 28). This view is implicit in the strategic actor of Goffman's (1959) *Presentation of the Self in Everyday Life,* and it is explicit in *Asylums:*

> The self . . . is not a property of the person to whom it is attributed, but dwells rather in the pattern of social control that is exerted in connection with the person by himself and those around him. This special kind of institutional arrangement does not so much support the self as constitute it. (Goffman, 1961, p. 168)

It is worth stressing the extremism of this approach, for it goes well beyond classical liberal environmentalism. John Locke (1902), in *Some Thoughts Concerning Education,* described the minds of children "as easily turned this or that Way, as water itself" (p. 2). But Locke qualified human malleability with the metaphor of the tabula rasa, a blank slate that accumulates durable impressions. In contrast, the actors of structural sociology, as it were, remain children, "easily turned this or that Way." Accumulating no history, they are literally looking glass selves, reflecting their contemporary settings. This view was implicit in the environmentalism of early liberalism (see Spragens, 1981, chap. 4) but fully emerged in Bentham's erasure of differences between individuals: "The only reason Washington did not act in America as Bonaparte acted in France, must be sought not in differences of motives, which were egoistic in both cases, but in the differences of political conditions" (quoted in Alexander, 1982, p. 100). In this view, the promptings of pain and pleasure rather than the traits of individuals control conduct.

Denial of the relevance of history appears at various levels of structural thinking. Wallerstein (1979) applies the logic of situational determinism to nations:

> One cannot reasonably explain the strength of various state machineries at specific moments of the history of the modern world-system primarily in terms of a genetic-cultural line of argumentation, but rather in terms of the structural role a country plays in the world economy *at that moment in time*. (p. 21. emphasis added)

Nations, like the structural self, have no ingrained history. As in real estate, what matters is location, location, location.

Again, this approach puts homo sociologicus close to homo economicus. As sketched in Chapter 3, neoclassical economics empties the self of all features—save the impulse to maximize—in order to stress the determinative role of costs and benefits. The belief that "attitudes are adaptive or fungible depending on their contribution to an abstract utility" leads to an emphasis on the "social pliability of the self" (Friedland & Robertson, 1990, pp. 24-25). Becker's (1979, p. 9) premise that tastes do not vary between individuals and that changes in price explain variations in behavior implies the interchangeability of persons.

This view also suggests that actors are forward-looking, little affected by their past:

> According to the game-theoretic model of choice, individually rational behavior is motivated by the expected causal consequences of individual acts. Expediency prevails at any instance of decision. Not only are bygones bygones . . . [actors] "must" react opportunistically to the exigencies of each choice situation. (Kliemt, 1990, p. 74)

Marginalist theory is similarly indifferent to the past: "The rational consumer continually looks forward" (Bucholtz, 1989, p. 159). Situational determinism reaches an apogee in rational expectations theory in which habits and memory are erased with a model of the actor who instantly reacts to new information, regardless of accumulated experience. Arthur Stinchcombe (1992) has noticed this convergence of seemingly disparate forms of sociology and economics:

> Theoretically Coleman and Goffman (and Simmel) have much the same thrust, to attach the core of social life to evanescent situations rather than to features of roles people occupy permanently. This is also characteristic of microeconomic theory, that both supply and demand for example depend on market price, a sit-

uational variable, rather than on any predispositions of persons or corporate bodies. (p. 199)

This approach has played a prominent role in psychology. Trait psychology and personality theory have been challenged by emphasis on situational forces. Noting the parallel with economics, Etzioni (1988) characterizes those who "argue that the evidence shows that there are no (or only very weak) personality traits" as "neoclassical psychologists" (p. 47). Kenneth Bowers (1972) cites studies purporting to show that honesty is situationally variable rather than a function of ingrained personality. Claiming that "when we know the objective conditions under which a given behavior characteristic occurs, we can explain any relevant behavior in terms of those conditions," I. E. Farber (1964) professed to "look forward to the day . . . when personality theories are regarded as historical curiosities" (p. 37). While rooted in the belief that organisms respond mainly to costs and rewards, radical situationism goes beyond behaviorism: the learning history of the organism is scanted in favor of an ongoing plasticity. Walter Mischel (1968) has argued that there are no personality traits and hence "behavior is specific to every circumstance" (quoted in Frank, 1988, p. 234).

Situationism in psychology is not confined to behaviorism. Evoking Goffman's portrayal of the self as contextual, Harry Stack Sullivan's (1950) interpersonal psychiatry is based on the belief—contra Freud—that "no such thing as the durable, unique, individual personality is ever clearly justified. For all I know every human being has as many personalities as he has interpersonal relations" (p. 329).

This perspective is most developed in economic psychology in which personality traits are explained as adaptations to the environment of costs and benefits. Richard Posner (1995) interprets various traits of the elderly—such as parsimony, garrulousness, risk aversiveness, and so on—as rational responses to alternations in their cost-benefit situation. The elderly tend to be poor listeners, not because of the personality dynamics of aging, but because they "invest less in the creation of human capital and therefore have less to gain from receiving inputs of information from other people" (p. 57). As the life span shortens, the "returns" on investments in new information diminishes. Swidler's (1986) sociological structuralism echoes this conception of personality traits as investments. Traditionalism among the old is explained in terms of "the costs of learning new cultural skills" (p. 283). Despite their apparent extremism, these views are extensions of the standard assumption of equal preferences and cost-benefit sensitivity, which leads to what Friedland and Robertson (1990) describe as the neoclassical reduction of "the self to a form of human capital, whose hard-wired emotions and deep values are functional for exchange" (p. 25).

Cultural theorists, of course, see actors as freighted with training rather than as mirrors of contemporary forces. But like structuralism, radical culturalism denies the importance of presocial traits. Like the environment of costs, the cultural environment is considered to determine behavior. This conception of the self derives from Hegel's belief that there is no enduring human nature. Rather, human traits are historical, a perspective retained by Marx. Similarly, Durkheim (1950) claimed that human nature is "merely the indeterminate material that the social factor molds and transforms" and contended that even filial love is "far from being inherent in human nature" (p. 106).

The claim that there is little to the self that is not trained is expressed in Richard Rorty's (1989) widely cited aphorism that socialization "goes all the way down" (p. 185). This has been the guiding principle of the postmodern assertion of the "social construction" of nearly all human characteristics, especially the "essentialisms" that legitimate systems of domination. For some feminists, "Womanhood and manhood are seen as neither a natural fact—nor a settled social fact but as part of a ceaseless, contested struggle among various groups to establish a gender ordering of human affairs" (Seidman, 1991, p. 141). Like Foucault, Judith Butler denies the possibility of a philosophical anthropology that can define human nature and regards all such efforts as implicated in a struggle for domination. As Martha Nussbaum (1999) describes her view, "Our ideas of what women and men are reflect nothing that exists eternally in nature. Instead they derive from customs that embed social relations of power" (p. 40). The evolutionary psychologists John Tooby and Leda Cosmides (1992) characterize the belief that culture overrides biology as the "Standard Social Science Model."

But whittling persons down to a function of their cultural training or cost-benefit situation, while of heuristic value, cannot offer complete explanations. Implying that some notion of a presocial self is not just empirically evident but *theoretically* necessary, Dennis Wrong (1994) argues that "hyperstructural approaches" neglect "discussion of human motivation, of the human wants, feelings, and impulses that undergird and set in motion the whole process of social interaction" (p. 59). As mentioned in Chapter 1, Elster (1990) claims that "there are really just two basic motivations of human behavior—rationality and social norms." But this is wrong or badly put because rationality and norms are not *motivations*: they *shape* behavior, which must be otherwise motivated. Contrary to Burt's (Ricardian) belief that "the network is its own explanation of motive," opportunities are not a sufficient explanation because we must explain why persons respond to them—that is, what they are opportunities *for*. Similarly, we must account for the human traits that induce normative compliance and explain why norms are often rejected or modified.

The dialectical process described in the last chapter is thus incomplete: something about persons must set it in motion. Indeed, this is implicit in Durkheim. Contradicting his claim that persons are "indeterminate material that the social factor molds and transforms" (1950, p. 106), his concern about anomie was provoked by the "inextinguishable thirst" (Durkheim, 1966, p. 242) of individuals who are insufficiently restrained. And his belief that "liberty is the fruit of regulation" (Durkheim, 1961, p. 53) implies that there is something about persons that needs to be regulated.

Despite strenuous and sometimes bitter resistance, the notion that there is indeed some sort of human nature is gaining wider acceptance. Emirbayer and Mische (1998) note the sociological neglect of "psychical structures" (p. 970, n. 5) and "of such categories as 'desire' " (p. 974). Goodwin (1997), in a study of guerilla fighters of the Philippines, tries to remediate this by incorporating the role of libidinal forces in maintaining commitment and solidarity.

The leading edge of this "rediscovery of human nature" (Wright, 1994, p. 8) is evolutionary psychology, which argues that various psychological dispositions, in humans and other animals, are not only abundantly documented but indispensable. For example, it is hard to imagine the survival of a species without certain inclinations, such as a tendency to care for infants, being genetically imprinted. The applicability of this view to humans is supported by what social constructionists deny: the universality of various human traits such as "gratitude, shame, remorse, pride, honor, retribution, empathy, love, and so on" (p. 8).[1] Under the assumption that the brain, like other organs, is a product of evolution, evolutionary psychologists argue that the key to these human universals is the logic of reproductive advantage: those animals with inclinations that enhance survival tend to out-reproduce those that do not. For example, Wright argues that apes "with an ounce of extra love for their offspring, love that translates into slightly more assiduous nurturing," have a reproductive advantage over their rivals (p. 25). This logic readily applies to humans, genetically nearly identical to the higher apes. Characterizing emotions as "stratagems of the genes" (p. 88), Wright emphasizes the reproductive edge offered by various senti-ments. For example, the natural feeling of affection for those who provide help may be "fortuitous genetic mutations" (p. 198) that facilitate the for-mation of bonds of mutual aid.[2]

Evolutionary psychologists further argue that norms and institutions must be understood as partly shaped by the imperatives of reproduction. For example, humans could not flourish absent values and institutions to provide care for the young, which is why "In every human culture on the an-thropological record, marriage—whether monogamous or polygamous, permanent or temporary—is the norm, and the family is the atom of social organization" (Wright, 1994, p. 57). The formation of such values and insti-tutions is founded on psychological dispositions that emerge from the im-peratives of biological survival. The extended helplessness of human, and primate, infants requires the resources a family can provide. Thus, culture reflects precultural traits, which is why we find foreshadowings of "family values" among gorillas, not leopards. Contrary to Durkheim's belief that love is a cultural artifact, men and women naturally tend to fall in love and form durable bonds in part because of "the genetic payoff of having two par-ents devoted to a child's welfare" (Wright, 1994, p. 59). The offspring of parents who do not bond are less likely to survive.

If it is indeed the case that humans are not the ciphers of the "Standard Social Science Model," there must also be psychological variation between individuals. In addition to the abundant examples of individuals responding differently to the same structural situations, however structure is defined, there is accumulating research on the genetic foundations of individual dif-ferences in behavioral dispositions, such as nervousness and extroversion (see Tooby & Cosmides, 1990). A striking example of the role of such dispo-sitions is the finding that the criminal records of adopted children more closely resemble those of their biological than their adoptive parents. The overwhelming preponderance of men in criminal violence in all known societies also suggests a genetic factor. Another challenge to radical situationalism emerges from studies of the enduring impact of early childhood.[3] Bourdieu and Wacquant's (1992) description of individuals as "pregnant with history" (p. 124) is more multifaceted than was likely intended.

There are various grounds for hostility to the idea that persons have traits that precede social experience. Some fear that concessions to the idea of human nature threatens the viability of the sociological perspective. It is implied that sociology is in a zero-sum game with emphasis on the importance of presocial traits, an attitude often reciprocated by biological determinists who, like economists, often see culture as marginally important or epiphenomenal. But this fear is exaggerated. By maintaining a dialectical logic, presocial individual traits can be theorized in a way that retains a robust situationalism that *requires* a sociological perspective.

A dialectical understanding of the relationship between presocial traits of persons—desires etc.—and the social context is suggested by research on the social construction of emotion. In this approach, emotions are seen as deeply cultural. In contrast to "traditional theories of emotion as natural phenomena" (p. 34), Claire Armon-Jones (1986) argues that "emotions are learnt as part of the agent's introduction to the beliefs, values, norms and expectations of his/her culture" (p. 33). This view was developed by cultural anthropologists but has entered the sociological literature. Challenging the "organismic" view that biology dictates emotions, Arlie Hochschild (1979) contends that "conventions of feeling" (p. 552) lead us to do "emotion work" so that we experience what is normatively appropriate. Thus, we "actively try to manage what we feel in accordance with latent rules" (p. 571).

Various aspects of "inner" experience are subject to cultural mediation. A considerable literature has followed Howard Becker's (1963) pioneering work on the role of learning in shaping reactions to chemical intoxicants. A study of the cultural component of drunkenness found that not only the incidence but the *experience* of drunkenness varies considerably. A major difference in the cultural construction of drunkenness is that alcoholism-prone groups, such as Irish Americans and Native Americans, invest alcohol with great effect, believing that individuals are powerless to control its influence. In contrast, groups with low incidence of alcoholism, such as Jews and Chinese Americans, reject drunkenness as an excuse for antisocial behavior. As a consequence, even in a population of assimilated Jews, it was found that alcoholism was one-hundredth the rate reported for some other ethnic groups. Among the 17,515 arrests reported for New York's Chinatown for the period 1933 through 1949, not one reported violent or disorderly drunkenness (Peele, 1990, p. 58).

A deficiency of social constructionism is that inner experience is seen as mainly shaped by culture. The risk in this approach is that the actor becomes a cultural dope, feeling what is taught or socially expected. Durkheim claimed that "mourning is not a natural movement of private feelings wounded by a cruel loss; it is a duty imposed by the group. . . . It is a ritual attitude which [a person] is forced to adopt out of respect for custom, but which is, in a large measure, independent of his affective state" (quoted in Levy, 1984, p. 215). Hochschild (1979) also suggests cultural determinism by describing her work as demonstrating "the power of the social" (p. 558). In her view, "Since culture directs our seeing and expecting, it directs our feeling and our naming of feeling" (Hochschild, 1983, p. 223).

This emphasis on the cultural character of emotions has largely shaped their sociological study. But the actor should not be conceived as simply following "conventions of feeling." In the first place, the effect of culture must be qualified because if "it directs our feeling and our naming of feeling," something is there for it to shape. Secondly, space should be left for the role of calculation in emotional life emphasized by economic psychology. The arguments in Chapter 4 that rules are subject to interpretation in light of practical exigencies implies that cultural rules about emotions can be strategically deployed.

Following Bentham's dictum that "passion calculates, more or less, in every man," Robert Frank (1988) contends that actors can *manage* their emotions, not simply conform to cultural dictates. In *Passions Within Reason,* he challenges the conventional conception of emotions as subverting rationality by showing how they can provide instrumental advantages. His argument is mainly based on a paradox: the strategic value of noninstrumental behavior. For example, numerous experiments on the division of resources have shown that unfair shares of money are often rejected even when this decision results in *no* reward. But this is not simply the triumph of emotions, such as anger, or norms of fairness. Individuals who are willing to sacrifice immediate gains tend to do better in the long run because they are usually treated more fairly than those who take the "rational" course of preferring something to nothing—which encourages exploitative treatment. Similarly, an inclination to angry retaliation, such as paying a lawyer $2,000 to retrieve a $1,000 loss, can induce cautious treatment by others. Payoffs often accrue to the emotionally charged when their irrational dispositions are perceived by others, as considerable research shows they usually are. We are more willing to enter business relations with the guilt-ridden than with the inveterate calculator, and those capable of love beyond reason are more likely to inspire reciprocal commitments in others. In each case, signs of passion profit the passionate.

Emotions are crucial in this process because the prospect of greater rewards in the future is often too feeble to resist a bird in the hand, a well-documented inclination called the "matching law." But an angry impulse to retaliate for unfair treatment provides a *present* motivation to forgo the temptations of *present* material advantage. Similarly, the tendency to discount future for present benefits means that present guilt or shame is a better resource for resisting a harmful addiction than rational understanding of its eventual, and often uncertain, costs. Emotions thus provide an alternative to, or reinforcement of, the discipline of moral training and/or rational restraint.

Frank's account of the origins of such emotions is two-pronged. Part of the story draws on evolutionary psychology, what Wright (1994) calls the "stratagems of the genes." Because others are inclined to choose the guilt-ridden business partner, to defer to the angry, and to marry the devoted lover, natural selection leads to their advantage over the relentlessly rational. But Frank (1988) introduces a more specifically economic argument by contending that emotions are, in some measure, subject to intentional control. That is, we more or less consciously cultivate useful emotional dispositions. The *appearance* of honesty may be strategically superior in that we gain its advantages without bearing the costs of being invariably honest. But like anger and love, honesty is difficult to fake. Frank describes the various clues by which emotional states are judged (such as the "Pinocchio effect": lying causes the nose to swell and redden slightly) and concludes that it is a rare individual who can reliably simulate the appropriate tones of voice, body language, facial expressions, and so on that communicate emotional states.

Because authentic honesty is more reliable than its simulation, "In order to *appear* honest, it may be necessary, or at least very helpful, to *be* honest" (Frank, 1988, p. 18). A prudent person will thus cultivate traits of character that inspire trust. A familiar puzzle for rational choice theory—tipping in restaurants that will not be revisited—can be solved by recognizing the strategic value of emotion:

> The motive is not to avoid the possibility of being caught, but to maintain and strengthen the predisposition to behave honestly. My failure to tip in the distant city will make it difficult to sustain the emotions that motivate me to behave honestly on other occasions. It is this change in my emotional makeup, not my failure to tip itself, that other people may apprehend.(p. 18)

Frank thus introduces an economic element to the evolutionary account to conclude that emotions are subject to prudential management. In Wright's (1994) metaphor, "the knobs of human nature" (p. 9)—that is, the behavioral dispositions that have emerged through evolution—can be "tuned" not only by variations in individual training but by calculating actors.

Some of Hochschild's (1979) findings belie her emphasis on "the power of the social." For example, she cites a college athlete who had lost interest in the game: "I did everything I could to get myself 'up.' I would try to be outwardly 'rah rah' or get myself scared of my opponents—anything to get the adrenalin flowing" (p. 563). She also quotes a student controlling her romantic feelings because she was "afraid of being hurt" (p. 562). Hochschild's interpretation stresses "obeisance to rules not completely of [the actor's] making" (p. 563). But these cases seem to be, more than conformity with "conventions of feeling," an effort to *manage* feelings. One of the appeals of armed robbery, according to Jack Katz (1988), is the challenge of staying cool in situations where others panic: "The hardman seizes on chaos as a provocation to manifest transcendent powers of control" (p. 206).

Sociologists have been reluctant to acknowledge nonsocial traits of individuals. But a fully multidimensional approach should incorporate features of the actor, the "personality system," as more than epiphenomena of culture or structure. If desires etc. can be understood in relation to structures of opportunity and culture, it is dogmatic sociologism to deny their significance.

There is an additional advantage in recognizing presocial human traits. It has been argued at several points that the problem of collective action resists a rational choice solution. But the claim that the normative solution is ad hoc and does not explain why norms compel behavior, is telling. This puzzle can be solved by introducing a natural sociability that antedates training and that motivates contributions to public goods independently of, or even contrary to, individual advantage. The notion of "inclusive fitness" (see Ridley, 1997) means that animals who risk their own survival—by, for example, crying out at the sight of a predator—to increase the chances of their close relatives are more likely to reproduce their genes than the inveterately selfish. It would take a "New Creationism" to dismiss out of hand a tendency for humans to similarly contribute to group survival. Even Hobbes (1985) did not ground sociability in social contract alone; it derives from "complaisance, that is to say, that every man strive to accommodate himselfe to the rest" (p. 209). Adam Smith (1976)—the "other" Adam Smith of *The Theory of Moral Sentiments*—stressed the essential sociability of persons: "Nature, when she formed man for society, endowed him with an original desire to please, and an original aversion to offend his brethren. She taught him to feel pleasure in their favourable, and pain in their unfavourable regard" (quoted in Robinson, 1962, p. 162). This reference to "Nature" would fit comfortably within an evolutionary view.

WITTGENSTEIN ON FEELINGS

It was argued earlier that an agential and synthetic understanding of culture and social structure requires that each be reconceptualized. That is, agency and synthesis cannot be theorized strictly in terms of the actor. Similarly, the relationship of desires etc. and the social context should be underpinned with a conception of "inner" experience that allows agency and synthesis. This can be found in Wittgenstein's thought. In his critique of Descartes's mind-body dualism—the view that mental experience is "private"—that is, unconnected or only contingently connected to visible behavior—Wittgenstein (1970) argued that emotions are not inner sensations—such as pain—because they are conceptually, or dialectically, tied to the context in which they appear and the behaviors with which they are associated. To illustrate the importance of the behavioral criteria of feelings he says, " 'I am completely exhausted'—if someone said that, but moved as briskly as ever, we should not understand him" (para. 589). This suggests that "being exhausted" is not just a feeling: it entails appropriate behavior, the absence of which raises doubt about the claim.

Behavioral criteria are particularly relevant to emotions. We often miss this because the language of, for example, pain and love are partially parallel. Like pain, feelings of love can be described as intense or mild, lasting or fleeting, and so on. But these similarities obscure important differences. For example, Wittgenstein (1970) claims that "love is not a feeling. Love is put to the test, pain not. One does not say: 'That was not pain, or it would not have gone off so quickly' " (para. 504). The point of this gnomic, but then plausible, claim is that *whatever* goes on "inside us" cannot be called love unless it matches appropriate conduct and occurs in a suitable context. Just as there are criteria for professing doubt (see Chapter 4), use of the word *love* is a language game, or social practice, not merely the naming of a "private" inner sensation, and whether or not the game is played rightly depends on various considerations.

For example, although we can feel a sharp pain for a moment, Wittgenstein (1953) asks, "Could someone have a feeling of ardent love or hope for the space of one second—*no matter what* preceded or followed this second? What is happening now has significance—in these surroundings. The surroundings give it its importance" (para. 583). Ardent love, unlike intense pain, is simply not the sort of thing that quickly evaporates. Indeed, constancy is a criterion of "true" love. Hence, determining "what goes on in us" cannot be made by introspection. Similarly, Wittgenstein (1970) argued that "fear is not a sensation" (para. 492) because whatever a person might feel, we can only predicate fear in fearful circumstances. The strange sensation in the pit of one's stomach that can be called fear in some situations might be called excitement, or perhaps even love, in others.[4] The concept of dialectics applies exactly to emotions in that their character is established in relation to their context.

The Cartesian model of inner experiences as phenomena to be discovered by introspection is shared by otherwise disparate approaches. B. F. Skinner (1964) claimed that the verbal community

> cannot teach a child to call one pattern of private stimuli "diffidence" and another "embarrassment" as effectively as it teaches him to call one stimulus "red" and another "orange," for it cannot be sure of the presence or absence of the

private patterns of stimuli appropriate to reinforcement or lack of reinforcement. (p. 85)

Speaking for phenomenological psychology (and, seemingly, common sense), Carl Rogers (1964, p. 111) claimed that "it is only by referring to the flow of my experiencing that I can determine my feelings: 'Do I love her?' It is only by reference to the flow of feelings in me that I can begin to conceptualize an answer" (p. 110). In contrast, Wittgenstein claimed that "private patterns of stimuli" or "the flow of feelings in me" cannot be the criteria for using the word. In Norman Malcolm's (1970, p. 15) interpretation, Wittgenstein suggests that we need to look "horizontally," at the context rather than "vertically," or introspectively, in determining the character of inner experience. Children often misuse the language of emotion and are corrected by reference to their situation.

Many aspects of the context establish the character of "feelings" such as love and fear. Jeffrey Coulter (1979) emphasizes social conventions: "What distinguishes grief from remorse and disappointment from shame is not a determinate inner feeling but responses, actions, appraisals and situations in the social world" (p. 127). Remorse cannot be distinguished from grief in terms of nuances of inner feelings. Rather, it is conceptually tied to features of the situation in which it occurs: one must have done something wrong to feel remorse, but not grief. The context rather than the "sensate" character of emotions allows us to distinguish between anger, indignation, and annoyance:

> The decision to say that the driver of a car which has broken down for lack of water is indignant, or merely annoyed, or angry, depends on whether the radiator is empty through the carelessness of a garage mechanic . . . or through his own carelessness ("annoyed with myself" but not "indignant with myself"). (p. 128)

The "grammar" of indignation, the conventional social practices—or language games—that constitute the meaning of the word, not its peculiar feel, dictates that it cannot be used reflexively. We designate one feeling "embarrassment" and another "diffidence," not through introspection, but through an appraisal of the context. I can feel embarrassment only if I, or someone I identify with, have done something untoward. Rom Harre (1986, p. 6) illustrates the relevance of the social context to emotions. If I see a man enjoying lunch with his wife I might feel envious; if he is enjoying the company of my wife, the feeling is more likely jealousy. Paralleling his theory of the ambiguity of rules (Chapter 4), Wittgenstein stresses the *indeterminate* character of inner feelings. They are, in large measure, *constituted* by actors, not *reported* on. Just as we cannot say what the rule means apart from an interpretation, there is no internal "ding an sich."

Wittgenstein (1953) appears to deny what seems undeniable: that we feel fear, love, anger, and so on: "And now it looks as if we had denied mental processes. And naturally we don't want to deny them" (para. 308). Wittgenstein recognizes that we have inner feelings: "*Certainly* all these things happen in you" (para. 423). He even acknowledges Rogers's claims: "It makes sense to ask: 'Do I really love her, or am I only pretending to myself?' and the process of introspection is the calling up of memories; of imagined possible situations and of the feelings that one would have if . . ." (para. 587). Wittgenstein claims that our inner sensations *are* cases of hoping, embarrassment, love, grief, and so on in their (dialectical) relations with a context: *what* we feel is dependent on its context. I cannot tell if I love her "*only* by reference to the flow of feelings."

The ability to appropriately label emotions is in large part a product of cultural training: adolescents must be taught to distinguish between love and lust or infatuation. But Wittgenstein's emphasis on the role of practical exigencies in determining the meaning of rules applies to his conception of inner feelings. That is, a strategic element can be introduced into the determination of emotions. The college student cited by Hochschild might well decide that she was not in love on practical grounds.

The intrication of desire and context can be illustrated by a recent analysis of sexual orientation. Reviewing the deficiencies in the literature on the biological determinants of sexual orientation, Byne and Parsons (1993) argue for an interactive approach that emphasizes "the active role of the individual in constructing his or her identity" (p. 236). Criticizing approaches in which "the individual is passive and sexual orientation is thrust upon him or her either by constitution or by parental treatment," they propose "an interactional model in which genes or hormones do not specify sexual orientation per se, but instead bias particular personality traits and thereby influence the manner in which an individual and his or her environment interact as sexual orientation and other personality characteristics unfold developmentally" (pp. 236-237). They show how in different situations traits believed to be heritable—such as novelty seeking, harm avoidance, and reward dependence—can lead to either heterosexual or homosexual orientation. In ordinary situations, a boy high in novelty seeking and low in reward dependence might be disposed to choose the thrills of an unconventional sexual lifestyle. But in the context of, say, an absent father and an overly protective mother who discouraged sports, the same traits might encourage emphatic masculinity. Byne and Parsons conclude that sexual orientation involves both biologically based temperamental traits and "a cascade of choices made in the context of changing circumstances in one's life and enormous social and cultural pressures" (p. 237).

In this analysis, sexual drive is seen to be amorphous and to take form in relation to environmental factors: "Sexual orientation emerges from an interaction between the environment and personality characteristics of the individual" (p. 237). It is reasonable to specify culture and opportunity as the environment within which emotions are labeled. Sexuality is not determined by introspection. If indeed a "genital itch" even qualifies as "sexuality," its nature is constituted by the actor in light of cultural resources and practical exigencies.[5]

THE (PARTIAL) AUTONOMY OF DESIRES ETC.

In earlier chapters, it was argued that while culture and opportunity interpenetrate, they must not be conflated. While open to interpretation, rules have a partial autonomy and opportunities are not entirely cultural constructs. This logic applies to desires etc.: although subject to interpretation in light of culture and social structure, we are not "socialized all the way down," and feelings are not infinitely malleable.

In the study of emotions, there is an ongoing debate between "constructionists" and "positivists." The former conceive of emotions as entirely sociocultural phenomena, whereas positivists believe that there is a biological core, such as anger, fear, and disgust, around which cultural interpretations develop. Defending the second position, Steven Gordon (1990) argues that "we cannot assume human emotional nature to be infinitely malleable, and must search for any biological or psychological limiting conditions that constrain the social construction of emotions" (p. 152). According to Neil MacKinnon (1994), "Positivists suppose the existence of a small number of culturally universal 'primary' emotions associated with specific physiological changes, onto which are grafted an indefinite number of culturally defined 'secondary' emotions during affective socialization" (p. 125).

In contrast, constructionists squeeze the biological element down to vanishing. Robert Solomon's (1984) "cognitive theory of emotions" argues that "an emotion is not a feeling (or a set of feelings) but an interpretation . . . a system of concepts, beliefs, attitudes, and desires, virtually all of which are context-bound, historically developed, and culture specific" (pp. 248-249). In contrast to Theodore Kemper's (1987) conception of anger as a primary emotion, Solomon argues that "anger is not just a physiological reaction cum sensation *plus* an interpretation. . . . It is *essentially an interpretation*" (p. 249). Because anger is a social construct, Solomon suggests that some societies may not even have the emotion. In a sense, not much hangs on this debate. Positivists predicate only a few primary emotions and they allow ample room for the role of culture. The gap is further narrowed by the constructionist concession that some emotions, even though culturally constructed, may be universal. But there are good reasons to maintain a dialectical logic and resist cultural reductionism by recognizing the partial autonomy of desires etc. Certain desires and emotions are resilient and cannot be redefined or defined away in light of culture and/or their "cost."

Wright (1994) recognizes the autonomy of desires etc. by qualifying his adaptive theory of emotions. He points out that guilt and depression, for example, "can misfire: feeling bad about yourself for too long, without relief, may lead to suicide" (p. 389). Solomon (1984) claims that the Utka Eskimos not only do not express anger: "They do not "feel" angry" (p. 244). But this remarkable claim is qualified: "They do feel annoyed, even hostile, and they can display raw violence, for example, in the beating of their dogs" (p. 244). And since infants and animals display behavior that seems of a piece with anger, there is good reason to believe that certain emotions, although subject to cultural mediation, are biologically rooted. Moreover, Solomon's claim that anger is "an interpretation" implies that there is *something* there to interpret. This is not to deny that there are cultural variations in how basic emotions are treated: Perhaps the Utka are aversive to speaking of anger or make great efforts to suppress it. But it is scarcely imaginable that they do not experience anger. One wants to ask if Solomon can imagine a society in which no one felt *fear.*

Drawing on diaries and autobiographies, Gerald Linderman (1997) has described the ways in which soldiers struggle to cope with the terrors of combat: they pray, concoct magical rituals, cultivate emotional numbness and fatalism, and so on. Although each of these techniques provides some respite, "In the end, none of these efforts succeeded in providing the assurance that soldiers sought" (p. 70). They remained "susceptible to sudden flashes of tumultuous feeling" (p. 79) and ultimately found that "battle was a disintegrative experience" (p. 361). With prolonged combat, most soldiers were finally overwhelmed by fear.

Flexibility is surely the best approach. While some emotions, such as anger and fear, are clearly universal, others are culturally contrived. For example, the Japanese experience an emotion—*amae*—unknown to other societies. To *amae* is to "presume upon another's love; behave like a spoilt child; play the baby; to be coquettish . . . take advantage of another's kindness" (Morsbach & Tyler, 1986, p. 290). This feeling plays a prominent role in Japanese culture; it is central to intimate relationships, and many domains of Japanese society, including politics and work relations, are shaped by *amae.* But even here, a culturally unique emotion is related to universal feelings, which is why non-Japanese can at least roughly understand *amae.*

Although evolutionary and economic psychology partially coincide, there are important differences. While the latter emphasizes the strategic adaptability of emotions, the former argues that they can be resistant to manipulation, even *mal*adaptive. Wright (1994) points out that various emotional dispositions emerged in the "ancestral environment" and may no longer be appropriate in new settings. But they persist. For example, the females of most species are more selective than males in the choice of mates. Female choosiness has two sources. First, because of the "costs" of gestation, the female investment in offspring is greater than that of males who can produce many offspring and thus "afford" some that have less chance of survival. But a second source of *human* female selectivity is contingent. In the ancestral environment, women were unable to sustain themselves in the latter stages of pregnancy or to single-handedly support a dependent infant. Under such conditions, a preference for and the ability to discern and attract devoted males was an asset. In modern times, these exigencies have faded. But Wright argues that the ancestral trait, greater selectivity, persists. The resilience of "obsolete" emotions is illustrated by the "primitive" fear that many people have of snakes and spiders, whereas few have such reactions to the far more real threat posed by automobiles.

As indicated earlier, Wittgenstein (1953) did not deny that we have, for example, feelings of love, nor did he discount their resistance to interpretation. His emphasis on cultural training and practical considerations did not obviate the importance of what he described as "the primitive, unreasoned reaction on which the system of *rules* and reasons is grafted" (p. 81). In speaking of reactions to the pain of others, he allowed that there are "natural, instinctive, kinds of behavior towards other human beings" (Wittgenstein, 1970, para. 545) such as "a primitive reaction to tend, to treat, the part that hurts when someone else is in pain" (para. 540). While granting considerable scope to cultural training, he argued that "our language-game is an extension of primitive behavior" (para. 545). His belief that "the common behavior of mankind" (Wittgenstein, 1953, para. 206) is the starting point for interpreting behavior suggests that his social constructionism is not incompatible with the claims of evolutionary psychology.[6]

Because there are "primitive" reactions, there are limits to the cultural or strategic interpretability of emotions: it is hard to imagine, say, that nausea could be interpreted as love. A striking example of the resistance of emotional reactions to training can be found in a nineteenth century description of scalping. One observer found that Native American fighters sometimes balked before the task: "Twice he saw a brave pause during the operation in order to vomit" (Connell, 1984, p. 165). Just as there are limits to the interpretation of texts, we cannot make whatever we want of our feelings. And like culture, they can have a "grip on the mind." In a famous experiment, Schacter and Singer (1969) concluded that the inner sensations that occur with the experimental administration of adrenaline are subject to social definition. Subjects surrounded by stooges evincing euphoria became euphoric and so on. But while Schachter's stooges could inspire either euphoria or fear, it is unlikely that they could induce, say, boredom in adrenalin-saturated subjects. While the experience of alcohol is culturally mediated, believing that one can drive competently while drunk does not make it so.

Dennis Wrong (1994) also argues that emotions are shaped by, but never fully subordinated to, social influences. In contrast to utopian—or dystopian—visions of a resolution of tensions between the individual and society, he argues, "Motives, emotions, even affect-laden ideas, possess a 'compulsive' or 'obsessive' quality that cannot be willed away" (p. 155). B. F. Skinner's (1948) utopian novel *Walden II* suggested that antisocial impulses, such as envy and jealousy, could be eliminated through a system of reinforcements. In contrast, Wrong cites Freud's description, in *Civilization and Its Discontents,* of the superego's imperfect grip on emotional life: "Civilization . . . obtains mastery over the individual's dangerous desire for aggression by weakening and disarming it and by setting up an agency within him to watch over it, like a garrison in a conquered city" (quoted in Wrong, 1994, p. 144). The importance of resisting cultural reductionism is suggested by the ample role of recalcitrant human emotions in social life that overcome both training and calculations of benefit.

Still, we must not underestimate the power of training to subvert "natural reactions." Evolutionary psychologists argue that, amidst considerable cultural variety in standards of human beauty, there is a universal preference for symmetry that is detectable in infants and even animals. The logic of this is that the symmetrical are more likely to be robust and so those attracted to lopsided lovers are at a reproductive disadvantage. But there are anomalies in preferences suggesting that a culturally derived aesthetic sense can transcend its original evolutionary logic. "Heroin chic"—the attraction to sallow, emaciated, emphatically *unhealthy* lovers—shows how far we can wander from the importunings of our genes. Denis de Rougement's *Love in the Western World* (1956) described another contradiction to the exigencies of genetic reproduction: the near cultic preference in Medieval courts for *unconsummated* love.

To this point I have discussed the bearing of culture and calculation on desires etc. Maintaining a dialectical perspective requires that the reciprocal process be considered—that is, the ways in which desires etc. mediate culture and opportunity. Because most work on the sociology of emotions has emphasized the bearing of culture on emotions, this process is not as easily illustrated. But some preliminary observations are possible. As suggested earlier, evolutionary psychologists argue that culture and institutional arrangements partly reflect ingrained emotional dispositions: The family emerges from a natural bonding. In *Civilization and Its Discontents* (1962), Freud portrayed culture as, in large measure, a response to instinctive drives. But this formulation does not yet capture a dialectical relationship— that is, the ways in which desires etc. *constitute* opportunity and culture. This can be suggested by showing how, just as culture is open to variable interpretation in light of opportunity, the passions mediate cultural meanings. While masculine culture in part reflects the nature of men, Donald Dutton's (1995) analysis of domestic violence emphasizes its complexity and the ways in which violent men find cultural themes that legitimate their impulses. Arguing that the personalities of abusive men are formed mainly by dysfunctional childhoods, he contends that the violent man will "cast about desperately for aspects of the culture that will reaffirm or justify his abusiveness" (p. 121). His point is that abusive men are not formed by cultural training—no medals have been struck for Jack the Ripper. Rather, such men read cultural values to find support for their ingrained dispositions. The openness of rules to idiosyncratic interpretation facilitates this process. Similarly, Jack Katz (1988) and Matza (1964) show how conventional notions can be twisted to support deviant acts. Those who find violence thrilling can cite codes of honor to legitimate retaliation for trivial affronts.

So too, desires etc., like appropriate cultural resources, can be crucial to the constitution of opportunity. Boxing presents opportunity for those with the suitable habitus *and* heart. Cloward and Ohlin (1960) illustrate the role of emotions in opportunity by explaining drug addiction as an alternative for juveniles temperamentally unsuited to participation in violent gangs.

AGENCY

The interpenetration of desires etc. with culture and opportunity bears on the issue of agency. Because the actor can read feelings in light of opportunities and cultural resources, a measure of autonomy is possible. The actor *has* but is not, as it were, *filled with* emotions. Sartre (1957) sketches an agential theory of emotions that stresses choice in determining both the character of feelings and the actions they impel:

A mock feeling and a true feeling are almost indistinguishable: to decide that I love my mother [in the context of an ethical dilemma] and will remain with her, or to remain with her by putting on an act, amount somewhat to the same thing. In other words, the feeling is formed by the acts one performs: so, I cannot refer to it in order to act upon it. Which means that I can neither seek within myself the true condition which will impel me to act, nor apply to a system of ethics for concepts which will permit me to act. (p. 27)

Like Wittgenstein, Sartre limits the role of introspection in the determination of emotional states and, drawing on his core claim that "existence precedes essence," he emphasizes the role of the actor in constituting them: "The feeling is formed by the acts one performs." But again, Sartre's perspective is insufficiently tied to the social context of emotion and the role of cultural training emphasized by Wittgenstein.

A problem with Sartre's theory of emotions is that, like economic psychology, it fails to recognize limits to agency. An implication of the (partial) autonomy of emotions means that, just as cultural and structural dopes are possibilities, sometimes desire rules and we become, for example, fools for love or anger or narcotic stimulation. Elster (1989d) speaks of "counter-adaptive preferences"—that is, those that "no one could choose to have . . . and so they can only be explained by some kind of perverse drive of which it can be said, metaphorically speaking, that it has the person rather than the other way around" (p. 174). Failure to recognize this again results in an actor either oversocialized or unrealistically instrumental. In his zeal to argue the strategic role of the passions, Frank underplays their capacity to overwhelm instrumental considerations. In contrast, while Wright explains emotions and values in terms of their evolutionary value, he allows that guilt, depression, etc. can be maladaptive. DeTocqueville's comment on "the passion for equality" (quoted in Elster, 1989a) was cited in Chapter 5 to emphasize how norms overwhelm instrumental calculation. It also illustrates the autonomy of emotions. Indeed, desires etc. can directly defy reason and culture. Those who find the grass on the other side of the road to be greener value exactly what they cannot have and the enchantment of forbidden fruit is provoked by cultural taboos.

It was argued earlier that rather than binding agency to culture or instrumental reason, a theory of agency should recognize its situational contingency. Desires etc. can be incorporated in this approach. Each element of action can, depending on circumstances, support or subvert autonomy. Opportunistic calculation can protect actors from cultural dopery and the grip of emotions; but cultural training protects from domination by the main chance, as well as emotional impulses. Weber portrayed traditional societies as so custom-bound that conduct barely breaks the threshold of genuine action. In such a context, reason can liberate, which is why Descartes saw custom as a drag on autonomy and reason as its source. But this does not mean that the triumph of reason is necessarily the triumph of agency. Weber's (1958) argument that both traditionalism and the Protestant ethic have been replaced by the "mechanism" of "technical and economic conditions of machine production" (p. 181) suggests that the "iron cage" of modern capitalism is inhabited by structural dopes, driven by market forces: "The Puritan wanted to work in a calling: we are forced to do so" (p. 181). He described capitalism as a "masterless slavery" that "enmeshes the worker or the debtor" and where conduct is "essentially prescribed by objective situations" (p. 58). Similarly, although desires can enslave the addict, they can also liberate from surplus repression, whether instrumentally or culturally derived: busting loose can be liberation. Each component of action can allow agency in relation to the others via the mediating actor.

It was argued in Chapter 7 that the role of culture and opportunity in behavior can vary across situations and actors. Similarly, there can be individual, contextual, and historical variation in the role of desires etc. Considerable research finds that "impulse control" varies across individuals (Wilson & Herrnstein, 1985, chap. 7). Some societies allow a freer expression of emotions than others. A sports fan, or a lover, while never free of culture and calculation, may be more fully in the grip of emotion than a stockbroker, although the latter is hardly free of passion.

9

A Truly Multidimensional Sociology

The schema introduced in Chapter 1 can now be better explained (see Figure 9.1.):

1. The actor appraises and interprets *culture* through desires etc. and opportunities.
2. The actor appraises and interprets *desires* etc. through opportunities and culture.
3. The actor appraises and interprets *opportunities* through culture and desires etc.

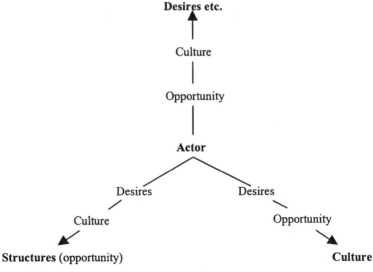

Figure 9.1.

The actor depicted here is a theoretical construct—an entity somehow "outside" of features that are integral to real persons. There is, of course, no such thing as a person without desires and culture or not shaped by opportunities. But insofar as desires, beliefs, and opportunities are in some sense what we act on, it is helpful to theorize a self separate from constituent aspects of real selves. Similarly, I have argued that each component of behavior is interpenetrated with the others. Just as "actor" is a theoretical construct, culture, opportunity, and desires etc. cannot be disentangled from their interrelations. The limitations of this scheme emerge from the difficulty of dialectical thought that tries to articulate autonomy and interpenetration simultaneously. Also, while the focus here is on individuals, it is important to remember that actors are typically socially situated: for example, the Mississippi Chinese (Loewen, 1988) drew on collective resources to constitute opportunities.

What I mean to illustrate is that the components of action are indeterminate and mediated by the others. This results in a sort of trialectic in which each is subject to two *interactive* pulls. But each has a certain autonomy that can lead to dominance. The privileging of the elements of action can be allowed in concrete situations. But the reductive view that "in the final analysis" a preferred factor is determinative and the others are epiphenomenal should be resisted.

Reductionism is particularly evident in the structural attempt to reduce moral rules to instrumental tools. Wright (1994) adds the voice of evolutionary psychology to this view. For example, because submissiveness encourages future abuse, "a genetically based aversion to submission makes evolutionary sense. In our species, we call this aversion a sense of honor" (p. 255). Echoing Marxism, economism, and the various other sources of skepticism about the authenticity of morality, he contends that "cultural values are expedients to social success. People adopt them because other people admire them" (p. 261). Our feelings of the "rightness" of our actions are "just window dressing" (p. 340) in the pursuit of advantage.

But as argued earlier, there are limits to the interpretation of rules, and they can bind behavior even when they subvert self-interest. Furthermore, as has been argued at several points, the instrumentalist view of morality is incoherent because moral "window dressing" works as a manipulative tool only if someone takes it seriously. And Wright (1994) ultimately backs away from this view. For example, while compassion originally facilitated the survival of the family or small band, "In the thought of reasoning beings, it takes on a logic of its own which leads to its extension beyond the bounds of group" (p. 372). Wright does well to qualify his skepticism, because the last chapter of his book is a plea to expand moral reasoning beyond its original instrumental boundaries.

Similarly, although resources are open to various readings, there are limits. Marx is right to say that a machine can be incorporated into various systems of social practices (see Chapter 6). But his claim that "the way in which machinery is used is *totally distinct* from the machinery itself" is a rhetorical excess. Although a bicycle can afford transportation, entertainment, exercise, and so on, it cannot be used as, say, a toothbrush. While Marx emphasized the variable social uses of technology, he would likely recognize that the introduction of gunpowder makes some sort of difference in how people live and the possibilities are limited: we cannot eat it. And while gunpowder can be used to "wound a man or to dress his wounds," its primary use will likely be to wound. So, too, we cannot make *whatever* we like of inner feelings. We distinguish anger from indignation contextually. But the surge of feelings about a broken-down car cannot plausibly be interpreted as love. While opportunities, culture, and desires etc. are interrelated, each has a certain autonomy. Marx's dialectical approach to natural objects captures this combination of interdependence and autonomy. Although the nature of the sun (see Chapter 7) is in part established by its relationship to the plant, and vice versa, each has traits that permit the emergence of certain relational properties—but not others. In discussing inner sensations, Wittgenstein (1953) suggests a precisely dialectical view: "It is not a *something,* but not a *nothing* either!" (para. 304).

Either out of true belief or in the name of explanatory parsimony, different theoretical traditions have emphasized the priority of a preferred variable. But the need for a multidimensional approach is widely felt. Beyond an "additive" multidimensionality, I have argued for a dialectical or synthetic view because a proper understanding of each variable requires recognition of its relation to the others. Because each component of action is articulated by the actor in light of the others, each is *essentially* agential and *essentially* synthetic.

The intrication of these elements of behavior results in complexity. It also threatens what Hollis (1983) (see Chapter 6) calls explanatory "chaos" because if the character of each component of action varies in its relation to the others, none has a determinate impact on behavior. The implications of this for a predictive science are not encouraging. But we cannot ignore the interactions of culture, opportunity, and desire etc., because each factor is implicated, not just in action, but in constituting the others. Hence, a unidimensional approach is not only inadequate. It is impossible.

My main objective has been to address some enduring theoretical issues of social science. But theoretical problems have empirical consequences and their solutions ought to suggest changes in sociological practices. Perhaps the main implication of these arguments is that the process whereby the components of action interpenetrate should be a primary subject of analysis. For example, culture ought to be seen dynamically as it is interpreted by actors engaging their opportunities and their desires. The new cultural studies, as well as symbolic interactionism and ethnomethodology, treat culture dynamically. But these approaches are insufficiently clear in specifying the role of opportunities and emotion in culture because such explanatory elements are typically seen as rivals.

A particularly apposite topic for this sort of analysis is the interpenetration of culture and opportunity. Numerous studies, like those described in Chapter 6, have highlighted the role of habitus in constructing opportunity. At the same time, structural sociology can show how values are shaped in light of opportunity. The explanatory weakness of the variables commonly employed in studies of status attainment suggests the need for the study of this process: the ethnography of status attainment implied by Simons' (1987) advice (see Chapter 6) that we must "understand the processes that the economic actor employs in making decisions" (p. 27). This kind of work can fill in the substantial gaps left by studies of status attainment that focus on the standard measured variables, such as family background, education, work experience, race, gender, and so on. It can also explain why "structural constraints" affect individuals so differently and leave so much variance unexplained. Much of what Jencks (1972) attributes to luck (p. 227) can perhaps be elucidated by ethnographic study of how actors engage standard sociological variables.

This scheme can be applied to other concerns of social theory. A *micro-macro* link can be established in terms of the relationship between emotional life and the larger social context. The sociology of emotions is well along in incorporating culture, but this field could be strengthened with the findings of economic and evolutionary psychology. Also, *social change* can be theorized insofar as alterations in any of the three dimensions of action ramify through the others. For example, as structuralists argue, change in opportunity will be echoed in culture and in individual desires and emotions. Each component of action follows its own dynamic but is also implicated in changes in the others. Much debate in the field of *deviance* has been about the role of opportunity, culture, or genetic dispositions, which are usually presented as rival foci of explanation. Their interactions can fill the gaps left by each factor alone. For example, the malleability of culture, emphasized by Matza (1964) and others, should be analyzed in light of opportunities and desires.

A primary goal in this book has been to recognize the constrained nature of action while avoiding the various types of social science dopes. Because the components of action interact in unpredictable ways, action, while constrained, is not, except in limiting cases, fully determined. That is, we cannot be certain how a rule, opportunities, or desires etc. will shape conduct insofar as each is constituted by the actor in light of the others. This is not the place to engage the extensive philosophical debate on whether reasons ought to be seen as the causes of action. But insofar as actors engage the components of action in light of one another, they are best seen as providing *grounds* for action rather than *causing* it. This implies a different sort of social science than some have hoped for because if the determinants of action are themselves indeterminate, the quest for strong causality must suffer.

Flexibility is surely the best approach. As suggested, there are limiting cases in which the components of action seem to act on us: persons can be oversocialized or overwhelmed by desires etc. And in some circumstances, opportunities are determinative: a starving man may overcome social taboos and the "natural reaction" of disgust certain objects provoke. But in more ordinary cases, rather than acting on us, there is a strong sense in which we act on them. This might explain the failure of social science to establish strong causality in the explanation of action.

THE POLITICS OF STRUCTURAL EXPLANATION

It has been suggested at various points that there are political aspects to the issues under consideration. The oddity of the sociological adoption of homo economicus and the difficulty of incorporating this adoptee into a sociological perspective suggest that extra-theoretical motives are involved. This suspicion is reinforced by the stubbornness with which this position is maintained, often against the evidence developed by its advocates. Elijah Anderson (1990) is frank in his description of ghetto pathologies. But he remains convinced that the solution is to open the blocked opportunities that cause them: "Legal employment for idle youths would improve the quality of life for all of us who inhabit the inner city" (p. 254). He is certain that "the overwhelming majority would work if they could find gainful employment" (p. 101).

But like other studies cited here, Anderson's data contradict his interpretations. One of his respondents, an "old head" of the sort who once provided moral leadership in black communities, challenges Anderson's interpretation in comments on the success of Asian businesses in the ghetto: "Colored folks got the same opportunity to do that, if they want to. They don't wanta do that, though. Onliest thing they wanta do is sell crack, stand on the corner, sell ten bags" (p. 63). Such observations are common in Anderson's data: "These young boys today just don't want to work. They could work if they wanted to. There's plenty of work to do. Today they just want somethin' give to them, wanta get on welfare . . . there are a lot o' guys out here who just don't wanta work" (p. 72). At points, Anderson concedes that there is "a lack of motivation to work in certain jobs when they are available" (p. 57). Still, he faults old head's inclination to "blame the victim for 'not wanting to work' " (p. 101). Commenting on a respondent's claim that "There are jobs out there for people who want to work. . . . Many of them don't know the value of work" (p. 110), Anderson chastises his moral harshness: "Many of the employed consider the jobless to be personally at fault, their condition the result of their own character flaws—a comfortable perspective" (p. 111).[1]

EGALITARIANISM

One of the main attractions of structural explanation is its egalitarian implication. Attributing attainment to culture or personality suggests that there are individual differences between persons and between groups. But if these differences, and skill itself, can be explained as adaptations to opportunity, inequality can be attributed to "external" factors.[2] Indeed, inequality becomes nearly synonymous with injustice as unequal *outcomes* are seen as a measure of unequal *opportunity*. Boudon (1974), for example, equates "inequality of educational opportunity" with "differences in level of educational attainment according to social background" (p. xi). For many sociologists, inequality of outcome is used as a handy measure for various inequalities of treatment. Michael Reich (1994) argues:

> The ratio of median black to median white incomes thus provides a rough, but useful, quantitative index of the economic consequences of racism for blacks as it reflects the operation of racism in the schools, in residential location, in health care—as well as in the labor market itself. (pp. 469-470)

In an early work, James Coleman argued that "the difference in achievement at grade 12 between the average Negro and the average white is, in effect, the degree of inequality of opportunity" (quoted in Flew, 1981, p. 52).

It is not contentious to attribute a political element to the structural perspective because its advocates often champion this feature. As noted earlier, Baron and Hannon (1994) attribute sociologists' "tendency to attribute unequal outcomes to unfair social advantages" to their "strong ideological egalitarianism" (p. 1118). Arguing for an allocation model of inequality, Beck et al. (1978) contend that

> rather than interpreting group differences in earnings or poverty as due to differential rates of individual "failure" in a competitive market, the theory suggests that such group differences may be the outcome of differential assignments of group members within the sectoral structure [the dual economy] of the economic order. (p. 707).

Kanter (1977) is explicit about the exculpatory and reformist agenda of structural explanation: "Use of versions of the individual model inevitably leads to the conclusion that 'women are different' and . . . leads women to believe that the problem lies in their own psychology, and gives the organization a set of excuses for the slow pace of change" (p. 261). Gerson's (1985) book closes with policy recommendations, mostly a program of affirmative action for women. Elliott Currie (1985), speaking for opportunity theory, is also explicit about the politics of structural explanation:

> By shifting the explanation of crime onto an amorphous, ill-defined realm of
> culture or values detached from the social and economic context that nourishes
> or undermines them, such reasoning conveys a vague sense—more a mood than
> an argument—that the roots of crime are beyond human control, thus encour-
> aging inaction and passivity. (p. 47)

Wellman (1983) drops the scientist rhetoric of network theory to praise its
ideological advantages over normative explanation: "Analysts often seize
upon these norms to explain social behavior. This tendency can easily lead
to blaming the victim—as when analysts attribute lower-class shiftlessness
to normative forces rather than to structural constraints" (p. 167). Conceding that "ideas or cultural themes" carry "a significant residue of truth"
Barrington Moore (1966) is frank about his aversion to such explanations:
"My objection is to the way they are put into the explanation, which in my
estimation, creates a strong conservative bias under the color of scientific
neutrality and objectivity" (p. 485). Stinchcombe's (1986) interpretation
of the rejection of cultural explanation by dependency and world systems
theory applies to much sociology: "Poor countries still differ from rich ones
in the ways identified by the modernization theorists of the 1950s and
1960s, though we are now professionally committed to ignoring that fact"
(p. 135).

The sociological adoption of a neoclassical model of action seems in-
congruous because of the ideological differences between these disciplines.
Indeed, as argued in Chapter 3, the concept of structure, especially in its emphasis on the role of power in inequality, is meant to *challenge* the neoclassical portrait of social order, human capital explanations of inequality, and
implicitly and sometimes explicitly, the fairness of capitalism. But there is an
egalitarian kernel in the theory of situational explanation because it minimizes differences between individuals. The egalitarian optimism implicit in
neoclassical theory is expressed by the Peruvian novelist and champion of
capitalism Mario Vargas Llosa (1992): "There are no such things as lazy or
hard-working classes or cultures; what there are, rather, are systems—rules
of the game, laws, practices—which stimulate effort and initiative or stifle
them" (p. 27). Structural sociologists are not usually enthusiasts of laissez
faire. But they are attracted to the neoclassical premise that variations in
costs and benefits, rather than individual differences, explain different outcomes.

Indeed, belief in equal potential is at the core of the philosophical seed-bed of neoclassical economics: liberalism. Descartes (1960), a progenitor of liberalism, believed that "the power of judging rightly ... (which is generally called good sense or reason) is equal by nature in all men" (p. 37). Hobbes (1985) argued that social conflict is unavoidable in part because "Nature hath made men so equall, in the faculties of body, and mind" (p. 183) that unequal outcomes cannot be easily legitimated. And Marx (1963a) quoted Adam Smith's claim that street porters and philosophers were more alike than the different breeds of dogs (p. 182). In the liberal tradition, differences in ability were seen as socially produced. Locke thought that "of all the Men we meet with, nine Parts of ten are what they are, good or evil, useful or not, by their Education" (quoted in Spragens, 1981, p. 100). The eighteenth-century philosopher Claude Helvetius was emphatic about the power of training: "There is nothing impossible to education. . . . it makes the bear dance" (p. 100). Despite various ideological differences, the assumption of equal potential combined with environmental explanation of inequality draws structural sociologists to liberal neoclassical thought. The belief that the potential for reason is equal and that training makes us unequal leads the egalitarian to emphasize the priority of the former over the latter in action.

But neoclassical theory presents problems for the structural perspective. As a result, its incorporation is selective. For example, the assumption of equal preferences is not sustained. As pointed out in Chapter 3, while criminals, women, the poor, and others are seen as rational maximizers, the social order is controlled by persons with very different motivations. Merton's "innovators" turn to crime because they are victims of class and ethnic bigotry. Cloward and Ohlin (1960) claim that there is "no evidence" that delinquents "are objectively less capable in basic endowments" including "intelligence" (p. 117, n. 110), and hence their exclusion from legitimate opportunities cannot be rational.[3] While denying the cultural roots of Chinese success, Loewen (1988) emphasizes the traditionalism and racism of Mississippi whites. Professing, at one point, that "everyone is rational" (p. 291), Kanter (1977) explains men's refusal to hire competent women in terms of Freudian dynamics and group loyalty (p. 233). Marini (1989) attributes the exclusion of women to "sex stereotypes that are inaccurate" (p. 360) and men's "nonpecuniary group loyalties" (p. 369). Wilson weaves rational choice and culture in and out of his work. Portraying the culture of poverty as adaptive, he rejects rational choice explanations of "racist culture" (Wilson & O'Sullivan, 1988, p. 227) and argues that it is *mal*adaptive because "greater benefits would be secured from intergroup alliances" (p. 229). Wilson (1987) also argues that the rise in separation and divorce for white women is "mainly due to the increased economic independence of white women *and* the related social and cultural factors embodied in the feminist movement" (p. 145, emphasis added).

The social science penchant to "rationalize the irrational" (Elster, 1984, p. 185) is thus selectively applied. Generally, the *dominated* are portrayed as guided by rational responses to opportunity, whereas the *dominant* are seen as motivated by irrational prejudices and loyalties. Michael Katz (1989) adopts Wilson's view of the culture of poverty as "a response to structural constraints and opportunities" (p. 207). But his explanatory lexicon is expanded when he describes cultural explanations of poverty as "a justification for mean and punitive policies" (p. 17). Wacquant (1993) argues that ghetto thieves "got to" burglarize their neighbors and so on. But the language of compulsion is dropped when he speaks of "the political will of urban elites" whose "decision to abandon the ghetto" (p. 24) has "intentionally packed and trapped poor blacks" (p. 28) in "hyperghettos." Although there may be an instrumental element in such decisions, they are not portrayed as situationally compelled, and their motivation includes "racial enmity" (p. 15). While racism is often portrayed as rational, no structural sociologist would portray the Ku Klux Klan as situationally *compelled*.

There are several related reasons for this dualism in which the dominated are portrayed as "materialists" and the dominant as "idealists." As mentioned in Chapter 7, Holmes (1990) finds that traditional thinkers attributed crass self-interest to commoners and nobler motives, such as devotion to the common good, to religious and political elites. The liberal claim that everyone is motivated by self-interest was "a by-product of modern egalitarianism," because "to say that *all* individuals were motivated by self-interest was to universalize the status of the common man" (p. 284). But the liberal homogenization of motive is abandoned in structural sociology. Indeed, the traditional dualism is resurrected but *reversed:* values—perverse values—drive the dominant, whereas the dominated are rational maximizers. This shift emerges because in a utilitarian culture, the attribution of rationality, even in the form of self-interest, is a means of exculpation, even praise, whereas nonrational motives are grounds for indictment.[4]

There are additional reasons for a dualistic view of the dominant and the dominated. As argued in Chapter 3, the free rider problem requires that most exclusionary alliances must be sustained by motives other than rational self-interest. The key structural claim that social power, rather than human capital differences, explains inequality thus requires that employers are not acting to maximize. Indeed, if the dominant were modeled as homines economici it would be difficult to portray the excluded as victims of discrimination. Rational employers will hire on the basis of ability, which would imply that the excluded lack desired attributes and, indeed, undercut the very idea of structured inequality. The egalitarian cum structural thesis requires that the dominant and the dominated be cast in fundamentally different terms. In this way, the dominant can be held responsible for the plight of the dominated.

SOCIAL REFORM

Perhaps the primary attraction of structural explanation is that it suggests a convenient means of social reform. Eliminating objectional inequalities does not require changing cultures and persons but simply equalizing opportunities. For there *are* no deep differences in abilities or values between criminals and the law-abiding, men and women, the rich and the poor, developed and undeveloped nations, and so on. The suitability of structural explanation for a program of reform or, more precisely, social engineering is highlighted by the emphasis on "immediate" (Wacquant, 1993) circumstances and the "present situation" (Granovetter, 1985) rather than on "the dim past" (Kanter, 1977). Arguing that "neither chance circumstances nor individual personalities determined the paths these women took" Gerson (1985) believes that "constraints and opportunities in the *immediate* social environment limited the range of possible options and channeled motivation to select one option from this range" (p. 192, emphasis added). The conception of persons as mirrors—that is, lacking history and memory, suggests a perfect malleability. If opportunity structures control not just attainments but also personalities, values, and even skills, then problematic social outcomes are easily remediated. If "organizations make their workers into who they are" (Kanter, 1977, p. 263), new structural arrangements can re-make them. This belief in the redemptive power of opportunity forges an-other link between structural sociology and economics. The confidence that expanded opportunities will solve the problems of the poor replicates the classical economists' assumption "that the labouring classes would readily seize any opportunities to adopt middle class attitudes, standards, and patterns of behavior" (Coats, 1971, p. 178).

The *engineering* implication of structural sociology is reinforced with the conception of culture and personality as situationally constrained. What people want and believe merely reflects their immediate circumstances and thus carry little moral weight. This is illustrated by Gerson's (1985) treat-ment of one of her subjects who, when asked how she would feel about working while her husband stayed home with the children, responded, "There might be a little bit of jealousy in there—his being able to be home and my having to go off to work" (p. 130). But this straightforward prefer-ence for a domestic life is dismissed as inauthentic: "Given the limited op-portunities these women encountered in the paid labor force, such a stance is hardly surprising" (p. 130). For Gerson, a preference for domesticity is a *symptom*: "Domestically oriented women faced an opportunity structure that motivated them to reproduce both a traditional sexual division of labor and an ideology to justify that arrangement" (p. 132). While Gerson prefers the term "perceived interests" to "false consciousness" (p. 201), she accords little respect to adaptations made "without full conscious awareness of the structural forces impinging on them or the overall logic of their choices" (p. 193).

The notion of culture as a structure also undermines the authenticity of expressed preferences. If values and beliefs are stamped in by socialization or the "culture industry," if like the Azande, persons cannot think their own thoughts, their preferences are tokens of their domination. Mark Lilla (1994) has noticed the challenge that structuralism poses to liberalism:

> If autonomous individuals as conceived by the Enlightenment and the liberal tradition do not exist independently, if it is structures that produce them—whether those structures are linguistic, symbolic, cultural, psychologi-cal, ideological, "logocentric," or simply those of "power." . . . If "man" and the "author" were dead, then clearly so was man as the author of his political acts. (p. 13)

Finally, the warrant for social engineering is certified with the "Standard Social Science Model" of persons as having no presocial nature. If "what appear to be 'sex differences' in work behavior emerge as responses to structural conditions" (Kanter, 1977, p. 262), nature, like culture, can present no serious obstacle to reform: what is socially constructed can be readily reconstructed.

In "Two Concepts of Liberty," Isaiah Berlin (1969) described "negative" freedom as freedom from restraint by others. But this traditional liberal notion is deemed insufficient by advocates of "positive" freedom. For one can be free of coercion but still rendered unfree by being subject to one's own "lower" nature. Unbridled passions and desires can enslave the true, ideal, or real self as surely as external restrictions. The political implications of this conception of freedom are considerable, for now expressed wants can be dismissed as inauthentic: "Once I take this view, I am in a position to ignore the actual wishes of men or societies, to bully, oppress, torture them in the name, and on behalf, of their 'real' selves" (p. 24). Coercion can be construed as liberation, for the liberator can see himself as acting on the authentic will of his subjects, "for their own sake, in their, not my, interest."[5]

The situational self of structural sociology is uncomfortably well suited to the notion of liberation described by Berlin's concept of negative freedom. Since expressed preferences reflect constrained opportunities or imposed culture, the actual self can be deemed inauthentic or delusory, and changed circumstances will allow the emergence of the authentic self. What the dominated want need not be taken seriously by those who know what they would want were their opportunities expanded.

It may seem excessive to compare Berlin's critique of nascent totalitarianism with the modest reforms proposed by Kanter, Wilson, and others. Nothing in their rhetoric suggests a desire to bully or torture anyone to achieve utopia. I have argued that elements of culture are subject to variable interpretations, and this surely applies to the claims of social theory. But I have also argued that rules and the like do affect conduct. In this light, the logic of structural determinism can reveal a sharp edge. If habitus constrains "all the thoughts, all the perceptions, and all the actions" the possibility of agency can be displaced by a warrant for social engineering. This tendency is manifest in Althusser's determinism which, Steven Smith (1985) argues, destroys the concepts of "freedom, autonomy, dignity, or rights" and thus provides "a sophisticated way of justifying the dominance of the Marxist intelligentsia" (p. 655).[6]

A hint of coercive liberation can be found even in more moderate programs of reform. Thomas Spragens (1981) argues that "Moral Newtonianism" is implicit in the foundational notion of the person as a tabula rasa. When combined with claims of social science expertise, this concept can lead away from John Locke's and Adam Smith's minimal state and toward expansive schemes of social reform. Helvetius declared that "man is a machine" and portrayed scientific study as a means "to guide the motions of the human puppet" (quoted in Spragens, 1981, p. 98). This conception of persons as perfectly explainable and perfectly reformable can erode the respect for liberty and individual rights that was at the core of liberalism. Bentham's zeal for reform led him to dismiss the idea of rights as "nonsense upon stilts" (quoted in Spragens, 1981, p. 111). A contemporary example of determinism eroding the grounds of autonomy is the helplessness and passivity that some structural theorists attribute to those they want to help. Elliott Currie (1985) describes the poor as victims of "unemployment and financial dependency," which are characterized as "often beyond any *imaginable* control by individuals" (p. 214, emphasis added). Noticing this tendency, Michael Katz (1989) admonishes liberals for taking the path from compassion to technocratic politics: "By defining dependent people as passive, in the 1960s liberal social science enhanced its own role. Without the assistance of liberal intellectuals, dependent people would remain mired in their own degradation" (p. 22).

But the pull of this outlook is illustrated in Katz's adoption of the very posture he warns against. Criticizing conservative arguments that dependency induced by the welfare state can disable those it purports to help, he argues that "minorities and working people *no matter how competent,* cannot without the power of the state reduce discrimination or improve their wages and working conditions" (p. 161 emphasis added). The dualistic view of the dominant and the dominated thus extends to their capacity for agency. For Katz, Wacquant, and others, although the motives of the elite are perverse, they are more agential than are the dominated whose "rational" sensitivity to costs and benefits renders them uniquely malleable. The exculpatory thrust of situational explanation thus opens the door to control.[7]

This dualism also appears in the implicit contrast between the theorists and their subject matter. The enterprise of theorizing implies that advocates of cultural and/or structural determinism cannot be as passive as those they purport to explain: what would be the point of Evans-Pritchart's (cited in Archer, 1988) intellectual endeavors if, like the Azande, he could not think his own thoughts? And how can Durkheim (1966) reflexively apply his belief that "it is society which, fashioning us in its image, fills us with religious, political, and moral beliefs that control our actions" (p. 212). Marx's Third Thesis on Feuerbach nicely summarizes both the limitations of determinism and the paradox its advocates create:

> The materialist doctrine that men are products of circumstances and upbringing, and that, therefore, changed men are products of other circumstances and changed upbringing, forgets that it is men that change circumstances, and that the educator himself needs educating. Hence this doctrine necessarily arrives at dividing society into two parts, of which one is superior to society (in Robert Owen, for example). (Feuer, 1959, p. 244)

The final sentence shows that Marx was well aware of the manipulative implication of Moral Newtonianism.

But if persons—all persons—are agents, if they are more than trager of opportunity, culture, or their desires, efforts at remaking them will fall short. There is good and bad news in this: the Moral Newtonians will never develop a deterministic social science that will allow them to devise the social order they seek. But the reason for this is that persons cannot be reduced to puppets of a technocratic elite.

Because persons are not structural dopes, social reform requires more than changing economic incentives: it requires attention to the beliefs and values that constitute opportunities. But the conservative emphasis on values—now designated as "family values"—is sociologically and philosophically naive. As structural sociologists argue, elements of culture are interpreted in light of practical circumstances, a process Wittgenstein shows to be unavoidable. Hence, training in values alone is of limited effect. Unless circumstances are altered, cultural messages will be interpreted in ways unforeseen by their advocates. For example, if medieval barriers to trade and enterprise had not been dissolved in early-modern Europe, if opportunities for capitalist endeavor had not opened up, it is unlikely that the Protestant ethic would have been interpreted to encourage entrepreneurialism. This means that changing values requires changing the circumstances in light of which they are received. A dialectical understanding of culture and structure suggests that social reform is a more multifaceted project than ideological advocates of left and right have recognized.

NOTES

Preface

1. Twin studies are surveyed by Lawrence Wright (1997) and Steven Pinker (1997, n. 4).

Chapter 1

1. Economism runs the gamut from Marx to Milton Friedman. The Marxist Antonio Gramsci and Edmund Burke, the progenitor of conservative thought, stress the priority of culture in action.

2. Tomlinson (1991, p. 4) counts 150 definitions of culture.

3. While Simmel's (1965) "formal" sociology is often cited by structuralists, he denied that structural variables could be separated from culture: "In the Kantian view which we follow here, the unity of nature emerges in the observing subject exclusively. . . . By contrast, the unity of society needs no observer. . . . The consciousness of constituting with the others a unity is actually all there is to this unity" (p. 338). Indeed, the very idea of separating the social scientific idea of society from ideas in society is preposterous. Insofar as social events such as signaling, promising, accusing, and so on are *constituted* by the ideas of social actors, describing social order without reference to culture would be like describing the game of chess without reference to its rules. This is not to say that the ideas of the social scientist must *replicate* the ideas of social actors. As Marx (1967a) said in *The Eighteenth Brumaire,* one differentiates between what a man thinks and says of himself and what he really is and does" (p. 43).

4. While Karl Mannheim's (1971) sociology of knowledge was based on some sort of distinction between "existence" and "consciousness," he emphasized the implication of ideas in substructure and spoke of "two 'mental' spheres, the mutual relationship of which is that of substructure and superstructure." He considered "mind-in-the-substructure" to be "the more massive factor." But he maintained that "economy would not exist without mind' (p. 88).

Chapter 2

1. Two different senses of *adaptive* are often glossed over. An action or attitude can be psychologically adaptive—violence can make poor males feel better about themselves—while being instrumentally maladaptive: a reputation for violence puts off employers and can lead to injury and prison.

2. Mickelson's (1990) claim is contradicted by the finding of Ainsworth-Darnell and Downey (1998) that with controls for parents' education, occupational status, income, and so on, "African American students are significantly more likely than white students to report that education is important to getting a job later on and to have more optimistic occupational expectations than white students" (p. 540).

3. Kenneth Waltz's *Theory of International Politics* (1979) similarly argues that position in international structures of power, rather than the internal characteristics of states, determine foreign policy decisions.

Chapter 3

1. Paul Samuelson (1979) grants 35 lines to the issue of culture in a section titled "Superficial Theories of Development." While listing various cultural prerequisites of development—the work ethic, thrift, and so on—he concludes, obscurely, that "putting stress on these non-economic factors does not solve the problem of *explanation*. It poses new problems" (p. 718).

2. The backlash against functionalism's alleged inability to theorize conflict has resulted in the dominance of conflict theory. In a recent survey of American sociologists, 41% identified themselves as conflict theorists or Marxists, exceeding the popularity of all other theoretical orientations (Sanderson & Ellis, 1992).

3. Atomism was central to the utilitarian view of social order. According to Jeremy Bentham (1988), "The community is a fictitious body, composed of the individual persons who are considered as constituting as it were its members. The interest of the community then is, what?—the sum of the interests of the several members who compose it. It is vain to talk of the interest of the community without understanding what is the interest of the individual" (p. 3).

4. Some theorists have tried to deal with the problem of collective action with the notion of "collective" reason. In his study of the self-destructive oppositional culture of the British working class, Paul Willis (1977) acknowledges that because individual mobility in a capitalist society is possible, "conformism may hold a certain logic for the individual" (p. 128). But because although "few can make it, the class can never follow" (p. 128), Willis argues that "the counter-school culture makes a real penetration of what might be called the difference between *individual* and *group* logics" (p. 128). But in moving the locus of rationality to the group level, Willis abandons any ordinary sense of the term:

> We have, therefore, in the informal group a relative suspension of individual in-
> terests and a commitment to the reality of the group and its aims. . . . In this sense
> the group, can, therefore, be considered as a subject in its own right. It has an in-

ternal impulse to find an objective specific to its own level. . . . This is not to assert that any such intention . . . is actually in any one person's head. . . . We are
dealing with the unit of the group, and the specific level of cultural 'insight.' "
(p. 124)

It is to avoid such reification that Marxists, such as Adam Prezworzski (1985),
have concluded that revolution requires nonrational commitments.

5. Structural sociologists are, however, too eager to attribute exclusion to the
exercise of collective power. Individual prejudice often produces results that are
mistaken as evidence of exclusionary alliances. The homely, the short, and the
overweight suffer significant disadvantage in the labor market (Ruane & Cerulo,
2000, pp. 80-81). It is implausible that the handsome, the tall, and the slim collude to
produce these outcomes. Also, explaining success and failure in terms of power
differentials implicitly, and often explicitly, aims to delegitimate achievement by
attributing it to manipulative means rather than talent and effort. When applied to
examples not ordinarily intended—such as Jews—this claim carries unpleasant
nuances. As Lieberson (1980) notes, it is also false: Jews were not disproportionately
involved in politics.

6. Abundantly documenting his claim that "The utilitarians did not employ an
action model composed merely of atomistic individuals pursuing material ends with
rational means" (p. 536), Camic (1979), contends that Parsons's indictment of
utilitarianism is "so selective that it is inaccurate on nearly every detail" (p. 542).

7. Explaining wage differences between groups is an endlessly complicated task
because so many factors can bear on earnings. When controls are added, gaps tend to
fade. George Farkas and Keven Vicknair (1996) contend that "with the measure of
cognitive skill controlled . . . the finding of race discrimination against Black men is
gone!" (p. 557). June O'Neill finds that "measurable characteristics—including
region of residence, years of schooling, potential and actual work experience, scores
on the Armed Forces Qualification Test, industry of employment, and skill
associated with the reported occupation—explain essentially all of the variations
between hourly wages of black and white workers in 1987" (quoted in Aaron, 1990,
p. 5). But even this list is far from the whole story. Suggesting the importance of the
various *un*measured, and perhaps unmeasurable, factors that bear on employment,
Christopher Jencks (1992) concludes that "Most employers now pay blacks who
can talk, act, and think like whites almost as much as they pay 'real' whites" (p. 128).
William J. Wilson (1996) finds that this preference is not racial: "In our study,
74 percent of white employers expressed negative views of inner-city workers;
80 percent of the black employers did so as well" (p. M3).

Chapter 4

1. It is hard to know what to make of this claim: countless actions, like swatting
a bug, leaping across a puddle, etc. are intentional and purposive acts that may have

nothing to do with norms. Even social actions, such as hitting someone, may be autonomous of norms.

2. Archer (p. 47) notes the affinity of Parson's and Althusser's view of action.

3. Throughout his work, Wittgenstein (1953) challenged the notion of meaning as a mental accompaniment of action—that is, the idea that some sort of mental events distinguish intentional action from mere behavior. He argued that "nothing is more wrongheaded than calling meaning a mental act" (p. 172). A sense of his argument can be found by considering whether the difference between a knee-jerk reflex and an intentional kick is something like thinking "move, leg." Wittgenstein uses such examples to argue that intentional action cannot be distinguished by looking "inside" the mind. Similarly, intentional speech is not ordinarily accompanied by an internal monologue: "If God had looked into our minds he would not have been able to see there [what] we were speaking of" (p. 217). His "contextual" approach to meaning will be elaborated in Chapter 8.

Chapter 5

1. In a recent editorial piece the Dalai Lama (1998) interprets Buddhism to counter the claims that "Asian values" are incompatible with democracy. Arguing that "at the heart of Buddhism lies the idea that the potential for awakening and perfection is present in every human being and it is a matter of personal effort to realize that potential," he analogizes this with the democratic belief "that all human beings are essentially equal, that each of us has an equal right to life, liberty and happiness. Thus, not only are Buddhism and democracy compatible, they are rooted in the same understanding of equality and the potential of the individual" (p. 18).

2. In the movie *Quiz Show,* the Charles Van Doren character makes this point nicely: "If you think money is just money, you'll never have much of it."

3. An acquaintance of mine sadly discovered the constraints of norms. He and his sister jointly purchased a summer cottage that was to be shared. His sister then married and sold her permanent home. She and her new husband began to live in the cottage between their frequent travels. Despite his sister's reassurances, the cottage effectively became her home, and my friend discovered that he had become an occasional guest. He saw this happening but found no culturally legitimate way to resist the process. To deny his sister the use of a home that was empty most of the year would have been stingy. Unwilling to be a dog in the manger, he lost his equal access to the cottage. He was not, however, a victim of his sister for she too was impelled by cultural rules such as, "Of course one should use an underutilized home."

4. Inspired by this ideology, the famously neurasthenic Franz Kafka took up weight lifting.

5. The pains of cultivating a new habitus in pursuit of social advancement has been a frequent subject of novels. Fitzgerald's *The Great Gatsby* closes with Gatsby's father's account of his son's efforts to cultivate the cultural prerequisites of high status. This process is especially common among immigrants. Mordechai Richler's *The Apprenticeship of Duddy Kravitz* portrays the pains of those who struggle to remake their cultural endowment to get ahead.

Chapter 6

1. After decades of research focused mainly on the role of peer groups, neighborhoods, and the economy in crime, evidence has recently accumulated on the importance of family structure, especially the presence of a father. Galston and Kamark argue that "the relationship is so strong that controlling for family configuration erases the relationship between race and crime and between low income and crime. This conclusion shows up again and again in the literature" (quoted in Popenoe, 1996, p. 144).

2. Shelby Steele (1990) finds an "aversion to opportunity" in contemporary urban ghettos: "In black communities the most obvious entrepreneurial opportunities are routinely ignored. It is often outsiders or the latest wave of immigrants who own the shops, restaurants, cleaners, gas stations, and even the homes and apartments" (p. 50).

3. This tradition seems to persist. Katherine Newman (1999) found that employed ghetto blacks are sometimes hazed on the job by friends to provoke a reaction that will get them fired. In a review of the book, Alan Wolfe (1999) describes this as a way of "guaranteeing a kind of primitive equality" (p. 51). This is sometimes called the "crab-bucket" syndrome—that is, pulling those about to escape back to the bottom. The difference is that crabs pull others down, not out of envious resentment, but incidental to their own efforts to rise.

4. Redding's study of Chinese entrepreneurs, cited in Chapter 3, casts doubt on Loewen's claim that the Chinese success in Mississippi is contingent on the peculiar circumstances of the setting. Chinese merchants flourish in almost any environment.

5. The threat of free riding to collective action (see Chapter 3) applies with particular force here. A "rational" Mississippi white would exploit the opportunities enhanced by the lack of competition from other whites. The problem is especially troublesome for the category "men." Even if men in general might benefit from the exclusion of women from the labor market, most men are emotionally and/or financially tied to some women. A "rational" man will not harm the well-being of his wife, daughter, mother, and so on—and ultimately his own—for the benefit of "men."

6. This conception of crime as a path to honor is encouraged by social critics such as Norman Mailer:

> It takes little courage for two strong eighteen-year-old hoodlums ... to beat in the brains of a candy-store-keeper. ... Still, courage of a sort is necessary, for one murders not only a weak fifty-year-old man but an institution as well, one violates private property, one enters to a new relationship with the police and introduces a dangerous element into one's life. The hoodlum is therefore daring the unknown, and so no matter how brutal the act, it is not altogether cowardly" (quoted in Magnet, 1993, p. 160). Social science explanations can be criminogenic by providing "forms of assessment" that dignify crime by showing it to be rationally compelling. Sociological

explanations can thus be a kind of teaching and, as they enter the cultural repertoire, they may become self-fulfilling.

7. Willy Sutton denied the story that he said that he robbed banks "because that's where the money is." He robbed banks "because I enjoyed it. I loved it. I was more alive when I was inside a bank robbing it, than at any other time in my life ... to me the money was the chips, that's all. The winnings. I kept robbing banks when, by all logic, it was foolish. When it could cost me far more than I could possibly gain" (quoted in Nettler, 1984, p. 320).

8. Weber's discovery of the irrational religious core in capitalism can be seen as a riposte to Marx's search for the rational nuggets in irrational behavior, such as his (1963a) interpretation of religion as "an expression of real suffering and a protest against real suffering" (p. 43). Katz (1988) shows that there is much to be gained by following Weber's lead. Similarly, Norman Cohn's (1962) *The Pursuit of the Millennium* finds the apocalyptic visions of early Christianity behind "scientific socialism." As Sahlins (1976) argues, reason has pride of place in our culture and is commonly used to legitimate behavior that is otherwise motivated. Voters whose votes will make no difference typically say, and may believe, that they are acting out of self-interest because this rhetoric has such cultural power. Mary Douglas and Aaron Wildavsky (1982) analyze the extra-rational motivations of environmentalism, such as the urge to self-purification. Photographed amidst equipment described as "Desert Camouflage Ranger Gear," an assault rifle is described in a firearms magazine as "one of the finest general-purpose sporting, hunting, and recreation firearms in the world today. It is not an 'assault rifle,'. . . . It is nothing but a fine, useful shooting tool with tremendous utility to a wide range of law-abiding sportsmen, landowners, and U.S. citizens" (*Shooting Times*, August 1991, p. 53). As was pointed out in Chapter 3, identifying the extra-rational motives behind actions legitimated as instrumental is complicated by the fact such actions may indeed provide "material" benefits. The assault rifle may be a "useful shooting tool," but one suspects that other sorts of motives are involved. Even if, for example, vegetarianism is advocated as healthful and does enhance health, this may not be its motive. The costly and luxurious sports *utility* vehicle that will never leave pavement or haul more than groceries illustrates the "conspicuous utilitarianism" of our culture.

9. Elijah Anderson (1994) finds that "many less alienated young blacks have adopted a street-oriented demeanor as a way of expressing their blackness" (p. 4). Prison-style jumpsuits have recently become a popular ghetto fashion (Crockett, 1999)

10. The early utilitarians emphasized the "moral" dimension of material acquisitiveness far more than their critics have recognized. As Weber (1958) pointed out in *The Protestant Ethic*, early defenders of capitalism often saw it as a venue to cultivate virtues, such as prudence and thrift.

11. In a TV documentary about a program designed to reform juvenile offenders, one of the hard cases characterized the project this way: "They want me to be a geek." The implication of values in interests has been a key problem for John Rawls's (1971) attempt to find distributive justice behind the "veil of ignorance."

This is a thought experiment in which individuals choose a distributive scheme without bias—that is, not knowing their identities, values, skills, and so on. As critics such as Robert Paul Wolff (1979, p. 71) have noted, a person in the "original position" might well ask, How can I say what I want unless I know who I am? Values, beliefs about the good life, and the like are the necessary foundation of choice.

12. In a magazine article I have lost track of, an advocate for the deaf said that he would refuse remediative surgery in order to maintain a "deaf identity."

13. Lucy Dawidowicz (1975) argues that many German Jews failed to respond adequately to the holocaust because they reacted to Nazism in terms of strategies that had worked in the past, such as waiting for cooler heads to prevail. They did not know, until it was too late, that Nazism was not like traditional anti-Semitism.

14. Paul Johnson's (1987, pp. 285-286) account of the retail success of European Jews makes a similar point. Jews were customer rather than guild oriented and were willing to advertise and aggressively promote cheap goods for small profits, practices that violated guild notions of dignity.

15. It was argued in Chapter 3 that mobility rates challenge the claim that opportunity is "structured" by group power. This is emphatically the case for blacks. Wacquant (1993) acknowledges that the black middle class in Chicago increased fivefold between 1950 and 1980 (p. 19).

Chapter 7

1. As indicated earlier, Marx (1969) emphasized the role of the complex of collective practices implicated in constituting economic resources: "A Negro is a Negro. He only becomes a slave in certain relations. A cotton spinning jenny is a machine for spinning cotton. It becomes capital only in certain relations. Torn away from these relations it is no more capital than gold is in itself money, or sugar the price of sugar" (p. 159).

2. Ordinarily, elements of nature are portrayed as "externally" related—that is, as conceptually independent of one another. In this view, the truth of an empirical proposition is thought to be independent of any other fact in the world. In contrast, an internal relation is established in the logical relations of ideas. Its truth is not empirical but conceptual, or *a priori*. For example, the relation of equality in the proposition, "The sum of the three interior angles of a triangle is equal to the sum of two right angles" is analytically true—independent of matters of fact. As David Hume put it, "Tis from the idea of a triangle that we discover [this] relation of equality" (quoted in Ollman, 1971, p. 69). In contrast, external relations are contingently true or false. Hume believed that mathematics and logic are about internal relations, whereas the empirical sciences deal exclusively with external relations of fact that are logically independent of one another. The belief that empirical inquiry is confined to externally related facts is a canon of positive science: "It is assumed by philosophers of science who think that the goal of explanation is the production of causal generalizations . . . that it is always possible to describe any fact or event in the natural order in such a way that its description is logically

independent of the description of any other fact or event" (Ryan, 1970, p. 130). The reason for this is that it is not possible to affirm a causal relation of elements unless they are logically independent. We can say that x causes y only if each can be identified independently. The concept of affordances violates this distinction. Facts, the properties of things, are seen to exist in relation to other things.

3. Alexander (1988a) is persuasive about Bourdieu's equivocation on this issue. But his own ambivalence is as striking. At times he advocates a dialectical view: "By conceptualizing reciprocity and conflict between the ideal and material dimensions of society—indeed, their *symbiosis and fundamental interpenetration,* Parsons transformed the dichotomous orientation that has polarized and diminished the social structural approach" (p. 32). But in the same volume, he retreats to an additive approach: "An action is made with reference to two environments: norms (ideal elements) and conditions (material elements). . . . Every end is a compromise between individuals' effort, their objective possibilities, and their normative standards of evaluation" (p. 308). It was argued in Chapter 4 that "normative standards" are implicated in "objective possibilities."

4. The awkwardness of subordinating schemas to resource accumulation is revealed by the difficulty, noted by Parsons and others, of *defining* resources, or costs and benefits, autonomously of schemas. Schemas cannot be seen as adapting to resource accumulation—as though they were separate things—if, as Sahlins (1976) says, "culture constitutes utility." That is, insofar as costs and benefits are defined by schemas, judgments about the former are not autonomous of the latter. Of course, "the bottom line" can tell us if we are "maximizing profit." But that judgment appears from within an established schema. Sewell fails to sustain a dialectic by, first, separating schemas and resources and then by granting the latter priority over the former.

5. The loss of dialectical interplay between culture and social structure is signaled by a shift in the conception of what Archer (1988) calls the "fallacy of central conflation." In the Emirbayer and Goodwin (1994) article, central conflation meant the conception of culture and social structure as "mutually constitutive" so that the interplay "between cultural and social structural formations" (p. 1444) becomes invisible. But in the Emirbayer and Mische (1998) article, central conflation means "the tendency to see structure as so closely intertwined with every aspect of practice that [quoting Archer] 'the constituent components [of structure and agency] *cannot* be examined separately' " (p. 1003). In the first article, the "fallacy" was described as the conflation of *culture* and structure; in the latter, it is of *agency* and structure. While admitting that "strictly speaking," Archer warned against "an elision of" the "Cultural System" and "sociocultural interaction" (Emirbayer & Mische, 1998, p. 1003, n. 22), the authors shift her meaning. In doing so, they adopt the conflation of culture and social structure that Archer warns against. The result is that the disaggregated notion of structure, which allowed Emirbayer and Goodwin (1994) to conceptualize the "interplay" of culture and structure, has been abandoned. Perhaps the most

important cost of the conflated notion of structure is that disaggregating structure into "the cultural context" and "network patterns of social ties" facilitates empirical study of the dialectic of social structure and culture by highlighting how it occurs. In the examples of Chapter 6, we can see that the Mississippi Chinese brought a specific set of cultural values that expanded their opportunities. Maintaining an analytical distinction between culture and structure reveals the ways in which Mormon theology was adapted to their opportunities.

6. Craig Calhoun (1993) describes Bourdieu's work as attempting to "do justice both to objective material, social, and cultural structures and to the constituting practices and experiences of individuals" (p. 3) and specifically at overcoming the dichotomy between Sartre's voluntarism and Levi-Strauss's structural determinism (p. 8). Similarly, Ira Cohen (1987) portrays Giddens as aiming at the "reconciliation of action and structure" (p. 297).

7. Drawing parallels between behaviorism and economics, George Homans (1987) cites Richard Herrnstein's experiment showing that pigeons are efficient maximizers: "If it gets 20 percent of its rewards from the left disc, it allocates 20 percent of its pecks there. If it gets 50 percent of its rewards from the left, then half the pecks will go there too" (p. 196).

8. The emphasis on collective cultural values as the source of voluntarism evokes Rousseau's (1950) conception of freedom as being subject not to the individual but to the General Will.

9. One might suspect that freedom is allowed only to a gifted few who can somehow transcend the determinations of ordinary people.

Chapter 8

1. Evolutionary psychology supports a doctrine found in Aristotle and prominent in Catholic thought: natural law philosophy. This approach contends that humans have natures to which ethical and political principles must be adapted. Just as knowledge of their natures allows us to say what a dog or a horse needs to flourish, a proper understanding of persons dictates certain conceptions of the good and precludes others. The natural law philosopher John Finnis (1980) surveys the anthropological literature to find that, contrary to Rorty's (1989, p. 185) claim that "socialization goes all the way down," all human societies "show a concern for the value of human life . . . restrict sexual activity . . . display a favour for the value of co-operation . . . know friendship . . . have some conception of *meum* and *tuum* . . . treat the bodies of dead members of the group in some traditional and ritual fashion different from their procedure for rubbish disposal," and so on (p. 83).

2. There are hints of an evolutionary understanding of persons in Marx. His cryptic descriptions of humans as "inhaling and exhaling all the powers of nature" and of nature as "the inorganic body of man" (Marx, 1963a, p. 206) suggests that persons are formed in interaction with nature: "The cultivation of the five senses is

the work of all previous history" (p. 161). This interpretation gains plausibility in light of Marx's admiration of Darwin.

3. Wilson and Herrnstein (1985) survey extensive data relating the criminality of adoptees to parents, concluding that "the criminality of the biological parents is here more important than that of the adoptive parents, suggesting genetic transmission of some factor or factors associated with crime" (p. 96; see also Mednick et al., 1984). Anne Fausto-Sterling (1992) argues against genetic determinism by showing that the brain is importantly shaped by early environmental inputs. But insofar as training hardwires the nervous system, this still contradicts the thesis of situational determinism: persons are more than intersections of present environmental forces. David Popenoe (1996) draws on numerous studies that demonstrate the enduring effect of early training.

4. Some people have phobias—that is, they are afraid in nonfearful situations. This would seem to break the connection between context and feelings. But these are considered to be deviant *because* of their contextual inappropriateness.

5. Goodwin's (1997) conception of libidinal drives is what I have called "additive." That is, he makes no effort to show how desires etc. are intricated with culture and social structure.

6. It might seem that evolutionary psychology might threaten Wittgenstein's emphasis on cultural training. That is, if animals have fear and anger, it would seem that humans need not learn the language games of these emotions. Wittgenstein might respond that not all human emotions are continuous with those of animals and those that are shared are more complex and culturally elaborated. Apes and other animals form enduring bonds that resemble, and likely foreshadow, human love. But they do not distinguish between love and infatuation. Also, Wittgenstein's warning about doing philosophy on a one-sided diet of examples applies: *some* emotions are deeply cultural while others may rely on "primitive reactions."

Chapter 9

1. Christopher Jencks (1992) cites findings that 46% of unemployed 16- to 24-year-old black males thought it would be "very easy" to find work and 25% thought it would be "somewhat easy." He concludes that "a lot of idleness is voluntary" (p. 127).

2. Richard Felsen (1991) contends that "those who wish to protect the poor will emphasize opportunity—an external factor—over ability—an internal factor, in explaining class differences" (p. 13). This sentiment also leads to "rejection of a 'cultural' approach in the explanation of the persistence of poverty" (p. 11).

3. Travis Hirschi and Michael Hindelang (1977) find that delinquents have substantially lower IQs.

4. Richard Felsen notes that while cultural explanations are not applied to "protected groups," "a cultural argument is acceptable in explaining why offending groups engage in discrimination," because "to say that prejudice is the result of culture and learning implies that prejudice reflects ignorance, which assigns racists

and sexists the blame they deserve" (p. 12). Felsen cites many examples of theoretical dualism. While poor criminals are seen as "victims of labeling and lack of opportunity" (p. 15), these exculpatory explanations are not extended to dominant groups. Explanations of men's violence against women that emphasize interaction effects are shunned, while "it is acceptable to analyze homicide committed by battered women against their husbands in terms of victim precipitation" (p. 16).

5. Lionel Trilling (1950): "Some paradox of our natures leads us, when once we have made our fellow man the objects of our enlightened interest, to go on to make them the objects of our pity, then of our wisdom, ultimately of our coercion" (p. 221). Anthony Arblaster's (1984) (left-wing) critique of liberalism also emphasizes the tendency of reformists to reduce men to objects of manipulation by the enlightened legislator (pp. 186-188, 306). Coercive liberation reaches an apogee in Rousseau's (1950) suggestion that "whoever refuses to obey the general will shall be compelled to do so" and by this "he will be forced to be free" (1950, p. 18).

6. There is debate over Marx's commitment to rights. Steven Seidman (1983, p. 110), among others, argues that he was a committed democrat. But the anarchist Michael Bakunin saw in Marxism the potential for "the despotism of a governing minority" which is "all the more dangerous in that this minority appears as the expression of the so-called people's will" (quoted in Singer, 1980, p. 76).

7. William O'Neill (1981), author of the phrase "blaming the victim," similarly follows the path from sympathy to attributions of helplessness that approach benign contempt:

> Our own individual characteristics, our plans, our efforts, and our attempts to follow the rules of the American dream have very little influence on whether we do well or poorly in life. Diligence or laziness, intelligence or stupidity, thriftiness or extravagance, ambition or inertia—these personal traits, often defined, in various combinations, as "merit," account for very little of what happens" (p. 25).

The technocratic aspirations of B. F. Skinner, Frank Lester Ward, George Lundberg, and others are discussed in Spragens (1981), especially Chapter 5.

REFERENCES

Aaron, Henry. (1990). Symposium on the economic status of African Americans. *Journal of Economic Perspectives, 4*(4), 3-7.

Ainsworth-Darnell, James W., & Downey, Douglas B. (1998). Assessing the oppositional culture explanation for racial/ethnic differences in school performance. *American Sociological Review, 63,* 536-553.

Alexander, Jeffrey C. (1982). *Theoretical logic in sociology: Positivism, presuppositions and current controversies.* Berkeley: University of California Press.

Alexander, Jeffrey C. (1984). Social-structural analysis: Some notes on its history and prospects. *Sociological Quarterly, 25,* 5-26.

Alexander, Jeffrey C. (Ed.). (1987a). *The micro-macro link.* Berkeley: University of California Press.

Alexander, Jeffrey C. (1987b). *Twenty lectures.* New York: Columbia University Press.

Alexander, Jeffrey C. (1988a). *Action and its environments.* New York: Columbia University Press.

Alexander, Jeffrey C. (Ed.). (1988b). *Durkheimian sociology: Cultural studies.* Cambridge, UK: Cambridge University Press.

Alexander, Jeffrey C. (1988c). The new theoretical movement. In N. Smelser (Ed.), *Handbook of sociology.* Newbury Park, CA: Sage.

Alexander, Jeffrey C. (1990). Understanding the relative autonomy of culture. In J. C. Alexander & S. Seidman (Eds.), *Culture and society: Contemporary debates.* New York: Cambridge University Press.

Alexander, Jeffrey C. (1995). *Fin de siecle social theory.* London: Verso.

Althusser, Louis, & Balibar, Etienne. (1970). *Reading capital* (B. Brewster, Trans.). London: New Left.

Ambercrombie, Nicholas, Hill, Steven, & Turner, Bryan. (1980). *The dominant ideology thesis.* London: Allen & Unwin.

Anderson, Elijah. (1990). *Streetwise.* Chicago: University of Chicago Press.

Anderson, Elijah. (1994, May). The code of the streets. *Atlantic Monthly*, pp. 81-84.

Anderson, Perry. (1976-77). The antinomies of Antonio Gramsci. *New Left Review*, *100*, 5-80.

Ang, Ien. (1985). *Watching Dallas: Soap opera and the melodramatic imagination*. London: Methuen.

Arblaster, Anthony. (1984). *The rise and decline of Western liberalism*. London: Basil Blackwell.

Archer, Margaret S. (1988). *Culture and agency*. Cambridge, UK: Cambridge University Press.

Armon-Jones, Claire. (1986). The thesis of constructionism. In R. Harre (Ed.), *The social construction of emotions*. New York: Basil Blackwell.

Banfield, Edward. (1970). *The unheavenly city*. Boston: Little, Brown.

Baron, James, & Hannon, Michael. (1994). The impact of economics on contemporary sociology. *Journal of Economic Literature*, *32*, 1111-1146.

Barry, Norman. (1987). *On classical liberalism and libertarianism*. New York: St. Martin's.

Barthes, Roland. (1977). The death of the author. In R. Barthes (Ed.), *Images, music, text*. New York: Hill & Wang.

Bartov, Omer. (1999, October 4). The lost cause. *The New Republic*, pp. 47-53.

Bauer, P. T. (1979). *Dissent on development*. Cambridge, MA: Harvard University Press.

Beck, E. M., Horan, Patrick, & Tolbert, Charles. (1978). Stratification in a dual economy: A sectoral model of earnings data. *American Sociological Review*, *43*, 704-720.

Becker, Gary. (1976). *The economic approach to human behavior*. Chicago: University of Chicago Press.

Becker, Gary. (1979). Economic analysis and human behavior. In L. Levy-Garbona (Ed.), *Sociological economics*. London: Sage.

Becker, Gary. (1981). *A treatise on the family*. Cambridge, MA: Harvard University Press.

Becker, Gary, & Stigler, George J. (1977, February-March). De Gustibus Non Est Disputandum. *American Economic Review*, *67*, pp. 76-90.

Becker, Howard. (1963). Becoming a marijuana user. In *Outsiders: Studies in the sociology of deviance*. Glencoe, IL: Free Press.

Belluck, Pam. (1999, July 24). When the heart sings, part of the cortex gets busy. *New York Times*, pp. B7-B9.

Bentham, Jeremy. (1963). *An introduction to the principles of morals and legislation*. New York: Hafner.

Bentham, Jeremy. (1973). An introduction to the principles of morals and legislation. In *The utilitarians*. Garden City, NJ: Anchor.

Bentham, Jeremy. (1988). *The principles of morals and legislation*. Buffalo, NY: Prometheus.

Berger, Bennett M. (1991). Structure and choice in the sociology of culture. *Theory & Society, 20,* 1-19.

Berlin, Isaiah. (1969). *Four essays on liberty.* New York: Oxford University Press.

Berne, Thomas. (1981). Thomas Hobbes. In L. Strauss & J. Cropsey (Eds.), *History of political philosophy.* Chicago: University of Chicago Press.

Bhagwati, Jagdish. (1998, May 25). The explanation. *The New Republic,* pp. 32-36.

Bibb, Robert, & Form, William. (1977). The effects of industrial, occupational, and sexual stratification on wages in blue collar markets. *Social Forces, 55*(4), 974-996.

Bielby, Denise, & Bielby, William. (1988). She works hard for the money: Household responsibilities and the allocation of work effort. *American Journal of Sociology, 93,* 1031-1059.

Bielby, William. (1980). More inequality: Christopher Jencks on the path of success. *Contemporary Sociology, 9*(6), 754-762.

Bielby, William. (1981). Models of status attainment. In D. Treiman & R. Robinson (Eds.), *Research in social stratification and mobility.* Greenwich, CT: JAI.

Blau, Peter. (1974). Parameters of social structure. *American Sociological Review, 39,* 615-636.

Blau, Peter. (1977). A macrosociological theory of social structure. *American Journal of Sociology, 83*(1), 26-54.

Blau, Peter. (1982). Metropolitan structures and violent crime. *American Sociological Review, 47*(1), 114-129.

Blau, Peter. (1987). Contrasting theoretical perspectives. In J. Alexander (Ed.), *The micro-macro link.* Berkeley: University of California Press.

Blau, Peter. (1994). *Structural contexts of opportunity.* Chicago: University of Chicago Press.

Blau, Peter, & Duncan, Otis Dudley. (1967). *The American occupational structure.* New York: John Wiley.

Blumer, Herbert. (1969). *Symbolic interactionism: Perspectives and methods.* Englewood Cliffs, NJ: Prentice Hall.

Boudon, Raymond. (1974). *Educational opportunity and social inequality.* New York: John Wiley.

Boudon, Raymond, & Bourricaud, Francois. (1989). *A critical dictionary of sociology* (P. Hamilton, Trans.). Chicago: University of Chicago Press.

Bourdieu, Pierre. (1977). *Outline of a theory of practice.* Cambridge, UK: Cambridge University Press.

Bourdieu, Pierre. (1993). *Sociology in question.* Thousand Oaks, CA: Sage.

Bourdieu, Pierre, & Passeron, Jean-Claude. (1977). *Reproduction in education, society, and culture.* London: Sage.

Bourdieu, Pierre, & Wacquant, Loic. (1992). *An invitation to reflexive sociology.* Chicago: University of Chicago Press.

Bowers, Kenneth. (1972). Situationism in psychology. *Psychological Review, 80*(5), 307-336.

Bowles, Samuel, & Gintis, Herbert. (1976). *Schooling in capitalist America*. New York: Basic Books.

Brantingham, Paul, & Brantingham, Patricia. (1984). *Patterns in crime*. New York: Macmillan.

Breines, Paul. (1990). *Tough Jews*. New York: Basic Books.

Buchanan, Allen. (1980). Revolutionary motivation and rationality. In M. Cohen, T. Nagel, & T. Scanlon (Eds.), *Marx, justice, and history*. Princeton, NJ: Princeton University Press.

Bucholtz, Todd. (1989). *New ideas from dead economists*. New York: Penguin.

Burt, Ronald. (1992). *Toward a structural theory of action*. New York: Academic Press.

Byne, William, & Parsons, Bruce. (1993, March). Human sexual orientation: The biologic theories reappraised. *Archives of General Psychiatry, 50,* pp. 228-238.

Calhoun, Craig. (1993). Habitus, field, and capital. In C. Calhoun, E. LiPuma, & M. Postone (Eds.), *Bourdieu: Critical perspectives*. Chicago: University of Chicago Press.

Callinicos, Alexander. (1985). Anthony Giddens: A contemporary critique. *Theory and Society, 14*(2), 133-174.

Camic, Charles. (1979, November). The utilitarians revisited. *American Journal of Sociology, 85,* 516-549.

Campbell, Richard. (1983). Status attainment research: End of the beginning or beginning of the end? *Sociology of Education, 56,* 47-62.

Clark, Kenneth. (1965). *Dark ghetto: Dilemmas of social power*. New York: Harper & Row.

Cloward, Richard, & Ohlin, Lloyd. (1960). *Delinquency and opportunity*. New York: Free Press.

Coats, A. W. (1971). *The classical economists and economic policy*. London: Methuen.

Cohen, Albert. (1955). *Delinquent boys*. Glencoe, IL: Free Press.

Cohen, Ira J. (1987). Structuration theory and social praxis. In A. Giddens & J. Turner (Eds.), *Social theory today*. Stanford, CA: Stanford University Press.

Cohen, Jean. (1985). Strategy or identity: New theoretical paradigms and contemporary social movements. *Social Research, 52*(4), 663-716.

Cohn, Norman. (1962). *The pursuit of the millennium*. New York: Harper.

Cole, Steven. (1975). The growth of scientific knowledge. In L. Coser (Ed.), *The idea of social structure*. New York: Harcourt Brace Jovanovich.

Coleman, James S. (1966). *Equal educational opportunity*. Washington, DC: Government Printing Office.

Coleman, James S. (1974). Inequality, sociology, and moral philosophy. *American Journal of Sociology, 80*(3), 739-765.

Coleman, James S. (1986). *Individual interests and collective action*. Cambridge, UK: Cambridge University Press.

Coleman, James S. (1990). *Foundations of social theory.* Cambridge, MA: Harvard University Press.

Collins, Randall. (1975). *Conflict sociology.* New York: Academic Press.

Collins, Randall. (1986). Is 1980s sociology in the doldrums? *American Journal of Sociology, 91*(6), 1336-1355.

Collins, Randall. (1988). The Durkheimian tradition in conflict sociology. In J. Alexander (Ed.), *Durkheimian sociology: Cultural studies.* Cambridge, UK: Cambridge University Press.

Collins, Randall. (1993). Emotional energy as the common denominator of rational action. *Rationality and Society, 5*(2), 203-230.

Connell, Evan S. (1984). *Son of the morning star.* New York: HarperCollins.

Coulter, Jeffrey. (1979). *The social construction of mind.* Totowa, NJ: Rowman & Littlefield.

Cox, Michael, & Alm, Richard. (1999). *Myths of rich and poor.* New York: Basic Books.

Crockett, Steven. (1999, May 7). Jump suits: Pro and con. *Washington Post,* p. 21.

Currie, Elliot. (1985). *Confronting crime.* New York: Pantheon.

Dalai Lama. (1998, December 7). The West's lessons for Tibet. *Wall Street Journal,* p. 22.

Dawidowicz, Lucy. (1975). *The war against the Jews.* New York: Bantam.

Derne, Steve. (1994). Cultural conceptions of human motivation and their significance for culture theory. In D. Crane (Ed.), *The sociology of culture.* Cambridge, MA: Blackwell.

Descartes, Rene. (1960). *Discourse on method* (A. Wallaston, Trans.). London: Penguin.

DeTocqueville, Alexis. (1961). *Democracy in America.* New York: Schocken.

DiMaggio, Paul. (1990). Cultural aspects of economic action and organization. In R. Friedland & A. F. Robertson (Eds.), *Beyond the marketplace.* New York: Aldine de Gruyter.

Dorfman, Ariel, & Mattelart, Armand. (1975). *How to read Donald Duck: Imperialist ideology in the Disney comic.* New York: International General Editions.

Dornbusch, Sanford, Steinberg, Lawrence, & Brown, Lawrence. (1996). *Beyond the classroom.* New York: Simon & Schuster.

Douglas, Mary, & Wildavsky, Aaron. (1982). *Risk and culture.* Berkeley: University of California Press.

Duncan, Gregory. (1984). *Years of poverty, years of plenty.* Ann Arbor: University of Michigan Press.

Durkheim, Emile. (1950). *Rules of the sociological method.* Chicago: Free Press.

Durkheim, Emile. (1958). *Professional ethics and civic morals.* Chicago: Free Press.

Durkheim, Emile. (1961). *Moral education: A study in the theory and application of the sociology of education* (E. Wilson & H. Schnurer, Trans.). Chicago: Free Press.

Durkheim, Emile. (1964). *The division of labor in society.* Chicago: Free Press.

Durkheim, Emile. (1966). *Suicide.* Chicago: Free Press.

Dutton, Donald G. (1995). *The batterer.* New York: Basic Books.

Eagleton, Terry. (1991). *Ideology.* London: Verso.

Edgarton, Robert B. (1992). *Sick societies.* New York: Free Press.

Ellis, John. (1987). *The social history of the machine gun.* London: Cresset.

Elster, Jon. (1979). Anomalies of rationality: Some unresolved problems in the theory of rational behavior. In L. Levy-Garbona (Ed.), *Sociological economics.* London: Sage.

Elster, Jon. (1984). Belief, bias, and ideology. In M. Hollis & S. Lukes (Eds.), *Rationality and relativism.* London: Basil Blackwell.

Elster, Jon. (1989a). *The cement of society.* Cambridge, UK: Cambridge University Press.

Elster, Jon. (1989b). *Nuts and bolts for the social sciences.* Cambridge, UK: Cambridge University Press.

Elster, Jon. (1989c). Social norms and economic theory. *Journal of Economic Perspectives, 3*(4), 99-117.

Elster, Jon. (1989d). Sour grapes—Utilitarianism and the genesis of wants. In J. Christman (Ed.), *The inner citadel* (pp. 170-188). New York: Oxford University Press.

Elster, Jon. (1990). [Interview]. In R. Swedberg *Economics and sociology.* Princeton, NJ: Princeton University Press.

Emirbayer, Mustafa, & Goodwin, Jeff. (1994, May). Network analysis, culture, and the problem of agency. *American Journal of Sociology, 99*(6), 1411-1454.

Emirbayer, Mustafa, & Mische, Ann. (1998). What is agency? *American Journal of Sociology, 1*(4), 962-1023.

Etzioni, Amitai. (1988). *The moral dimension.* New York: Free Press.

Farber, I. E. (1964). A framework for the study of personality. In P. Worchel & D. Byrne (Eds.), *Personality change.* New York: John Wiley.

Farkas, George, & Vicknair, Keven. (1996, August). Appropriate tests of racial wage discrimination require controls for cognitive skill: Comment on Cancio, Evans, and Maune. *American Sociological Review, 61,* 557-560.

Fausto-Sterling, Anne. (1992). *Myths of gender: Biological theories about women and men.* New York: Basic Books.

Feagin, Joe. (1989). *Racial and ethnic relations.* Englewood Cliffs, NJ: Prentice Hall.

Felsen, Richard, B. (1991, Spring). Blame analysis: Accounting for the behavior of protected groups. *American Sociologist,* pp. 5-23.

Feuer, Lewis. (1959). *Karl Marx: Basic writings on politics and philosophy.* New York: Doubleday.

Feuer, Lewis. (1969). *Marx and the intellectuals.* Garden City: Anchor Books.

Fine, Gary. (1992). Agency, structure, and comparative contexts: Toward a synthetic interactionism. *Symbolic Interaction, 15*(1), 87-107.

Finestone, Harold. (1957, July). Cats, kicks, and color. *Social Problems, 5*, 3-13.

Finnis, John. (1980). *Natural law and natural rights.* Oxford, UK: Clarendon.

Fiske, John. (1989). *Understanding popular culture.* Boston: Unwin Hyman.

Fitzgerald, F. Scott. (1953). *The great Gatsby.* New York: Scribner.

Flew, Anthony. (1981). *The politics of procrustes.* Buffalo, NY: Prometheus.

Foucault, Michel. (1980). *Power/knowledge* (C. Gordon, Ed.). Sussex, UK: Hassock.

Frank, Robert. (1988). *Passions within reason.* New York: Norton.

Freeman, Richard. (1983). Crime and unemployment. In J. Wilson (Ed.), *Crime and public policy.* San Francisco: ICS.

Freud, Sigmund. (1962). *Civilization and its discontents* (J. Strachey, Trans.). New York: Norton.

Friedland, Roger, & Robertson, A. F. (Eds.). (1990). *Beyond the marketplace.* New York: Aldine de Gruyter.

Friedman, Debra. (1983). Normative and rational explanations of a classic case: Religious specialization in academia. In M. Hechter (Ed.), *The microfoundations of macrosociology.* Philadelphia: Temple University Press.

Friedman, Milton. (1982). *Capitalism and freedom.* Chicago: University of Chicago Press.

Furchtgott-Roth, Diana, & Stolba, Christine. (1996). *Women's figures.* Arlington, VA: Independent Women's Forum.

Furchtgott-Roth, Diana, & Stolba, Christine. (1999). *Women's figures: An illustrated guide to the economic progress of women in America.* Washington, DC: AEI Press.

Galliher, John F., & Cross, John R. (1983). *Morals legislation without morality.* New Brunswick, NJ: Rutgers University Press.

Gans, Herbert. (1962). *The urban villagers.* New York: Macmillan.

Gans, Herbert. (1968). Culture and class in the study of poverty: An approach to anti-poverty research. In D. P. Moynihan (Ed.), *On understanding poverty: Perspectives from the social sciences.* New York: Basic Books.

Geertz, Clifford. (1973). *The interpretation of culture.* New York: Basic Books.

Gellner, Ernest. (1992). *Reason and culture.* Oxford, UK: Basil Blackwell.

Gerson, Kathleen. (1985). *Hard choices.* Berkeley: University of California Press.

Gibson, J. J. (1979). *The ecological approach to visual perception.* Boston: Houghton Mifflin.

Giddens, Anthony. (1976). *The new rules of sociological method.* New York: Basic Books.

Giddens, Anthony. (1977). *Studies in social and political thought.* New York: Basic Books.

Giddens, Anthony. (1981). *A contemporary critique of historical materialism.* London: Macmillan.

Gilligan, Carol. (1982). *In a different voice: Psychological theory and women's development.* Cambridge, MA: Harvard University Press.

Goffman, Erving. (1959). *The presentation of self in everyday life.* Garden City, NY: Doubleday.

Goffman, Erving. (1961). *Asylums.* Garden City, NY: Doubleday.

Goffman, Erving. (1963). *Stigma.* Englewood Cliffs, NJ: Prentice Hall.

Goodwin, Jeff. (1997, February). The libidinal constitution of a high-risk social movement: Affectual ties and solidarity in the Huk rebellion, 1946 to 1954. *American Sociological Review, 62,* 53-69.

Gordon, Steven. (1990). Structural effects on emotions. In T. Kemper (Ed.), *Research agendas in the sociology of emotions.* Albany: State University of New York Press.

Gouldner, Alvin. (1970). *The coming crisis of Western sociology.* New York: Basic Books.

Granovetter, Mark. (1981). Toward a sociological theory of income differences. In I. Berg (Ed.), *Sociological perspectives on labor markets.* New York: Academic Press.

Granovetter, Mark. (1985, November). Economic action and social structure: The problem of embeddedness. *American Journal of Sociology, 91,* 481-510.

Granovetter, Mark. (1988). Editor's statement for the series structural analysis in the social sciences. In B. Wellman & S. D. Berkowitz (Eds.), *Social structures: A network approach.* New York: Cambridge University Press.

Granovetter, Mark, & Charles Tilly. (1988). Inequality and labor process. In N. Smelser (Ed.), *Handbook of sociology.* Beverly Hills, CA: Sage.

Gray, John. (1987). The economic approach to human behavior: Its prospects and limitations. In G. Radnitzky & P. Bernholz (Eds.), *Economic imperialism.* New York: Paragon.

Griswold, Wendy. (1994). *Culture and societies in a changing world.* Thousand Oaks, CA: Pine Forge.

Gudeman, Steven. (1986). *Economics as culture.* New York: Routledge & Kegan Paul.

Hanley, James. (1999, November 29). [Correspondence] *New Republic,* p. 6.

Hannerz, Ulf. (1969). *Soulside: Inquiries into ghetto culture and community.* Stockholm: Almqvist & Wiksell.

Hanushek, Erik. (1996). School resources and student performance. In G. Burtless (Ed.), *Does money matter?* Washington, DC: Brookings.

Harre, Rom. (Ed.). (1986). *The social construction of emotions.* New York: Basil Blackwell.

Hays, Sharon. (1994, March). Structure and agency and the sticky problem of culture. *Sociological Theory, 12*(1), 57-72.

Hechter, Michael. (1983). Karl Polanyi's social theory. In M. Hechter (Ed.), *The microfoundations of macrosociology.* Philadelphia: Temple University Press.

Hechter, Michael. (1990). The emergence of cooperative social institutions. In M. Hechter, K-D Opp, & R. Wippler (Eds.), *Social institutions: Their emergence, maintenance, and effects.* New York: Aldine de Gruyter.

Hechter, Michael, & Friedman, Debra. (1988, Fall). The contribution of rational choice theory to macrosociological research. *Sociological Theory*, pp. 201-218.

Hechter, Michael, Opp, Karl-Deter, & Wippler, Reinhard. (Eds.). (1990). *Social institutions: Their emergence, maintenance, and effects*. New York: Aldine de Gruyter.

Hedges, Larry, & Robert Greenwald. (1996). Have times changed? The relationship between school resources and student performance. In G. Burtless (Ed.), *Does money matter?* Washington, DC: Brookings.

Heft, Harry. (1989). Affordances and the body: An intentional analysis of Gibson's ecological approach to visual perception. *Journal for the Theory of Social Behavior, 19*(1), 1-30.

Heritage, John. (1987). Ethnomethodology. In A. Turner & J. Turner (Eds.), *Social theory today*. Stanford, CA: Stanford University Press.

Himmelfarb, Gertrude. (1994, Fall). A demoralized society. *The Public Interest*, pp. 57-80.

Hindess, Barry. (1977). Economic action in the sociology of Weber. In B. Hindess (Ed.), *Sociological theories of the economy*. New York: Holmes & Meirer.

Hindess, Barry. (1984). Rational choice theory and the analysis of political action. *Economy and Society, 13*(3), 255-277.

Hindess, Barry. (1988). *Choice, rationality, and social theory*. London: Unwin & Hyman.

Hirsch, Paul, Michaels, Stuart, & Friedman, Roy. (1987). "Dirty hands" versus "clean models." *Theory & Society, 16*, 317-336.

Hirschi, Travis, & Hindelang, Michael. (1977). I.Q. and delinquency. *American Sociological Review, 42*(4), 571-587.

Hobbes, Thomas. (1966). In Sir W. Molesworth (Ed.), *The English Works of Thomas Hobbes*. London: John Bohm.

Hobbes, Thomas. (1985). *Leviathan* (C. B. MacPherson, Ed.). Harmondsworth, UK: Penguin.

Hochschild, Arlie. (1979). Emotion work, feeling rules, and social structure. *American Journal of Sociology, 85*(3), 551-575.

Hochschild, Arlie. (1983). *The managed heart*. Los Angeles: University of California Press.

Hollis, Martin. (1979). Rational man and social science. In R. Harrison (Ed.), *Rational action*. Cambridge, UK: Cambridge University Press.

Hollis, Martin. (1983). Rational preferences. *Philosophical Forum, 14*(3-4), 246-262.

Holmes, Steven. (1990). The secret history of self-interest. In J. Mansbridge (Ed.), *Beyond self-interest*. Chicago: University of Chicago Press.

Homans, George C. (1987). Behaviorism and after. In A. Giddens & J. Turner (Eds.), *Social theory today*. Stanford, CA: Stanford University Press.

Horan, Patrick, Beck, E. M., & Tolbert, Charles. (1980, September). The market homogeneity assumption: On the theoretical foundations of empirical knowledge. *Social Science Quarterly, 61,* 278-292.

Hume, David. (1978). *A treatise of human nature* (L. A. Selby-Bigge, Ed.). New York: Oxford University Press.

Huppes, Tjerk. (1976). Economic sociology or sociological economics? In T. Huppes (Ed.), *Economics and sociology.* Leiden, the Netherlands: Martinus Nijhoff.

Hurst, Charles. (1995). *Social inequality: Forms, causes, consequences.* Needham Heights, MA: Allyn & Bacon.

Hutchison, Terrence. (1984). Institutionalist economics old and new. *Journal of Institutional and Theoretical Economics, 140*(1), 20-29.

James, Susan. (1985). Althusser. In Q. Skinner (Ed.), *The return of grand theory in the human sciences.* London: Cambridge University Press.

Jencks, Christopher. (1972). *Inequality.* New York: Harper & Row.

Jencks, Christopher. (1973). Inequality in retrospect. *Harvard Educational Review, 40*(1), 138-164.

Jencks, Christopher. (1979). *Who gets ahead?* New York: Basic Books.

Jencks, Christopher. (1992). *Rethinking social policy.* New York: HarperCollins.

Jencks, Christopher. (1993). *Culture.* London: Routledge.

Joas, Hans. (1987). Symbolic interactionism. In A. Giddens & J. Turner (Eds.), *Social theory today.* Stanford, CA: Stanford University Press.

Johnson, Paul. (1987). *A history of the Jews.* New York: Harper & Row.

Jones, James. (1962). *The thin red line.* New York: Scribner.

Kahl, Joseph, & Gilbert, Dennis. (1987). *The American class structure.* Chicago: Dorsey.

Kahneman, Daniel, Knetsch, Jack, & Thaler, Richard H. (1987). Fairness and the assumptions of economics. In R. Hogarth & M. Reder (Eds.), *Rational choice: The contrast between economics and philosophy.* Chicago: University of Chicago Press.

Kalleberg, Arne. (1989). Linking macro and micro levels: Bringing workers back into the sociology of work. *Social Forces, 67*(3), 582-592.

Kane, Anne. (1991, Spring). Cultural analysis in historical sociology: The analytic and concrete forms of the autonomy of culture. *Sociological Theory,* pp. 53-69.

Kanter, Rosabeth. (1977). *Men and women of the corporation.* New York: Basic Books.

Katz, Jack. (1988). *The seductions of crime.* New York: Basic Books.

Katz, Michael. (1989). *The undeserving poor.* New York: Pantheon.

Keegan, John. (1993). *A history of warfare.* New York: Knopf.

Kemper, Theodore. (1987). How many emotions are there? Wedding the social and the autonomic components. *American Journal of Sociology, 93,* 263-289.

Kerckhoff, Alan. (1984, Spring). The current state of social mobility research. *Sociological Quarterly,* pp. 139-153.

Kliemt, Hartmut. (1990). The costs of organizing social cooperation. In M. Hechter, K-D Opp, & R. W. Wippler (Eds.), *Social institutions: Their emergence, maintenance, and effects.* New York: Aldine de Gruyter.

Knottnerus, David, & Prendergast, Christopher. (1994). *Recent developments in the theory of social structure* (Current Perspectives in Social Theory). Greenwich, CT: JAI.

Kornhauser, Ruth. (1978). *The social sources of delinquency.* Chicago: University of Chicago Press.

Kristal, Irving. (1983). *Reflections of a neoconservative.* New York: Basic Books.

Kubler, George. (1962). *The shape of time: Remarks on the history of things.* New Haven, CT: Yale University Press.

Ladurie, Emmanuel. (1978). *Montaillou: The promised land of error.* New York: Braziller.

Landes, David. (1998). *The wealth and poverty of nations.* New York: Norton.

Latsis, Spiro. (1972). Situational determinism in economics. *British Journal for the Philosophy of Science, 23,* 207-245.

Latsis, Spiro. (1976). A research program in economics. In S. Latsis (Ed.), *Method and appraisal in economics.* New York: Cambridge University Press.

Layder, Derek. (1985). Power, structure, and agency. *Journal for the Theory of Social Behavior, 15*(2), 131-149.

Leidner, Robin. (1993). *Fast food, fast talk.* Berkeley: University of California Press.

Leonard, Elmore. (1981). *Split images.* New York: Avon.

Levin, Michael. (1987, November). The return of human nature. *The World and I,* pp. 617-626.

Levi-Strauss, Claude. (1969). *The raw and the cooked* (J. Weightman & D. Weightman, Trans.). New York: Harper & Row.

Levy, Robert. (1984). Emotion, knowing and culture. In R. Shweder & R. Levine (Eds.), *Culture theory: Essays on mind, self, and emotion.* Cambridge, UK: Cambridge University Press.

Lieberson, Stanley. (1980). *A piece of the pie.* Berkeley: University of California Press.

Liebow, Elliot. (1967). *Tally's corner: A study of Negro streetcorner men.* Boston: Little, Brown.

Light, Ivan, & Bonacich, Edna. (1988). *Immigrant entrepreneurs.* Berkeley: University of California Press.

Lilla, Mark. (1994). *New French thought.* Princeton, NJ: Princeton University Press.

Lin, Chien. (1985). *The intergenerational relationships among Chinese immigrant families.* Unpublished dissertation, University of Illinois, Chicago.

Lin, Nan. (1982). Social resources and instrumental action. In P. Marsden & N. Lin. (Eds.), *Social structure and network analysis.* Beverly Hills, CA: Sage.

Lin, Nan. (1990). Social resources and social mobility: A structural theory of status attainment. In R. Breiger (Ed.), *Social mobility and social structure.* New York: Cambridge University Press.

Lindenberg, Siegwart. (1985). An assessment of the new political economy: Its potential for the social sciences and for sociology in particular. *Sociological Theory, 3*(1), 99-114.

Linderman, Gerald. (1997). *The world within war.* Cambridge, MA: Harvard University Press.

Lipset, Seymour Martin. (1976). Equality and inequality. In R. K. Merton (Ed.), *Contemporary social problems.* New York: Harcourt Brace Jovanovich.

Little, Daniel. (1989). *Understanding peasant China.* New Haven, CT: Yale University Press.

Little, Daniel. (1991a). Rational choice models and Asian studies. *Journal of Asian Studies, 50*(1), 35-52.

Little, Daniel. (1991b). *Varieties of social explanation.* Boulder, CO: Westview.

Llosa, Mario Vargas. (1992). The Miami model. *Commentary, 93*(2), 21-27.

Locke, John. (1902). *Some thoughts concerning education.* Cambridge, UK: Cambridge University Press.

Locke, John. (1952). *The second treatise of government.* New York: Bobbs-Merrill.

Locke, John. (1954). *Essays on the law of nature.* London: Oxford University Press.

Loewen, James W. (1988). *The Mississippi Chinese.* Prospect Heights, IL: Waveland.

MacKinnon, Neil. (1994). *Symbolic interactionism as affect control.* Albany: State University of New York Press.

MacLeod, Jay. (1987). *Ain't no makin' it.* Boulder, CO: Westview.

Magnet, Myron. (1993). *The dream and the nightmare.* New York: William Morrow.

Malcolm, Norman. (1970). Wittgenstein on the nature of the mind. Studies in the theory of knowledge. *American Philosophical Quarterly Monograph Series, 4,* 9-29.

Mannheim, Karl. (1971). *From Karl Mannheim* (K. Wolff, Ed.). Cambridge, UK: Oxford University Press.

Marger, Martin. (1999). *Social inequality.* Mountain View, CA: Mayfield.

Marini, Margaret Mooney. (1989). Sex differences in earnings in the United States. *Annual Review of Sociology, 15,* 343-380.

Marsden, Peter, & Lin, Nan. (Eds.). (1982). Purposive action in networks. In P. Marsden & N. Lin (Eds.), *Social structure and network analysis.* Beverly Hills, CA: Sage.

Marx, Karl. (1963a). *Early writings* (T. B. Bottomore, Ed. and Trans.). New York: McGraw-Hill.

Marx, Karl. (1963b). *The poverty of philosophy.* Moscow: International Publishers.

Marx, Karl. (1964). *Selected writings in sociology and social philosophy* (T. B. Bottomore, Ed. and Trans.). New York: McGraw-Hill.

Marx, Karl. (1967a). *The German ideology.* New York: International Publishers.

Marx, Karl. (1967b). *The eighteenth Brumaire of Louis Bonaparte.* New York: International Publishers.

Marx, Karl. (1969). Wage labor and capital. In *Marx and Engels: Selected works* (Vol. 1). Moscow: Progress Publishers.

Marx, Karl. (1971). *The Grundrisse* (D. McLellan, Ed. and Trans.). New York: Harper & Row.

Matza, David. (1964). *Delinquency and drift*. New York: John Wiley.

Matza, David, & Sykes, Gresham. (1957). Techniques of neutralization: A theory of delinquency. *American Sociological Review, 22*, 664-670.

Mayer, Susan. (1997). *What money can't buy*. Boston: Harvard University Press.

Mayhew, Bruce. (1980). Structuralism vs. individualism, Parts I and II. *Social Forces, 59*, (2,3), 335-375, 627-648.

McPherson, Michael. (1984). Limits on self-seeking. In D. Colander (Ed.), *Neoclassical political economy*. Cambridge, MA: Ballinger.

Mednick, S. A., Gabrielli, W. F., & Hutchings, B. (1984). Genetic influence in criminal convictions: Evidence from an adoptive cohort. *Science, 224*, 891-894.

Merton, Robert K. (1938). Social structure and anomie. *American Sociological Review, 3*, 672-682.

Mickelson, Roslyn. (1990, January). The attitude-achievement paradox among black adolescents. *Sociology of Education, 63*, 44-61.

Mill, John Stuart. 1895). *A system of logic* (Vol. II). London: Longman's Green.

Mischel, Walter. (1968). *Personality and assessment*. New York: John Wiley.

Monk, Ray. (1990). *Ludwig Wittgenstein: The duty of genius*. New York: Free Press.

Montgomery, James. (1990). *Is underclass behavior contagious? A rational choice analysis*. Unpublished manuscript, Department of Economics, Northwestern University.

Moore, Barrington. (1966). *The social origins of dictatorship and democracy*. Boston: Beacon.

Morsbach, H., & Tyler, W. J. (1986). A Japanese emotion: Amae. In R. Harre (Ed.), *The social construction of emotions*. New York: Basil Blackwell.

Neitz, Mary Jo, & Hall, John R. (1993). *Culture: Sociological perspectives*. Englewood Cliffs, NJ: Prentice Hall.

Nettler, Gwynn. (1984). *Explaining crime*. New York: McGraw-Hill.

Newman, Katherine. (1999). *No shame in my game: The working poor of the inner city*. New York: Knopf and Russell Sage.

Nielsen, Kai. (1985). *Equality and liberty*. Totowa, NJ: Rowman & Littlefield.

North, Douglass. (1984). Three approaches to the study of institutions. In D. Colander (Ed.), *Neoclassical political economy*. Cambridge, MA: Ballinger.

North, Douglass. (1986). A neoclassical theory of the state. In J. Elster (Ed.), *Rational choice*. New York: New York University Press.

Nussbaum, Martha. (1999, February). The professor of parody. *The New Republic, 22*, 37-45.

Ogbu, John U., & Fordham, Signithia. (1986). Black student's school success: Coping with the burden of "acting white." *Urban Review, 18*(3), 176-206.

Okun, Arthur. (1975). *Equality and efficiency: The big tradeoff.* Washington, DC: Brookings.

Ollman, Bertell. (1971). *Alienation: Marx's conception of man in capitalist society.* Cambridge, UK: Cambridge University Press.

Olson, Mancur. (1968). *The logic of collective action.* New York: Schocken.

Olson, Mancur. (1982). *The rise and decline of nations.* New Haven, CT: Yale University Press.

O'Neill, June. (1987). Discrimination and income inequality. *Social Philosophy and Policy, 5*(1), 169-187.

O'Neill, William. (1981). *Equality.* New York: Pantheon.

Orsagh, Thomas. (1980). Unemployment and crime. *Journal of Criminal Law and Criminology, 71*(2), 181-183.

Otto, Luther, & Haller, Archibald. (1979, March). Evidence for a social psychological view of the status attainment process: Four studies compared. *Social Forces, 57*(3), 887-914.

Outhwaite, William. (1985). Hans-Georg Gadamer. In Q. Skinner (Ed.), *The return of grand theory in the human sciences.* Cambridge, UK: Cambridge University Press.

Parsons, Talcott. (1937). *The structure of social action.* New York: McGraw-Hill.

Parsons, Talcott. (1966). *Societies: Evolutionary and comparative perspectives.* Englewood Cliffs, NJ: Prentice Hall.

Parsons, Talcott, & Kroeber, A. L. (1958, October). The concepts of culture and of social system. *American Sociological Review, 23,* 582-583.

Parsons, Talcott, & Shils, Edward. (Eds.). (1951). *Toward a general theory of action.* New York: Harper & Row.

Pease, John, Form, William, & Rytina, Joan. (1970, May). Ideological currents in American stratification literature. *American Sociologist,* pp. 127-137.

Peele, Stanton. (1990, August). Second thoughts about a gene for alcoholism. *Atlantic Monthly,* pp. 52-58.

Perrin, Noel. (1979). *Giving up the gun.* Boston: David Godine.

Pierce, C. S. (1934). Some consequences of four incapacities. In C. Hartshorne & P. Weiss (Eds.), *Collected papers* (Vol. 5). Cambridge, MA: Harvard University Press.

Pinker, Steven. (1997). *How the mind works.* New York: Norton.

Polanyi, Karl. (1957). *The great transformation.* Boston: Beacon.

Popenoe, David. (1996). *Life without father.* New York: Free Press.

Popkin, Samuel. (1979). *The rational peasant.* Berkeley: University of California Press.

Popper, Karl. (1950). *The open society and its enemies.* Princeton, NJ: Princeton University Press.

Popper, Karl. (1976). The logic of the social sciences. In T. W. Adorno et al. *The positivist dispute in German sociology.* (G. Adeny & D. Frisby, Trans.). New York: Harper & Row.

Porpora, Douglas. (1987). *The concept of social structure.* New York: Greenwood.

Porpora, Douglas. (1989). Four concepts of social structure. *Journal for the Theory of Social Behavior, 19*(2), 195-211.

Posner, Richard. (1995). *Aging and old age.* Chicago: University of Chicago Press.

Postone, Moshe, LiPuma, Edward, & Calhoun, Craig. (1993). Introduction: Bourdieu and social theory. In C. Calhoun, E. LiPuma, & M. Postone (Eds.), *Bourdieu: Critical perspectives.* Chicago: University of Chicago Press.

Press, Andrea. (1994). The sociology of cultural reception: Notes towards an emerging paradigm. In D. Crane (Ed.), *The sociology of culture.* Oxford, UK: Blackwell.

Prezworski, Adam. (1985). Marxism and rational choice. *Politics and Society, 14*(4), 379-409.

Rainwater, Lee. (1960). *And the poor get children.* Chicago: Quadrangle.

Rainwater, Lee. (1967, Summer). The lessons of Pruitt-Igoe. *The Public Interest,* pp. 116-123.

Rainwater, Lee. (1970). *Behind ghetto walls: Black families in a federal slum.* Chicago: Aldine.

Rapoport, Anatol, & Chammah, A. (1965). *Prisoner's dilemma.* Ann Arbor: University of Michigan Press.

Rawls, John. (1971). *A theory of justice.* Cambridge, MA: Harvard University Press.

Redding, Gordon. (1993). *The spirit of Chinese capitalism.* New York: Aldine deGruyter.

Reich, Michael. (1994). The economics of racism. In D. Grusky (Ed.), *Social stratification in sociological perspective.* Boulder, CO: Westview.

Renner, Karl. (1949). *The institutions of private law and their social function.* London: Routledge & Kegan Paul.

Richler, Mordecai. (1968). *The apprenticeship of Duddy Kravitz.* New York: Paperback Library.

Ridley, Matt. (1997). *The origins of virtue: Human instincts and the evolution of cooperation.* New York: Viking.

Ritzer, George. (1992). *Sociological theory.* New York: McGraw-Hill.

Robinson, Joan. (1962). *Economic philosophy.* Chicago: Aldine.

Rodman, Hyman. (1963). The lower-class value stretch. *Social Forces, 42,* 205-215.

Rogers, Carl. (1964). Towards a science of the person. In T. W. Wann (Ed.), *Behaviorism and phenomenology.* Chicago: University of Chicago Press.

Rorty, Richard. (1989). *Contingency, irony and solidarity.* Cambridge, UK: Cambridge University Press.

Rosenau, Pauline. (1992). *Post-modernism and the social sciences.* Princeton, NJ: Princeton University Press.

Rothman, Robert. (1978). *Inequality and stratification in the United States.* Englewood Cliffs, NJ: Prentice Hall.

Rougement, Denis de. (1956). *Love in the Western world.* New York: Pantheon.

Rousseau, Jean Jacques. (1950). *The social contract.* New York: Dutton.

Ruane, Janet, & Cerulo, Karen. (2000). *Second thoughts.* Thousand Oaks, CA: Pine Forge.

Rule, James. (1989). Rationality and non-rationality in militant collective action. *Social Theory, 7*(2), 145-160.

Ryan, Alan. (1970). *The philosophy of the social sciences.* New York: Pantheon.

Sahlins, Marshall. (1976). *Culture and practical reason.* Chicago: University of Chicago Press.

Sahlins, Marshall. (1981). *Historical metaphors and historical realities: Structure in the early history of the Sandwich Islands Kingdom.* Ann Arbor: University of Michigan Press.

Samuelson, Paul. (1979). *Foundations of economic analysis.* New York: McGraw-Hill.

Sanderson, L., & Ellis, L. (1992). Theoretical and political perspectives of American sociologists in the 1990s. *American Sociologist, 23*(2), 26-42.

Sartre, Jean Paul. (1957). *Existentialism and human emotions.* New York: Philosophical Library.

Sartre, Jean Paul. (1963). *Saint Genet: Actor and martyr.* New York: Braziller.

Schacter, Stanley, & Singer, J. (1969). Cognitive, social, and physiological determinants of emotional state. *Psychological Review, 69,* 379-399.

Schneider, Harold. (1974). *Economic man.* Chicago: Free Press.

Schnore, Leo. (1958). Social morphology and human ecology. *American Journal of Sociology, 63*(6), 620-634.

Schumpeter, Joseph. (1976). *Capitalism, socialism, and democracy.* New York: Harper & Row.

Schwartz, Joel. (1990, Spring). Anti-humanism in the humanities. *The Public Interest,* pp. 29-44.

Seidman, Steven. (1983). *Liberalism and the origins of European sociological theory.* Berkeley: University of California Press.

Seidman, Steven. (1991). The end of sociological theory: The postmodern hope. *Sociological Theory, 9*(2), 131-146.

Sen, Amartya. (1977, Summer). Rational fools: A critique of the behavioral foundations of economic theory. *Philosophy and Public Affairs,* pp. 316-345.

Sen, Amartya. (1997, July 14). Human rights and Asian values. *The New Republic,* pp. 33-40.

Sewell, William H. (1992, July). A theory of structure: Duality, agency, and transformation. *American Journal of Sociology, 98*(1), 1-29.

Simmel, Georg. (1965). *Essays on sociology, philosophy, and aesthetics* (K. Wolff, Ed.). New York: Harper & Row.

Simons, Herbert. (1987). Rationality in psychology and economics. In R. Hogarth & M. Reder (Eds.), *Rational choice: The contrast between economics and psychology*. Chicago: University of Chicago Press.

Singer, Peter. (1980). *Marx*. Oxford, UK: Oxford University Press.

Singer, Peter. (1981). *The expanding circle*. New York: Farrar, Strauss & Giroux.

Skinner, B. F. (1948). *Walden II*. New York: Macmillan.

Skinner, B. F. (1964). Behaviorism at 50. In T. W. Wann (Ed.), *Behaviorism and phenomenology*. Chicago: University of Chicago Press.

Smith, Adam. (1976a). *An inquiry into the nature and causes of the wealth of nations* (R. H. Campbell, A. S. Skinner, & W. B. Todd, Eds.). (2 vols.). Oxford, UK: Clarendon.

Smith, Adam. (1976b). *The theory of moral sentiments*. Oxford, UK: Clarendon.

Smith, Michael. (1990, December). What is new in new structuralist analysis of earnings? *American Sociological Review, 55*, 827-841.

Smith, Steven. (1985). Althusser's Marxism without a knowing subject. *American Political Science Review, 79*, 641-655.

Solomon, Robert. (1984). Getting angry: The Jamesian theory of emotions. In R. Schweder & R. Levine (Eds.), *Culture theory: Essays on mind, self, and emotion*. Cambridge, UK: Cambridge University Press.

Solow, Robert. (1995, September 11). *The New Republic*, pp. 36-39.

Sorensen, Aage. (1990). [Interview] In R. Swedberg *Economics and Sociology*. Princeton, NJ: Princeton University Press.

Sowell, Thomas. (1983). *The economics and politics of race*. New York: Quill.

Spragens, Thomas. (1981). *The irony of liberal reason*. Chicago: University of Chicago Press.

Steele, Shelby. (1990). *The content of our character*. New York: HarperCollins.

Stinchcombe, Arthur L. (1986). Economic sociology: Rationality and subjectivity in sociology. In U. Himmelstrand (Ed.), *Sociology: From crisis to science?* London: Sage.

Stinchcombe, Arthur L. (1992, April). Simmel systematized: J. S. Coleman and the social forms of purposive action in his foundations of social theory. *Theory and Society, 21*(2), 183-202.

Sullivan, Harry Stack. (1950). The illusion of personal individuality. *Psychiatry, 13*(1), 223-231.

Swidler, Ann. (1986, April). Culture in action: Symbols and strategies. *American Sociological Review, 51*, 273-286.

Sykes, Gresham. (1958). *Society of captives*. Princeton, NJ: Princeton University Press.

Szymanski, Albert. (1976). Racial discrimination and white gain. *American Sociological Review, 41*(3), 403-413.

Takahashi, Kamekichi. (1969). *The rise and development of Japan's modern economy*. Tokyo: JiJi Press.

Taylor, Charles. (1993). To follow a rule. In C. Calhoun, E. LiPuma, & M. Postone (Eds.), *Bourdieu: Critical perspectives*. Chicago: University of Chicago Press.

Tepperman, Lorne. (1988). Collective mobility and the persistence of dynasties. In B. Wellman & S. D. Berkowitz (Eds.), *Social structures: A network approach*. New York: Cambridge University Press.

Thompson, Michael, Ellis, Richard, & Wildavsky, Aaron. (1990). *Cultural theory*. Boulder, CO: Westview.

Tienda, Marta, & Stier, Haya. (1991). Joblessness and shiftlessness: Labor force activity in Chicago's inner city. In C. Jencks & P. Peterson (Eds.), *The urban underclass*. Washington, DC: Brookings Institute.

Toby, Jackson. (1989, Spring). Of dropouts and stayins: The Gershwin approach. *The Public Interest, 95*, 3-13.

Tomlinson, John. (1991). *Cultural imperialism*. Baltimore: Johns Hopkins University Press.

Tooby, John, & Cosmides, Leda. (1990). On the universality of human nature and the uniqueness of the individual. *Journal of Personality, 58*(1), 17-67.

Tooby, John, & Cosmides, Leda. (1992). The psychological foundations of culture. In J. Barkow, L. Cosmides, & J. Tooby (Eds.), *The adapted mind*. New York: Oxford University Press.

Trilling, Lionel. (1950). *The liberal imagination*. New York: Viking.

Tullock, Gordon. (1971, Fall). The paradox of revolution. *Public Choice, 11*, 89-99.

Turner, Jonathan. (1992). The production and reproduction of social solidarity: A synthesis of two rational choice theories. *Journal for the Theory of Social Behavior, 22*(3), 311-327.

Valentine, Charles. (1968). *Culture and poverty*. Chicago: University of Chicago Press.

Valenzuela, Samuel, & Valenzuela, Arturo. (1984). Modernization and dependency. In M. Seligson *The gap between the rich and the poor*. Boulder, CO: Westview.

Vanberg, Viktor. (1988). *Morality and economics*. Princeton, NJ: Transaction.

Wacquant, Loic. (1993). Redrawing the urban color line. In C. Calhoun & G. Ritzer (Eds.), *Social problems*. New York: McGraw-Hill.

Wallerstein, Immanuel. (1974). *The modern world system: Capitalist agriculture and the origins of the European world-economy in the sixteenth century* (Vol. 1). New York: Academic Press.

Wallerstein, Immanuel. (1979). *The capitalist world economy*. Cambridge, UK: Cambridge University Press.

Waltz, Kenneth. (1979). *Theory of international politics*. New York: McGraw-Hill.

Walzer, Michael. (1974). *The revolution of the saints*. New York: Atheneon.

Warriner, Charles. (1981). Levels in the study of social structure. In P. Blau & R. Merton (Eds.), *Continuities in structural inquiry*. London: Sage.

Weber, Max. (1946). Science as a vocation. In H. Gerth & C. Mills (Eds.), *From Max Weber: Essays in sociology*. New York: Oxford University Press.

Weber, Max. (1958). *The Protestant ethic and the spirit of capitalism*. New York: Scribner.

Weber, Max. (1966). *The theory of social and economic organization* (A. M. Henderson & T. Parsons, Trans.). New York: Free Press.

Wenglinsky, Harold. (1997). How money matters: The effect of school district spending on academic achievement. *Sociology of Education, 70,* 221-237.

Wellman, Barry. (1983). Network analysis: Some basic principles. In R. Collins (Ed.), *Social theory*. San Francisco: Jossey-Bass.

Wellman, Barry. (1988). Structural analysis: From method and metaphor to theory and substance. In *Social structures: A network approach*. New York: Cambridge University Press.

Wellman, Barry, & Berkowitz, S. D. (Eds.). (1988). Studying social structures. *Social structures: A network approach*. New York: Cambridge University Press.

White, Harrison. (1988). Varieties of markets. In B. Wellman & S. D. Berkowitz (Eds.), *Social structures: A network approach*. New York: Cambridge University Press.

White, Harrison. (1992). *Identity and control*. Princeton, NJ: Princeton University Press.

White, Harrison, Boorman, S. A., & Breiger, Ronald. (1976). Social structure from multiple networks: Parts I and II. *American Journal of Sociology, 81*(4,6), 730-781, 468-498.

Willis, Paul. (1977). *Learning to labour*. Aldershot, UK: Gower.

Willis, Paul. (1990). Masculinity and factory labor. In J. C. Alexander & S. Seidman (Eds.), *Culture and society: Contemporary debates*. New York: Cambridge University Press.

Wilson, James Q., & Herrnstein, Richard. (1985). *Crime and human nature*. New York: Simon & Schuster.

Wilson, William Julius. (1987). *The truly disadvantaged*. Chicago: University of Chicago Press.

Wilson, William Julius. (1996, November 3). Defending the safety net in the Welfare-Reform Debate [Interview]. *Los Angeles Times,* pp. M3.

Wilson, William Julius, & Katherine O'Sullivan. (1988). Race and ethnicity. In N. Smelser (Ed.), *Handbook of sociology*. Newbury Park, CA: Sage.

Winch, Peter. (1958). *The idea of a social science*. London: Routledge & Kegan Paul.

Winch, Peter. (1964). Understanding a primitive society. *American Philosophical Quarterly, 1*(4), 307-324.

Wippler, Reinhard, & Lindenberg, Siegwart. (1987). Collective phenomena and rational choice. In J. Alexander & B. Giesen (Eds.), *The micro-macro link*. Berkeley: University of California Press.

Wittgenstein, Ludwig. (1953). *Philosophical investigations*. New York: Macmillan.

Wittgenstein, Ludwig. (1958). *The blue and brown books*. New York: Harper & Row.

Wittgenstein, Ludwig. (1969). *On certainty*. New York: Harper & Row.

Wittgenstein, Ludwig. (1970). *Zettel*. Los Angeles: University of California Press.

Wolfe, Alan. (1989). *Whose keeper?* Berkeley: University of California Press.

Wolfe, Alan. (1999, May 10). Margaret Mead goes to Harlem. *The New Republic*, pp. 48-55.

Wolff, Robert Paul. (1977). *Understanding Rawls*. Princeton, NJ: Princeton University Press.

Wright, Lawrence. (1997). *Twins and what they tell us about who we are*. New York: John Wiley.

Wright, Robert. (1994). *The moral animal*. New York: Pantheon.

Wrong, Dennis. (1994). *The problem of order*. Cambridge, MA: Harvard University Press.

Wuthnow, Robert. (1987). *Meaning and moral order*. Berkeley: University of California Press.

Wuthnow, Robert, Hunter, James, Bergeson, Albert, & Kurzweil, Edith. (1984). *Cultural analysis*. Boston: Routledge & Kegan Paul.

Zeckhauser, Richard. (1987). Behavioral versus rational economics. In R. Hogarth & M. Reder (Eds.), *Rational choice*. Chicago: University of Chicago Press.

Index

ABOUT THE AUTHOR

David Rubinstein teaches at the University of Illinois at Chicago. He is author of *Marx and Wittgenstein: Social Science and Social Praxis* (1981) and numerous articles in journals of philosophy and sociology. He was awarded the Theory Prize from the American Sociological Association in 1980 for his paper *The Concept of Action in the Social Sciences*. He received his PhD from the University of Colorado at Boulder in 1974.